USA and POW/MIA Flags at Punchbowl Cemetery, Hawaii

M I A

(Missing In Action)

Printed by CreateSpace; an Amazon Company.
Second revision 3/6/2013

ISBN – 13: 978-1478197119
ISBN – 10: 1478197110

In reference to the citizens of Papua New Guinea, the following terms have been used: locals, nationals, villagers and, in cases referring to WWII time periods, natives or boys. No offense has been intended.

The opinions expressed in this book are those of the author alone.

Cover picture: Abandoned Japanese G3M2 bomber code named "Nell" at Gasmata airstrip. WNBP, PNG

Cover background picture: Nationals from Yumielo Village, WNBP, PNG

Cover graphics by: Mark Magno Design, Honolulu, HI.

http://www.mia-missinginaction.com
http://www.pacificwrecks.com/people/visitors/reichman/
http://www.youtube.com/watch?v=EiMfMvEOBbU
http://www.youtube.com/watch?v=hcr4emJBYxo

Who ever thought that I would someday write a book?
Each time I sat down to collect my thoughts and put
them on paper, I remembered the advice of one who
loved me and knew me from the beginning who said,
"Keep your notes and letters as one day,
you may write a book."

This book is dedicated to the loving memory of
my Mom for her prophetic encouragement.

Punchbowl Cemetery, Hawaii. Courts of the Missing on each side.

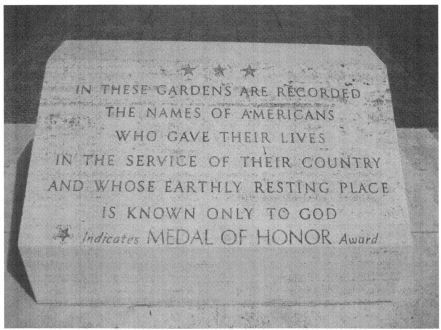

Punchbowl Cemetery, Hawaii. Monument to the Missing in Action.

M I A

That the Lost
May be FOUND

By Mark J. Reichman

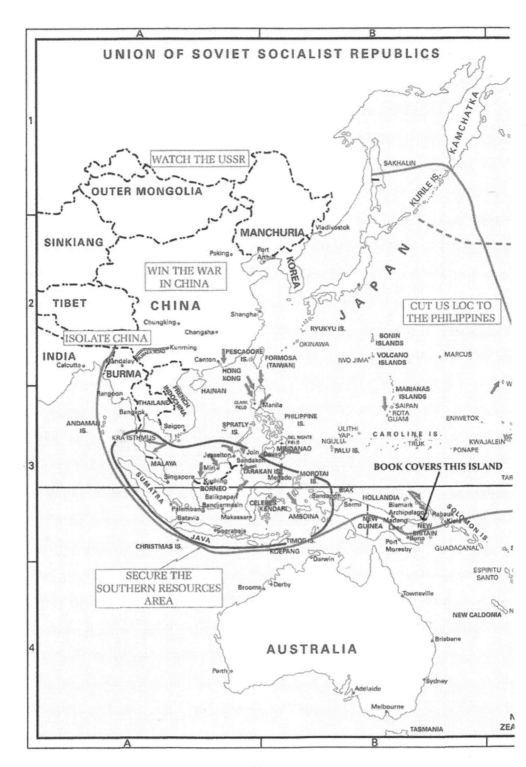

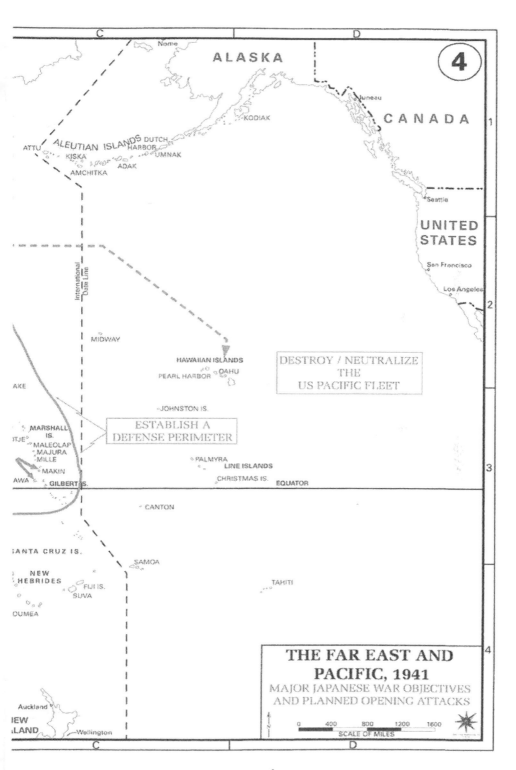

THE FAR EAST AND
PACIFIC, 1941
MAJOR JAPANESE WAR OBJECTIVES
AND PLANNED OPENING ATTACKS

ix

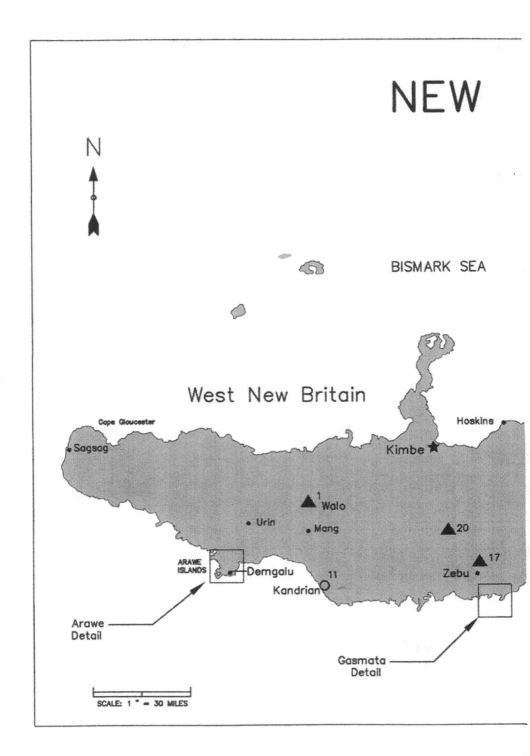

BRITAIN

Rabaul

GAZELLE PENINSULA

• Lemingi

• Tol

• Kol

▲23

• Korpun

• Matong

East New Britain

LEGEND

•	VILLAGE
○	TOWN
★	CAPITAL
▲	AIRCRAFT

SOLOMON SEA

ARAWE AREA

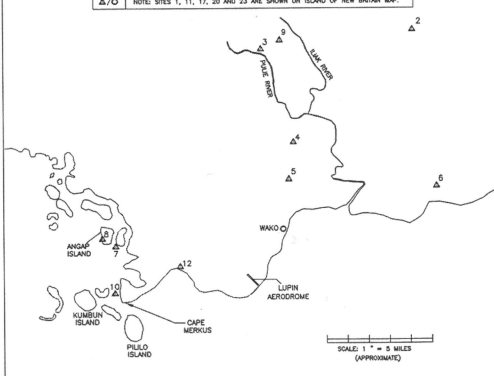

ID NO.	GEOGRAPHIC COORDINATE	MILITARY HARDWARE	MANAFACTURE NO./Name
NO. 1	S 05'49.711' E 149'29.964'	AIRCRAFT	D3A2 MN 3179
NO. 2	S 06'58.700' E 149'13.031'	AIRCRAFT	D3A2 MN 1520
NO. 3	S 05'59.118' E 149'07.680'	AIRCRAFT	D3A2 MN 3450
NO. 4	S 06'02.384' E 149'09.035'	AIRCRAFT	D3A2 MN 3487
NO. 5	S 06'04.029' E 149'08.827'	AIRCRAFT	D3A2 MN 3383
NO. 6	S 06'03.195' E 149'15.187'	AIRCRAFT	D3A2 MN 3373
NO. 7	S 06'06.722' E 149'01.865'	AIRCRAFT	D3A2 MN (NF)
NO. 8	S 06'06.601' E 149'01.118'	AIRCRAFT	D3A2 MN (NF)
NO. 9	S 05'58.975' E 149'08.593'	AIRCRAFT	P38 Regina Coeli
NO. 10	S 06'09.435' E 149'02.094'	JAPANESE SHIP	Taki Saki Maru
NO. 11	S 06'12.456' E 149'32.729'	TOWN	Kandrian
NO. 12	S 06'08.378' E 149'04.378'	VEHICLE	M3 STUART TANK
O	S 06'06.385' E 149'08.429'	VILLAGE	Wako
△/O	NOTE: SITES 1, 11, 17, 20 AND 23 ARE SHOWN ON ISLAND OF NEW BRITAIN MAP.

N

ILUK RIVER

PULIE RIVER

WAKO

ANGAP ISLAND

LUPIN AERODROME

KUMBUN ISLAND

CAPE MERKUS

PILILO ISLAND

SCALE: 1 " = 5 MILES
(APPROXIMATE)

GASMATA AREA

N

ID NO.	GEOGRAPHIC COORDINATE	MILITARY HARDWARE	MODEL/Name
NO. 13	S 06˚17.4701' E 150˚19.517'	AIRSTRIP	Gasmata Airstrip
NO. 14	S 06˚17.424' E 150˚18.507'	AIRCRAFT	HUDSON A16-165
NO. 15	S 06˚16.500' E 150˚19.410'	AIRCRAFT	B25G MITCHELL
NO. 16	S 06˚16.017' E 150˚18.824'	AIRCRAFT	BEAUFORT A9-204
NO. 17	S 06˚13.428' E 150˚18.002'	AIRCRAFT	HUDSON A16-91
NO. 18	S 06˚16.725' E 150˚18.112'	AIRCRAFT	HUDSON A16-101
NO. 19	S 06˚16.722' E 149˚01.865'	JAPANESE SHIP	ID NO. NOT FOUND
NO. 20	S 06˚04.811' E 150˚11.069'	AIRCRAFT	HUDSON A16-126
NO. 21	S 06˚16.253' E 150˚17.708'	ISLAND	UMBO ISLAND
NO. 22	S 06˚17.234' E 150˚17.059'	TOWN	OLD GASMATA
NO. 23	S 05˚25.092' E 151˚45.993'	AIRCRAFT	B17-TEXAS NO. 6
△/O	NOTE: SITES 1, 11, 17, 20 AND 23 ARE SHOWN ON ISLAND OF NEW BRITAIN MAP.		

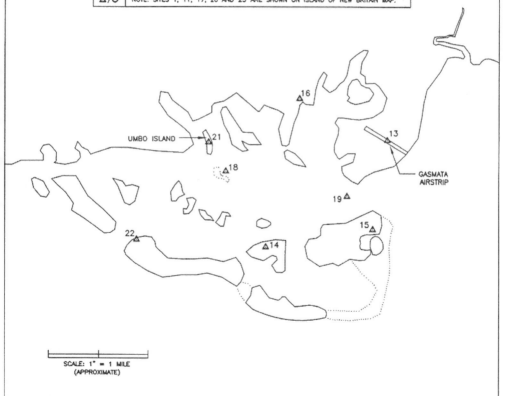

UMBO ISLAND

GASMATA AIRSTRIP

SCALE: 1" = 1 MILE
(APPROXIMATE)

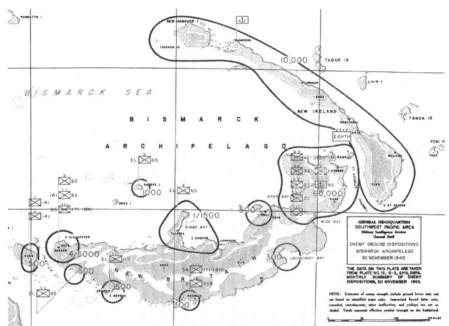

This map reflects Japanese troop strength and locations in the Bismarck
Archipelago, as of November 30, 1943. The data was originally compiled
by the Military Intelligence Section, General Headquarters,
Southwest Pacific Area.

Courtesy – U.S. Army Center of Military History

ACKNOWLEDGEMENTS

It has been said that a good meal takes time to prepare. If that holds true for a book, then this paperback should be a best seller, as it has taken 11 years to produce. Not so much because I am a slow writer, but because it took that long to live the exploits depicted here.

I am grateful to God for allowing me to have experienced these adventures with my family. Without Him sustaining me, the prayers of many, my children Micah, Jared, Mariko and Mieko by my side, and my wife, Joan, courageously "holding the fort" while we were gone on these explorations, I would not have been able to accomplish much, if anything. Appreciation likewise goes to our mission co-workers, Ryan and Nikki Coleman, Adam and Julie Martin, Randy and Diana Smyth, Paul and Robina Wolff, along with the countless Papua New Guinea nationals who assisted us, and Peter Stone for encouraging me to "go for it" when I first proposed the idea of writing this book.

Admiration goes to my band of researchers stretching from Australia to Japan via Papua New Guinea and over to America. Their assistance was invaluable. My Dad would always say, "If you do not know something, just ask, someone knows the answer." I have found that to be true with all the information I was fed from Cecilie Benjamin, Brian Bennett, Squadron Leader John Cotterell, John Douglas, Peter Dunn, Dr. David Forrester, James Forrester, Wing Commander Ian Honey, Hitoshi "Toshi" Kira, Daniel Leahy, Rod Pearce, my Japanese friend, John Stanaway, Lenore Tillitson, Sqn. Ldr. Gregory Williams and last, but not the least, as this guy was the inspiration that kept me going, Justin Taylan. Utilizing the vast knowledge of these researchers was far superior to "just googling it!"

The book in your hands would not have been enjoyable to read without my editorial team as well which consisted of Dr. Steve Wygle, Dr. Richard Perez, Pastor Robert Ohlson, Mrs. Lois Belcher and Mrs. Cheryl Goody. They did not know what they were getting themselves into when they agreed to "have a look" at my manuscript. I have never seen so much red ink in all my life! Their corrections, insights and advice were much appreciated and needed. Many hours were spent making the map and insets accurate and readable to which I am grateful for friends who assisted with these.

I also want to thank the Royal Australian Air Force for allowing me to accompany them as they conducted the remains recovery of Hudson A16-126. Lastly, my gratitude goes to the families of the missing crew who have allowed me to share their stories.

Dr. Barton David Forrester and Raewyn Pianta. Bita Paka, Rabaul, PNG

SERGEANTS

3210	ASHFORD	C.	A.
402844	BLACKMAN	R.	A.
406432	CASS	W.	I.
00552	CLAXTON	O.	G. F.
406773	COPPIN	W.	H.
405543	COUTIE	B.	I.
5219	DEWHURST	J.	E.
3470	FOX	R.	M.
406721	KORBOSKY	M.	R.
419203	McDONALD	R.	W.

FOUND – RAAF crewmen William Coppin and Barton "Bill" Coutie

CONTENTS

Bita Paka War Cemetery. Courts of the Missing. Rabaul, Papua New Guinea

Lady Columbia. National Memorial Cemetery of the Pacific. Honolulu, Hawaii

ILLUSTRATIONS

M I A

MAPS

INTRODUCTION

To have lost a loved one, a spouse, brother, daughter, father or son during a war is a tragedy. How can we really understand the pain? But to receive a report that they are "Missing in Action" (MIA) is equally, if not more, heart-wrenching. The agonizing thoughts of what might have happened never go away no matter how many years have passed. It affects many, not only the immediate family but also aunts and uncles, cousins and friends. They may not talk about the missing person because of the pain, but every now and then something jogs the memory and the hurt resurfaces. With unending hope, they imagine that their loved one had survived and resumed a life somewhere else. As they travel they check the local phone books in an attempt to locate them. Some sit for hours watching ships come into port and wondering if their loved one will finally come home. Their hope never diminishes, and the pain never goes away, even with the passing of time. Some, because of the emotional pain, choose not to talk about them. Others cannot think of anything else, as nothing is worse than not knowing. No matter how they deal with their emotions, their loved ones may be lost, but they have not been forgotten but they can only begin to mourn when they know the facts.

I have had the privilege, the rare opportunity, to have found the wreckage of a WWII military airplane in the jungles of Papua New Guinea. The four-man crew was listed as MIA. As you read my story, I hope you can get a sense of the excitement and euphoria after having found a lost airplane with its crew, and the humbling experience after hearing from the grateful families.

This book has not been written from a technical standpoint, although I have included a great amount of data and historical facts gleaned from many sources and especially from my experiences. My main goal is to bring hope to those that are still waiting to hear what happened to their own loved ones and to provide a view of what might have happened to these loved ones as they fought the war in the South Pacific. I have included people's names and village names with the hope that someone will be able to continue the search and carry on the mission that was started here.

Nearly every day, we hear of the recovery of remains of the

many American servicemen whose skeletal remains have been found in old war zones. Such activities reflect the degree of success with the ongoing recovery of the remains of many servicemen who perished during the various campaigns of the war.

World War II was the deadliest military conflict in history. An estimated 62 to 78 million people were killed.[1] So many people died in such a short period of time over a vast area; there was not enough time to keep track of them all. The following chart, categorized by just four countries, although impossible to be totally accurate, provides a minute picture of the human costs of WWII:

Country	Military Deaths	Civilian Deaths	MIA
USA	405,399[2]	1,700[3]	73,692[4]
Japan	2,400,000[5]	500k-1m[6]	1,135,000[7]
Australia	39,761[8]	700[9]	>12,000[10]
Papua/New Guinea		15,000[11]	

It is estimated that there are still over 500 aircraft with full crews missing in Papua New Guinea (about 300 American, 150 Japanese and 50 Australian), which means that there are more WWII aircraft missing in Papua New Guinea than in any other country.[12]

The memory and sacrifice of all casualties are honored and respected in the pages of this book. As for the Missing in Action, they are not lost or gone forever, just not found yet. For the four-man crew of Hudson A16-126, their recovery story starts here.

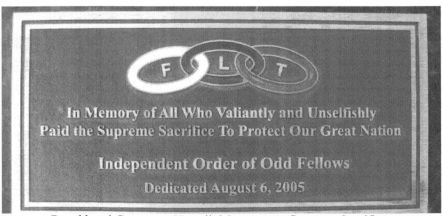

Punchbowl Cemetery, Hawaii. Monument - Supreme Sacrifice.

Chapter 1

THE MISSING HUDSON – A16-126

For Americans, December 7, 1941, is a "date which will live in infamy." This is the date when the Air Forces of the Japanese Empire (assisted by its Navy) bombed Pearl Harbor. Almost four weeks later on January 4, 1942, "the date that will live in infamy" occurred for the allies Down Under; it was on that date the town of Rabaul in New Guinea was attacked. New Guinea was a politically mandated territory under the League of Nations as a consequence of WWI and was the administrative responsibility of Australia. Therefore, an attack on New Guinea was an attack on Australia. The twenty-two "Nell" Mitsubishi bombers' high-altitude raid left twelve villagers dead and thirty wounded. WWII had reached the South Pacific.

The target, Rabaul, (See page xi) on the northeastern tip of the island of New Britain located north of Australia and northeast of New Guinea, (See page viii) continued to be "softened up" by constant attacks. For almost three weeks, the air power of the Japanese Imperial Forces dropped bombs in preparation for the invasion. The Royal Australian Air Force in Rabaul at that time was led by Wing Commander John Margrave Lerew of 24 Squadron.

The Australians were hopelessly under-resourced to meet the onslaught. On January 20, 1942, eight Wirraways were launched to face 80 Japanese bombers and over 40 Zeros. These Wirraways were only training aircraft without self-sealing fuel tanks and would catch fire easily if the tanks were hit. It was certain death for the courageous crews, a virtual suicide mission. Of the sixteen Australians who manned these hopelessly outmatched and outnumbered aircraft, six men were killed and five were wounded in action. Three of the eight Wirraways were lost, and three were totally destroyed. Within a matter of ten minutes of unyielding battering, only two Wirraways had miraculously survived.

Australia was left with one Hudson and two Wirraways to face the final Japanese landing. Lerew was ordered by his commanders to stay and give support to the Australian Army, a garrison of 1,400 men

1

that was left to defend Rabaul. His reply to his commanders is now enshrined in Australia's national history. The message in rough Latin, "Nos morituri te salutamus" was eventually translated in Australia with reference to the Gladiator's salute to the Roman Emperor when they fought to the death in the Coliseum. It translates, "We who are about to die, salute you." Disobeying orders, John Lerew, a true and inspiring leader, used the one remaining Hudson to send out his wounded men to Port Moresby and on to safety in Australia. In the ensuing retreat by the Royal Australian Air Force, Lerew managed to organize the escape of over 100 RAAF crew and personnel by truck, foot, dugout canoes and Sunderland flying boats. Only three RAAF men did not survive the Rabaul exodus; Wing Commander Lerew was never lauded nor reprimanded.

Then, in the early morning hours of January 23, 1942, the Japanese ground assault on Rabaul began. The small Lark Force garrison was no match for the 23,000 invaders; after putting up a good resistance for a few hours, the men from the garrison retreated into the jungle. Some reports have estimated that 1,500 to 2,000 Japanese were killed during the initial assault. Many of the retreating Aussie diggers made their way to the north coast while others headed to the south coast. Their tragic story of hunger, disease, surrender and merciless execution is told movingly in the book by Peter Stone, *Hostages to Freedom: The Fall of Rabaul*. I would do it an injustice to condense it here.

This period of January and February of 1942 was the darkest period in Australia's and Papua New Guinea's history. There has never been a time when the two countries were so threatened, facing so much danger, and so alone. Although Australia was a British dominion, England could not send help, and the USA, at war with Japan after the bombing of Pearl Harbor, was unable to provide air support in New Guinea for another two weeks.

The Japanese rapidly spread throughout New Britain Island after the invasion. The Australians attempted to slow the Japanese military's pace. On February 10, the Australians conducted three attacks on Gasmata, located approximately 241 kilometers (150 miles) west of Rabaul on the south coast of New Britain. The first attack departed Port Moresby at 3:30 A.M. consisting of five Lockheed Hudsons piloted by Wing Commander J. Lerew, Flight Lieutenant A.

Hermes, Flight Lieutenant K. Erwin, Flight Lieutenant W. Pedrina, and Flying Officer G. Gibson. Two airplanes dropped their bombs from high altitude. One airplane high-dived on a destroyer while another high-dived on a merchant ship. No hits were seen although near misses were reported. Hudson A16-126, piloted by F/O Gibson, never found the target and returned to Port Moresby almost an hour and a half behind the others. Later that morning, at 11:15 A.M., four of the Hudsons went out again. They concentrated their attack on shipping inside Gasmata Harbor, although again, no hits were observed. Wing Commander Lerew was not involved in this attack as he was diverted after the first attack and was picking up gold bullion at Salamaua. At 11:00 P.M. that night, three Catalinas (flying boats) departed Port Moresby and attacked Gasmata, dropping anti-personnel bombs on the runway, destroyers and merchant ships. Because of cloud cover, the result of the bombings could not be accurately observed. Although enemy fighter aircraft were seen, they did not attack.

Possibly because none of these attacks proved to be very successful, another attack was scheduled for the next day, Wednesday, February 11, 1942. For this sortie, only three Hudsons departed Port Moresby at approximately 12:30 P.M. headed for Gasmata again. Wing Commander John Lerew led the raid on the two Japanese merchant ships that were anchored in Gasmata Harbor. The plan for the bombing raid was to be a surprise attack designed to get in and out fast, but this time the raid was to be made at masthead height.[13] It was assumed that they wanted the determined attack to be totally unexpected since enemy fighter aircraft had previously been seen at the Gasmata airstrip. Actually, the Japanese had landed four or six Mitsubishi-built A5M fighters (later code named "Claude" by the allies) in Gasmata. Reports conflict as to the actual number of fighters. The single-seat "Claudes" were the predecessor to the famous and feared A6M-2, more notoriously known as the "Zero." Armed with only a pair of 7.7-millimeter (.303-inch) machine guns, like the "Zero," they had excellent maneuverability but with a fixed undercarriage they could only fly at a speed of about 237 kts (272 mph).[14]

Lerew was flying A16-91, followed by Flying Officer Graham Gibson piloting A16-126, and last in the formation was A16-103 piloted by Squadron Leader William Pedrina. The planes arrived at the target around 2:30 P.M. They flew at about 3,048 meters (10,000 feet) in clear skies; as they approached Gasmata, Lerew saw some fighters scrambling to take off. When they had reached approximately 914 meters (3,000 feet), they were attacked. Bill Watt, the second pilot told Lerew that his aircraft was on fire. He did not know if they had been hit by the fighter aircraft or anti-aircraft fire from one of the destroyers that was in the harbor. He handed a fire extinguisher to the second pilot who then broke the window and tried to extinguish the fire as Lerew flew down to 6 meters (20 feet) taking evasive action. Lerew felt they were doomed and was tempted to fly into one of the ships but instead released his bombs into the ship as he just cleared the mast. As the burning aircraft gained altitude, a frantic attempt to extinguish the engine fire was unsuccessful and the fire quickly grew in intensity with flames and smoke pouring into the cabin. Lerew gave the order, "Abandon the aircraft!" He last saw the crew disappear towards the rear, side door of the airplane.

Having forgotten about the escape hatch, Lerew tried to climb out through the pilot's window but became ensnarled in the window frame. The plane was now diving almost vertically and he could not get out. He returned to the cabin and pulled the control back with his foot. The plane leveled out at about 122 meters (400 feet); he then stood on the control column and forced himself through the window and jumped out sideways shielding his head to protect himself in the event he would make contact with the tail of the plane. As he tumbled through the air, he tried to find the rip cord for his parachute. On the way down, he saw another Hudson being pursued by three Japanese fighters. His parachute opened just before he crashed into a tree. He extricated himself from his harness and, to his horror, he realized he was still 24 meters (80 feet) in the air! To make matters worse, the tree did not have any branches other than the ones that had hung up the parachute. He had to wrap his arms and legs around the tree and shinny down like a fireman. As he was descending he picked up speed and nearly burnt his arms and legs off!

The Japanese saw him parachute from the airplane and were trying to find him. They had warned the natives that, if they assisted any soldiers that had escaped from Rabaul, they would be killed.[15] That threat would no doubt include assisting any downed airman as well. Lerew wandered in the jungle for several days and eventually met a young mission-trained native named Michael. Later, he met up with two Australian planters, Bill Douglas and Harold Koch, who had been hiding in a cave. These men had a coconut plantation called Aliwo that was close to the small outpost of Kandrian, (See page x – NO. 11) 80 kilometers (50 miles) west of Gasmata. Harold had a small dinghy that they paddled at night past Japanese ships as they made their way further west to Kumbun Island in the Arawes where an Anglican mission was located. This was another 56 kilometers (35 miles) west. The missionary stationed there, Father Bernard Moore, lent them his five and a half-meter (18-foot) boat with a small cabin and one-lung diesel engine. It is not known why the Father did not go with them; perhaps he felt a greater loyalty to his converts. Two local "boat boys" accompanied them, and they crossed the Vitiaz Straits in torrential rains and rough seas, bailing water as they went. Bill and Harold got seasick and were glad to see land by the next morning. This distance was approximately another 80 nautical miles (92 miles) west. So, all in all, Lerew had hiked, paddled and motored approximately 165 nautical miles (190 miles). As they approached Finschhaven on the mainland, they were met by two patrol boats but feared they had been found by the Japanese. One can image how relieved they must have been as the patrol boat pulled alongside and the Aussie sailors offered them "a cold one," which according to Lerew, "Made for a perfect day." Lerew again made his way safely back to Port Moresby, and Bill and Harold went on to become Coast Watchers.[16]

The other three crew members from Lerew's plane, for some unknown reason, did not bail out and went down with the airplane. Postwar RAAF search patrols, led by Squadron Leader Keith Rundle, found the Hudson A16-91 by Zebu Village, and the remains of the three airmen were recovered and buried in Bita Paka Commonwealth War Grave Cemetery in Rabaul, Papua New Guinea.

The Hudson aircraft last in line, A16-103, made its escape by keeping right down on treetop level. Subsequently, Squadron Leader William "Pedro" Pedrina was killed on December 14, 1942, while dropping ammunition supplies near Buna.[17] Ian Gibson, flying A16-126, may have sought cover in the clouds over the mountains as the three Japanese fighters attacked. Australian gunner "Bill" Coutie must have been firing feverishly from his newly installed twin-barreled 7.7 millimeter (.303 inch) Type C MKII Boulton Paul gun turret. He emptied over 400 rounds and it was reported by the Australians that one Claude was shot down. A twenty-four year old Japanese Pilot Officer Class 1, Satoshi Yoshino, reportedly returned to base claiming to have shot down two of the attacking Hudsons.

The Hudsons' historic mast-height mission was successful in that their bombs hit the *Kinryu Maru* and the *Kozui Maru*. Both ships took direct hits which left clouds of black smoke over the entire length of the ships, resulting in the deaths of several crew and the wounding of many others.[18] The *Kinryu Maru* eventually returned to Rabaul with 18 dead.[19]

Back at Port Moresby there was confusion as to the whereabouts of Hudson A16-126. Some assumed that it had gone down in the water, which is the story that was told to the families.[20] Postwar investigations revealed no information as to the fate of the crew of the Hudson. Wing Commander Lerew told one family he believed that it had gone down on a ridge. The mission report filed by Squadron Leader Pedrina, pilot of the third Hudson, stated that one plane, the A16-91, went down in flames, and the other was last seen flying inland being pursued and attacked by enemy fighters. That information, however, was shamefully never relayed to the families. Wherever it crashed, it was lost and the four missing crew were considered Missing in Action and presumed dead.

To the PNG (Papua New Guinea) nationals living at Asika Village some 28 kilometers (16.5 miles) northwest of Gasmata, it was no mystery. They knew where the plane lay; at the time, however, they did not even know what it was, having never seen an airplane, much less a downed airplane, before. After the war ended and they came to the coast and saw other airplane wreckage on the airstrip at Gasmata, they then realized that what lay in the jungle a two-hour hike from their village was indeed an airplane. For some reason, perhaps because nobody asked, they kept silent. Because of their fear of evil spirits, villagers did not disturb the wreckage although they continuously passed it at a distance. As a result, 66 years passed as the families and friends of Graham (Ian) Gibson, Frank Thorn, Barton "Bill" Coutie and Arthur Quail lived on with the unanswered questions they had regarding these fallen airmen. Had their loved ones parachuted from their airplane into the water or the jungle? Perhaps they had survived and were still alive! They had always held out hope for their return. As the years elapsed, their hopes diminished with the realization that their loved ones had indeed been lost. The questions of how and where plagued their minds and hearts. Would they ever be found? Was it even possible?

Japanese Mitsubishi G3M3 *Nell* Bomber.

Japanese Mitsubishi Ki-46 *Dinah* at Gasmata. WNBP, PNG

Gasmata Airstrip. New Britain, Papua New Guinea. Photo by Pacific Wrecks

Lockheed Hudson Bomber.

F/O Ian Gibson and Hudson crew. Photo provided by Tony Gibson.

Hudson waste gunner with Lewis machine gun. Photo provided by David Forrester.

Chapter 2

WWII STORIES OF MY DAD & VILLAGERS

My interest in World War II started when, as a child, I would listen to my dad tell of his Navy days. My father, Richard G. Reichman, served in the US Navy during WWII. He served mainly stateside driving a bus on the base but later was transferred to the USS *New Mexico* after it had been hit by a Kamikaze suicide plane on May 12, 1945. The attack killed 54 and wounded 119 of the crew.[21] My dad was one of the replacements who had met the ship at Leyte, Philippines; he arrived late in the evening and for some reason, he ended up sleeping on the deck. Something had poked him in the ribs during the night and, on the following morning, he realized that it was a piece of shrapnel from that kamikaze attack that had stuck in the wooden deck. When daylight emerged, he was shocked to see how mangled the ship had become as a result of that attack. As children, my sister Marilou, brother Dick and I heard many of Dad's war stories, such as how the 127-millimeter (five-inch) gun concussion had blown his shirt off as he stood in the mount's doorway. Dad's job after the gun fired was to catch the empty powder case as it was ejected from the chamber. He wore asbestos gloves as he carried the hot casing to throw it over the side. Each day, they would change from "flash" to flash-less powder depending upon whether it was for day or night shelling; this kept them busy while they practiced for the invasion of the Japanese homeland. He also had a favorite story that we never tired of hearing: how he "sank the Japanese fleet while riding on the back of a whale and going underneath their ships then pulling the bilge drain plugs." An interesting note here, my dad was later diagnosed with prostate cancer and I now wonder if it was instigated by those asbestos gloves.

The USS *New Mexico* was in Tokyo Bay on September 2, 1945, during the signing of the treaty: this was a tension-filled time. All the men were at their battle stations but someone on the bridge using the intercom was telling them what he was seeing and said, "I sure hope they aren't kidding" (about surrendering and signing the treaty). As he was looking at the battered hulks of the Japanese Navy in the bay he also commented, "No wonder we couldn't find their fleet; there's nothing left." From stories like these a fascination was instilled in us for the Navy and WWII. After high school, my brother and I joined the U.S. Navy. Dick served as a sonar technician on a fast attack submarine out of Charleston, South Carolina. I was a jet engine mechanic in a VAQ (Tactical Electronics Warfare) squadron out of Naval Air Station (NAS) Whidbey Island, Washington. Dick never did say where he had gone for his missions as his cruises were of a top secret nature. I eventually made two cruises, one to the Mediterranean Sea on the USS *Forrestal* in 1975 and the other to the Pacific Ocean on the USS *Enterprise* in 1976. During that Pacific cruise, I changed from a "pollywog" to a "shellback" after enduring a time-honored naval traditional ceremony when crossing the equator for the first time.[22] Little did I know then that someday I would be returning to live in the South Pacific.

During my navy enlistment, I became a Christian, and after my four years of active duty were completed, I returned home to Illinois and eventually moved to Port Charlotte, Florida. While attending a Christian and Missionary Alliance Church I was challenged to take the Good News message of Jesus Christ to people who had never heard that they could be saved from their sins. Shortly afterwards, I married a small, beautiful, long-haired girl from Wahiawa, Hawaii. My new wife of Japanese ancestry, Joan (Tanji), was shocked when I later suggested we become missionaries, and she probably wished that I had told her of my intentions *before* we were married! It took a while for her to get used to the idea, but she finally agreed and we both entered a four-year missionary training program. Toward the end of our training, our first son, Micah, was born. My father was German and my mom was Italian, so with Joan being Japanese, we jokingly said we had created an "Axis." Then in January of 1986, when Micah was only five months old, we departed from the Honolulu International Airport, and headed for the exotic yet primitive country of Papua New Guinea. Some thought we were crazy. Relatives of Joan were upset with me for taking her to a land that was known for tribal fighting and cannibalism.

We had not been in PNG long when I heard that some World War II airplane wreckages were located along the Japanese-built airstrip at Hoskins, West New Britain. (See page x) I found some trail guides and set out to investigate them. After a long and tedious wandering through the coconut plantation, we arrived at the sites of some aircraft relics. I did not know what they were, but there were a few broken airplanes and after I had dug around for awhile, I found several much desired bullet casings. These were historic findings!

Later, we moved to the south coast of West New Britain. Our job was to coordinate getting supplies in and transported to missionary teams who were establishing churches and translating the Bible deep within the interior. We built a house using bush material complete with a grass roof and lived in the village of Yumielo. The village was on the water's edge (Solomon Sea) located on a bright, white, sandy clearing. The thatch-roofed houses were lined up along the perimeter, and a large banyan tree stood tall in the center. The 75 inhabitants of the village were mainly Catholics. They were enormously helpful and seemed happy to have us live with them. We did add much activity to the mundane village routine with supplies and people coming and going frequently. We also held morning clinics and treated the people for malaria and infections; occasionally showing a movie which was a treat for all of us.

The first time I went to town to check the post office for mail I came upon a 20-millimeter (.79-inch) anti-tank rifle. It was lying on the ground near the administration building. It seemed to have been aiming right at me as I walked down the street. *That*, of course, sparked my interest. On the outskirts of Kandrian Town (which was two miles from our village), and almost covered by the encroaching jungle, was the cement-lidded grave of Private A.L. Robinson. He had been a bank clerk in Rabaul who had joined the New Guinea Volunteer Rifles and fought against the Japanese invasion of Rabaul on January 23, 1942. Overwhelmed by the number of invaders and his ammunition expended, he had escaped through the jungle along with Australian soldiers of the 2/22 Battalion and 2/10 Field Ambulance. He was one of the survivors of the Tol Massacre where approximately 158 Australian soldiers, hands tied behind their backs, were led into the jungle and bayoneted or shot to death. Pvt. Robinson and nine other soldiers were marched into the plantation by a "shooting party." As they marched around a bend, he dropped into the scrub and responded to the advice of the other men in line: "Lower, sport." Lying in the bush he went undetected by his captors and therefore survived. Another soldier miraculously survived after being bayoneted 11 times. The last piercing had entered his ear and exited his mouth.[23]

Six years after that incident and the end of the war, Robinson returned to PNG only to be killed by the natives in Poi'iong Village while recruiting men to work at Ring Ring copra (dried coconut) plantation. Apparently, the mother of a young native was fearful her son would be taken away and eaten by white men. She insulted the men of the village and in order to save face, they axed Robinson in the back of the head. Three men went to prison as a result of that murder.[24] Robinson's grave is on the outskirts of Kandrian; it was covered with a cement lid. The epitaph letters were made of lead and must have been stuck in the cement while it was still wet. Although now removed, their imprints were still visible. Robinson had been a strong Anglican who always carried a Bible in his pocket. His epitaph read: *"Go out into the darkness and put your hand into the hand of God – that shall be to you better than light and safer than to known [sic] why."*

Alongside his grave lay Harold Koch, the BP (Burns, Philp) coconut plantation manager at Aliwo[25] who had assisted Wing Commander John Lerew (the pilot and only survivor of Hudson A16-91 after his airplane was shot down over Gasmata). While making his way west along the coast, he joined up with Koch. Lerew, Koch and three other men escaped back to the safety of Port Moresby.[26] Harold Koch, too, returned to the south coast of New Britain after the war and resided there until he passed away of illness. The cement lid on his grave had no writing.

Even though Kandrian had been occupied lightly by the Japanese, interestingly enough many of the older local men could still sing a Japanese song they had been taught called *The Rabbit and the Turtle*.

Moshi Moshi Kame-yo, Kamesan-yo
Hello, Hey Mr. Turtle
Sekai no uchini Omae hodo
I know you are such
Ayumi no noroi Mono wa nai
a slow runner in the world
Doushite Son nani Noroino ka
I wonder why you are so slow [27]

I was to learn later that several older men throughout PNG were taught this exact same song, and it has continued to baffle me to this day as to why this song was taught. Some Japanese friends have suggested that perhaps it was because during that time, most songs had been replaced with only military songs. This is a song that the soldiers would have known from their childhood; it was sort of a Japanese equivalent of *Twinkle Twinkle Little Star* that many Americans have known since childhood.

Although no major battles were fought in the nearby area, there were still many war stories to be told and recalled by the old men, and being an oral society, these stories were passed down to the younger generation. One such story was about a native boy born off the shore of Kandrian but from the island of Apugi. He was born during the Japanese occupation and named "Kamano," after the Japanese Commander who was based in Kandrian.

After two years of living in the area, I realized that I really needed a boat. One day, I had blindly bid on a government dinghy that was up for auction. To my delight I was the highest bidder, but before paying for it, I wanted to see what I was about to buy. I hired our mission airplane to fly me to Gasmata where the boat was lying upside down on the shore with a hole in the bottom. I ended up buying it.

As we landed on the grassy airstrip at Gasmata and taxied to the apron, I was pleasantly surprised to see more Japanese airplane relics alongside the parking area. One was a rare Japanese Mitsubishi G3M Navy type-96 attack bomber code-named "Nell" by the allies. (See front and back cover) This was the type of bomber that first bombed Rabaul. It was still in pretty good shape although the nose and tail section were missing. Its bubble-framed, top-mounted gun turret was still intact. There are not many of these types of airplanes left in the world, and this one is considered to be in the best condition. But each time I visited Gasmata, I noticed the airplane had deteriorated more and more. On one occasion, a group of teenagers were breaking aluminum off the engine to be used for New Year celebrations. They take a small piece of aluminum about 6.4 millimeters (fourth of an inch) square and heat it up then quickly hit it with a hammer. It makes a loud noise just like a gun or fire cracker. I tried it too, and surprisingly, it works! The concept reminded me of when I was younger. We used to do a similar thing by hitting a roll of caps from our cap guns with a hammer. Being deaf in one ear from a childhood tumor, the loud bang would make my good ear ring. It continues to ring even today, but I contend it's from working around jet engines while I was in the Navy.

Another thing we used to do with those rolls of caps was to meticulously open each blister of gunpowder and pour it into a little pile. I am not sure what we planned to do with the powder, but every time before we completed the task, a spark would somehow be generated as we cut the blisters. It would ignite the little pile of powder causing it to flash up and scorch our finger nails leaving them white. It was always disappointing to see our hard work go up in smoke! This is probably not a safe thing to teach your children or grandchildren.

After ten years in the village, the termites destroyed our house making it unsafe. So, with the use of a chain saw and portable saw mill to cut our own timber, we cut down about 40 trees with the help of the villagers. We paid them for their labor and for the trees; in some cases the tree owners did not want pay. They preferred to take a portion of the timber we were milling to use to build their own houses. We actually had some square timber to frame the walls and to make flat floors: that was quite a novelty compared to using sticks for studding and curved palm bark for flooring. In October, 1996, with the assistance of work teams that came from churches in Washington and Hawaii along with our Australian co-workers, Gordon and Heather O'Toole, after one year of hard work, we completed our new house in the town of Kandrian. (See page x.- NO. 11) That was a much more convenient location as it was closer to the airstrip and where the barges pulled in with supplies.

When our family had grown to four children, I had three of them accompany me on my supply runs. Micah was now 15 years old and a chip off the old block. They say coconuts do not roll far from the tree and that was the case here. We even think alike so we would often bounce things back and forth to decide how something should be done. To an onlooker, it probably looked as if we were arguing. He was able to perform any task I sent him on as he was quite capable and independent, having been given responsibilities from an early age.

Our second son, Jared, was four-and-a-half years younger than Micah. We had hoped to have our children closer together in age, but for some reason, Joan had a difficult time getting pregnant. That may have been exacerbated by the difficulty of living in an unusually different and stressful cultural setting. We were not there because we liked it but rather because we believed that is what the Lord wanted us to do. Our life was anything but normal compared to life in the States;

14

originally, we lived in a kunai grass-roofed house which leaked. The walls were made from hand-hewn planks that the bugs loved to bore holes in making daily piles of dust on our floors. Micah's little Hot Wheels cars looked as if they had been in a snow storm! For lighting, we used two pressure kerosene lamps that I pumped up and lit every night. We had running water only because we collected rain and stored it in a big metal tank. We then pumped the water to a smaller tank on the roof which would gravity feed to the house. In the dry season, many times our water supply got nerve racking low (or depleted), so we had to conserve and that was always stressful for Joan as she had diapers to wash. We had a saying to remind us to safeguard the water supply that said, "If it's yellow, let it mellow. If it's brown, flush it down." There were only screens on the windows so living in a village along with 75 other people provided little or no privacy. To calm Joan's fears, I told her our mosquito net around the bed was sound proof. These and other factors may have contributed to her inability to get pregnant. Interestingly though, after living in PNG for over three years, when we started talking about going home for furlough, she then became pregnant!

We were so excited when Jared was born on April 18, 1990, in Hawaii. He was a great little guy but different from his brother. Instead of a vast flare of independence, Jared was more timid, but caring, and watchful of his sisters who were to come later. He had a lot of energy so we had to keep him busy or he would annoy all of us in one way or another. One job we gave him in order to keep him from irritating everybody was burying the dog poop from the many village dogs which would make deposits around our yard. It certainly kept him busy as there were several dogs. On one occasion, he commented that all he did was, "Dishes and doo-doo!" At the age of nine years, while we were on furlough in Illinois, his Aunt Teresa nicknamed him "Kenmore." She lovingly came up with that name after the Kenmore washing machine that had an agitator and she likened it to our Jared. And even now, if he is bored, one can rest assured that he is playfully poking his finger into someone's side.

Mariko arrived two years later. Try to visualize our exuberance when our little girl was born after 12 years of our marriage. She was born in the town of Kimbe at the government hospital and cost us five dollars. I call her "My five dollar baby," although that is not totally accurate because I tipped the midwife twenty dollars. Even as a baby,

15

she was always happy and cheerful. As she grew, she found happiness in everything, rain or shine. She was a real delight to be around and brightened up every day and everybody with her smile and witty comments. She grew to become very personable and optimistic.

We now had two boys but only one girl and the thought that we could lose them from disease or injury was always in the back of my mind. Then three years later (while on furlough), one night Joan said to me, "I think I'm pregnant." We were delighted and felt that was God's will for us so we excitedly awaited the arrival of our fourth child who had a fast heartbeat while in the womb – signaling the possibility of a girl. When we told the news to my mom, her first comment was, "Well, that's one more ticket." She knew how expensive it was for us to fly back and forth from PNG every four years, so that was the first thing that came to her mind.

The day finally arrived on February 22, 1996, when our second daughter was born at a private clinic in Lae. (Lae happened to be the last airport Amelia Earhart had taken off from.) My grandmother had started a family tradition and named her five daughters with names that all started with "Mar." My aunts had continued that tradition and now it was our turn to follow suit. Having already named our first daughter Mariko, we searched the books for another name that started with "Mar" and eventually settled on the name "Markie." Another family tradition from Joan's side was to have a Japanese middle name so her second name was "Mieko." That is the name we usually call her by. Having now two sons and two daughters made our family complete and we felt we were truly blessed with a full quiver.

Over the years, as I traveled around, my interest in WWII rose and fell as I discovered relics or heard stories. On one occasion, I saw an airplane engine resting on a reef at the mouth of the Apalik River. There was also the engine and the ribs of a Japanese ship that had been sunk in Arung Bay in Kandrian, WNBP. To my surprise, the ribs were made of cement and the stringers were made of wood.

On another occasion, I heard a story from a national named Langa, from Aviklo Island. He claimed to be an eye witness to the murder of the Australian Anglican Priest, Father John Barge. Father Barge had been taken from his mission station at the village of Pomete, two miles west of Kandrian, to the shore inside Arung Bay in Kandrian.

After being blindfolded, he was beheaded then quickly buried by the Japanese. Native friends of his came afterwards and gave him a proper burial.[28] I went to see his grave in the mangroves; it has a cemented deck with a cement table built by the Anglicans years later as a memorial.

On the island of Aviklo, one of the islands across from the Kandrian town center, I heard the account of a situation where a bomb had been dropped on the village. The explosion killed six men while they were having a traditional dance during the night. All their names are still remembered by the clan members.

In January of 2001, I started delivering supplies to a missionary, Paul Wolff, and his family, who were living on an island in the Arawes which is 56 kilometers (35 miles) to the west of Kandrian. One time while playing in the water, their son, Ben, had found something and when he picked it up, it started to smoke, fizzle and pop, leaving a 37 millimeter (one-and-a-half inch) diameter burn on his leg that took a long time to heal. This was probably a piece of white phosphorous from a bomb or mortar or perhaps, a flare. Alongside their house were three pits where his children had found bullets in the ground. On another exploration trek, I also saw what was left of a B-25 sitting on top of a reef and pieces of a plane in the mangroves.

The hearing of these stories and re-examining relics again wetted my appetite for information about WWII. Sometime later, I came across the US War Department movie, *Attack! The Battle for New Britain.*[29] The movie showed actual footage of the shelling and bombing on the morning of December 15, 1943, prior to the assault of Cape Merkus in the Arawes. US Army Texans of the 112th Cavalry Regiment and other reinforcements totaling 1,700 men were involved in the assault.[30] The task force, code-named "Director," was to seize and defend a suitable location for the establishment of a light naval facility. Actually, the Arawe assault was a diversionary tactic. Its goal was to divert the Japanese's attention from another more important landing planned for Cape Gloucester located on the northwestern tip of New Britain Island scheduled for Christmas Day ten days later where 310 marines would lose their lives.[31]

The movie also showed a small assault detachment that consisted of 15 rubber rafts carrying ten men each that were supposed to sneak to shore under cover of night. Unfortunately, the moonlight exposed them and, when they were almost to shore, Japanese machine guns opened fire on them, riddling 12 rafts with bullets and sinking them. Most of the men jumped overboard. One Sergeant did make it to the beach. Surprisingly, during searches for survivors, they found that only 16 of the original 150 men had been killed and 17 more had been wounded.[32]

Villagers from the area brought me a rusty U.S. bayonet, and I have often wondered if it was from one of those men who had given his life that morning. After viewing this movie, and as I passed by the Arawe's landing area, I became more acutely aware of what had taken place there on December of 1943. The movie added to my curiosity, and I began asking the villagers what they knew about the war.

The locals enjoyed guiding us all around; probably since our kids had accompanied us, it was like playtime. On one occasion they took us to the beach landing area at Arawe and showed us the amphibious Alligator or Buffalo tracks rusting in the water. These amphibious tractors were used to transport the assault force to the beach under cover of destroyer bombardment and rocket fire. The people also showed us one of the unexploded projectiles from the bombardment that was stuck in the mangroves. Understandably, fear kept them clear of that area.

When other villagers heard that we were interested in these things, some of the youth showed us a cave on the east side of Cape Merkus that had a wire running out of it. Inside we found an old radio tube and wire insulator. At another cave, we had to crawl on our stomachs through a small opening, and once inside, we found it to be full of cases of rations that had apparently been unused and discarded. As we walked down the 30-foot incline of rusted tins looking for "treasures," our feet would sink 15 centimeters (six inches) down as the rusted cans would give way under our weight. We found a couple of US helmets, a back-pack type of water filter and the real prize, some live bullets and empty cartridges. The Wikipedia article about the Arawe battle citing author John Miller's book *Cartwheel: The Reduction of Rabaul,*[33] describes a cave on the east side of the peninsula where 21 Japanese soldiers had been hiding and were eventually killed. I have always wondered if this was the same cave. On the side of the mountain, we found a small-arms clip and some bottles we supposed were once filled with "sake," a rice-based Japanese alcoholic drink. In another cave, we even found an old Coca Cola bottle which was made in Oakland, California. The kids really began to get into it even more than had their dad! Mariko still says that the cave was her best adventure. We all looked forward to the next trek with anticipation. One never knows what one can find. We were becoming involved in actual history! It was extremely exciting, like panning for gold or metal-detecting in a park in search of a lost diamond ring. These are things my dad used to enjoy doing, so I must have inherited my quest for adventure from him.

20 mm anti-tank rifle at the District Office, Kandrian. WNBP, PNG

Reichman family. (2002) Photo by Owen and Owen. Honolulu, HI.

USS *New Mexico* hit by Kamikaze May 12, 1945

Reichman's house. (1986) Yumielo Village. WNBP, PNG

Grave of A.L. Robinson, Kandrian. WNBP, PNG

Chapter 3

TROLLING FOR AIRPLANES – VAL #1

In my questioning of the locals about WWII relics, one of the young men from Pililo Island told me of an airplane he had seen in the water. On September 8, 2001, I went back to that area with my scuba diving gear and my two sons, Micah and Jared. We picked up our informant, Erimas, from Pililo Island, and went to the area where he had seen the airplane, ten years ago or earlier. We were somewhat close to where we had spotted the two B-25 engines that were on the reef. I let him jump into the water first to locate the airplane but after a half hour we sensed he was unable to find it. I sent my two sons in and they scoured the area, too, but did not see anything. A man came by in a dugout canoe and our guide talked to him. They moved away from the area where we were and continued to search along a reef edge. After a couple of hours, I became suspicious and felt that he was trying to lead us away from the airplane. I told my two boys to put on their masks and tie ropes to the back of the boat and I would drag them around using the GPS on the boat and, in that way, we could search in a grid pattern. We returned to the original area then trekked up and over, then back down again to make our grid. The water was fairly clear and ranged from three to nine meters (ten to 30 feet) in depth. I had been dragging the boys for 45 minutes when all of a sudden, I heard them yelling! It alarmed me since dragging your children behind a boat looks a lot like trolling. When they yelled, I did not know what had happened; I was quick to turn around. Fortunately, they were merely excitedly yelling, "We found it! We found it!" (See page xii - NO. 7)

I circled around and dropped anchor in 6 meters (21 feet) of water. Micah and I suited up with scuba-diving gear then went down to have a look. Our hearts were pounding as we descended. The airplane was there, and it was intact, lying on its back. The engine was missing; at least it did not appear to be where it should have been. We swam around the wreckage several times looking at the wings, the tail, the landing gear and peeked through the holes in the fuselage. We had dreams of finding a Samurai sword or dagger, pistol or anything! Since the plane was upside down with the cockpit opening flat on the sand, we were unable to look inside, and we did not think about digging underneath. We considered attempting to flip the airplane over, but we did not have the equipment and we did not really know how to do it. The thought that human remains might still be there entered our minds, but we realized that the silt upon which it was resting would cloud the water, and block our vision if we even touched it ever so lightly with our fins, so we did not do any digging around. We were content to restrict our search to only a visual examination of the airplane.

When we reached home again, we wracked our brains to remember some major characteristics of the design from details such as how the tail was shaped and how the back of the fuselage looked. We had noted the dive brakes on the underside of the wing and that the landing gear was not retractable. We dug through every book (two of them) we had on airplanes in our attempt to identify the type of airplane we had seen. Since we lived in a remote location, there was no library and we did not have many books, but my son Jared had what we called his "Bible." It was a book that he had almost memorized, the pilot's manual to *Combat Flight Simulator 2 (WWII Pacific Theater)*. From that book and a small book about Pearl Harbor, we determined that the airplane was a Japanese Aichi D3A Navy Type 99 Carrier Bomber, Allied reporting code name "Val." This two-seat model had an ability to carry a 550-pound bomb underneath in the center and four 132-pound bombs on its wings.[34] One hundred and twenty-six Vals were used during the bombing of Pearl Harbor and had a high success rate of more than eighty percent accuracy.[35] Only fifteen were shot down during the first-wave attack. Wow, what a find for us! We had found a renown historical airplane and could not wait to go back to see it again! But how were we to notify anyone about our find? How could we prove that we had indeed found a WWII Japanese bomber? How could we gain contact with a museum or government authorities to tell of our discovery? Does everyone know about it? Does anyone care? My wife was not too impressed when we told her about it. She was just glad we were back home safely again. She would worry at times while we were gone, especially in stormy weather when the seas were rough.

When we found the airplane, our guide acted confused about the plane's location and kept saying that "maybe someone tried to float it with 44-gallon drums and it got away from them." We considered the possibility that he was trying to cover his deception and that he was trying to lead us away from the sunken warplane. A couple years later however, he confided with me that the airplane we found was not the one that he had seen, and that is why he could only reason that someone had moved it. The one he had seen was on another nearby reef, so we returned to that site with our dive gear and tried to find that airplane as well. We swam along the reef edge in nine meters (30 feet) of water but to no avail. I still wonder if there is another airplane in that area.

A year later after finding the Val, I saw Rod Pearce, an avid historian and diver and told him of the find. He was interested, as he had heard of a plane in the water but had never found it. I gave him the GPS coordinates and he went to the crash site and later told me that the engine was still there but it had been tucked under the wing. Since I was new to these adventures, I had seen something there but could not tell what it was as it was covered with sponges and corals. Rod, being more experienced in this sort of thing, was able to find not only the engine but the pilot and crew's remains after he had dug under the cockpit. He was also able to confirm that, indeed, it was a Val and that he returned the remains to the fuselage where he had found them. He was hoping the Japanese Government would hire him to recover the remains.

Another man, Tim, who had accompanied Rod, told me later that they had brought the pilot's remains up on deck and laid them out. From their simple forensics it revealed the length of the skeleton. Oddly, it was longer than would have been expected and atypical for a Japanese person. The skull had a gash in the forehead and it was assumed that he must have hit the cockpit instrument panel or gun sight upon impact. They also found the sole of his shoe and said it too was rather large, probably a size thirteen. But who was this man? Could his family be notified that his remains had been located here?

ORDNANCE IN THE TAKA SAKA MARU

On another occasion, while talking with Rod Pearce about the Arawes, I told him that I had never found the Japanese cargo ship, the *Taka Saka Maru*, he had told me about. We tried to find it but our attempt, to our dismay, was unsuccessful. Fortunately, he shared the GPS coordinates that he had, so the next time I went to the Arawes, on December 29, 2002, we searched again. I took my son Micah, along with our dive buddies, Dave and Joy Mueller; we found the precise coordinates and dropped anchor. (See page xii - NO. 10) Dave was quick to get suited up and jumped into the water to see if we had, indeed, been accurate with our GPS tracking so as to place us close to the ship. To our surprise, Dave surfaced and presented us with a 75-millimeter (three-inch) ordnance shell which he had found below. It was totally encrusted and heavy; it was about 61 centimeters (two feet) long. A few locals were in their dugout canoes watching us and, since we did not want them to accuse us of stealing things from the wreckage, we nonchalantly gave them the projectile as a gesture of friendship and cooperation.

Micah and I anxiously prepared for our own dives. Our "open water" SCUBA training certification qualified us to dive to 18 meters (60 feet). We were pretty certain that this dive would exceed that. Knowing it would be close to a decompression dive, we hung a spare dive tank off the bow of the boat and lowered it down to nine meters (30 feet). Once the tank was in place, we then hopped in and made our descent. The anchor line, which appeared bright white, was our only point of reference because we could only see blue everywhere we looked. It was quite spooky as we descended deeper and deeper and our air bubbles began to get smaller and smaller. At 23 meters (75 feet), I started to see the shape of a ship, a big ship. This was it! It was the elusive *Taka Saka Maru* that I had sought for some time. It startled me at first, but I cannot explain what it was like seeing it for the first time. It was awesome, captivating and mysterious! To me, it was like what must have been felt by those who found the *Titanic*. You can imagine how fast my heart was pumping. This ship had sunk and had settled there for over 60 years.

The ship lay flat on the white sandy bottom. Our anchor had dropped right on top of the deck amidships at about 43 meters (140 feet). As mentioned, it was a "bit" deeper than our recreational diver certifications officially allowed. We knew that we only had 15 minutes or so before we would go into decompression so we did not want to waste any time. When you dive deeper than 30 meters (100 feet), there is a different feeling. You must still breathe slowly, but because the air in the tank is compressed so much, the air is used up more rapidly when you breathe. Consequently, your air supply does not last as long as it would if you were in shallower water. In addition, at lower depths, there is not much room for error, so it is necessary to make certain that the scuba gear is functioning at optimal performance. Actually, one look at my dive gear would not convince anyone that it was in "top shape," since it showed significant wear and looked faded and a bit tattered. Living in a remote area with no service centers, we maintained our own gear. However questionable it may have looked, it had worked well for me for a number of years. It was like a faithful friend. We also had a little gasoline-engine-powered air compressor that enabled us to refill our dive tanks, slowly, taking over a half hour for each one.

Micah hovered above the hulk as I went down for a closer look. The upper back section of the ship was gone, which I assumed must have been blown off. There were small chains lying on the deck which I thought may have held up sleeping bunks. I eased towards the bow past large ropes lying on the deck. I was startled by a huge fish that appeared to be one-and-a-half meters long and 46 centimeters (five feet long and 18 inches) wide as he came out from the shadows of the deep. With the giant wrasse out of the way, I then descended further into the rear cargo hold. It was considerably darker and a bit spooky too.

When I descended into the hold, there was a layer of silt everywhere, but even at that depth, the water was clear and I could see some rusted 55-gallon drums. Along the port and starboard bulkheads there was a one-meter (about three-foot) shelf which held several 75 millimeter (three-inch) diameter tubes about 61 centimeters (two feet) long and attached in groups of two. I assumed they likely contained an ordnance of some kind. After a few more minutes of looking around, I ascended out of the hold and swam farther forward. The wheelhouse had collapsed, and the windows were at about deck level. We looked into the windshield openings that did not have glass, but not much was in there. The wheel was also missing. We did not go down into the forward cargo hold as it looked spookily dark, and there was plenty to see elsewhere. A good, bright floodlight would have been handy, although Rod Pearce had advised against going inside the structure as it was starting to collapse and would not be safe. I have often wondered if there may have been human remains inside the ship.

It was such a unique sensation as we stood on the deck and beheld the scene. The wood had rotted away but there were still the support beams visible. The cable winches for the derricks were still identifiable, and they had cable wrapped around them. The chain railings were still slung along the deck's edge. There were stairways to the upper deck, and on top was a box of corroded bullets. It was not difficult to visualize someone taking his last shots at the airplane that had dropped bombs on this ship. We also found the eerie, empty lifeboat davits (hand-operated, winch-like devices for lowering the lifeboat). The ship had a straight bow which was angled sharply, and the anchor was lying in the sand on the starboard (right) side of the ship about 6 meters (20 feet) below. Another anchor lay on the deck on the starboard side just fore of the cargo hold. The raised foredeck was rotted away so we could look down into and through the ribbing into the forward cabin. On the deck lay a box with 24 detonating fuzes that could be screwed into the nose of the 75-millimeter (three-inch) ordnance shells I had previously seen while in the cargo hold.

After swimming the length of the ship, approximately 69 meters (225 feet) from stern to bow, our time was up all too soon. We returned amidships (midsection of the ship) to our anchor and adjusted it so it would not snag on anything as we pulled it up. It would have been a real hassle to have to go back down to release it if it had gotten stuck. We slowly ascended to the surface holding on to the bright white anchor line. As we ascended, our eyes were glued to our dive computers for any warning signals, such as, "too fast an ascent." Glancing left and right into the deep blue surrounding, we would see the occasional fish swim by but most of the time we could see nothing but blue vastness.

Once on the surface and into the boat, we stripped out of our gear, and again, as it was when we saw the Val, we recalled mental notes as to what we had seen. I could barely remember anything, I was so excited. Perhaps it was narcosis which caused my memory lapse; who knows? Micah, who had remained hovering above the ship, was able to watch me and said I was swimming all over the place while he was calmly taking in the entire scope of the ship.

After we explained the ship to Dave and Joy and made a sketch of it, they also dived down for their 20 minutes of excitement. Dave came up this time holding one of the detonating fuzes that screw into the top of the projectile. We did not know for certain what it was because it was totally encrusted. However, when we took it home and cleaned it up on the wire wheel, we could see the 15-centimeter (six-inch) long tapered brass fitting with threads, and it was fairly clear as to its purpose. I wondered afterwards if cleaning it with the wire wheel was such a good idea.

We spent a few nights in the Arawes with Paul and Robina Wolff (New Tribes Mission missionaries), and as we were celebrating New Year's Eve, we heard a loud explosion! Immediately we were fearful that the projectile we had given the locals had exploded. We were sort of worried during the night as to what had caused the loud distant sound. However, the next morning, no one came yelling at us so our fears were alleviated a bit. Had the explosion been from the projectile and someone had gotten hurt, in the local culture we would have probably been blamed and huge amounts of compensation demanded. One can only anticipate what other repercussions could have resulted from an event like that.

Still nervous and yet wondering what the loud boom was, we went to Pililo Island to enquire as to the explosion. The men told us some other villagers had found a bomb and dug a hole alongside a tree they wanted to knock down. They then lit a fire in the hole with the bomb (possibly mortar round) and returned to their village. Later, the bomb exploded, but to their disappointment, the tree had not fallen down. We then asked about the projectile we had given them and they brought it to us, all cleaned up! Apparently, someone spent the night scraping all the encrustation off of it, against the warnings from the older village "bigmen" (chiefs) that it could explode. These older men had seen bombs explode and knew the destructive power, so they had a healthy fear of them. We were of course relieved to see the projectile intact and recommended that we retrieve it for proper disposal. All were in agreement, so we took it to the middle of the passage and dropped it back in the deep water in plain sight for all to see. I slept better that night even though I certainly wish that I could have kept it. It was really an exciting relic and trophy, if you will, of our first *Taka Saka Maru* dive. Later, someone brought me a similar but shorter, and much corroded, 75-millimeter (three-inch) projectile which I did keep to show people who passed through our area.

When we all dove on the ship the second time on January 2, 2003, my son Micah and I went down second. We had planned to get one of those detonating fuzes. Like the first time, we had the same enthusiastic excitement diving down again to see this ship. On this dive, we went all the way down to the sandy bottom which was almost 49 meters (160 feet) deep. In the stern there were two large iron boxes on each side of the ship. They were totally sealed so there was no way to see inside. We noticed that the single propeller was still intact. After securing our prize of the detonating fuze, we got carried away; we did not want to leave the ship, so we spent an extra ten minutes looking things over. Those extra minutes at deep depths translated to having to spend 45 minutes at different depths while we ascended to allow our bodies to become decompressed. Divers need to decompress to avoid onset of the "bends," which portends a number of different symptoms including the possibility of death in some cases. Our buddies, Dave and Joy, were getting bored waiting for us on top. Because of the clear water, we could see them impatiently standing on the bow of the boat watching us, but we just had to wait and finish our safety stops.

Japanese Aichi D3A2 *Val*. US Naval Museum Aviation Photo.

Rear stabilizer of *Val* in 21 feet of water in Arawe Islands. Photo by Rod Pearce

Val undercarriage. Photo by Rod Pearce

Diving to sunken Japanese Merchant Ship - *Taka Saka Maru.*

Sunken Japanese Ship - *Taka Saka Maru* starboard deck.

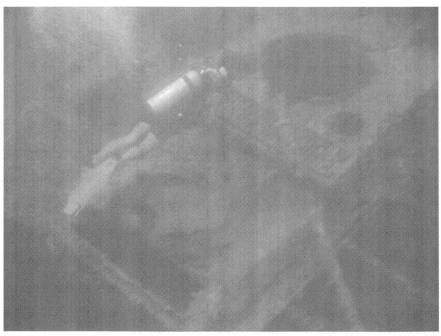

Sunken Japanese Ship - *Taka Saka Maru* amidship.

CHAPTER 4

THE LITTLE KNOWN ARAWE BATTLE

There were no more leads about wrecks in the water, but we started getting reports of wrecks on land. On March 3, 2003, my sons and some fellow enthusiasts explored a USA M3A Stuart tank with a 38-millimeter (one-and-a-half inch) gun at Demgalu Village; I stayed with the boat. (See page xii - NO. 12) They told me that there was one fairly complete tank and another with a turret that had separated and was lying about nine meters (30 feet) away from the main body. There were also some truck tires, frames and rusted leaf springs nearby. In addition, an unexploded bomb was in the area that the people were concerned about. Although they were told of a jeep not far away from this site, because of time restraints, they did not go see it.

These tanks and trucks were the remains of Company B, 1st Tank Battalion, of the 1st Marine Division, and 2nd Battalion, 158th Infantry. These units had been called in to break the stalemate after ground troops were unable to drive the Japanese out of position in the Arawes. These tanks had been hopelessly bogged down in the mud, and after the pocket of resistance was overrun, they were destroyed and abandoned. In all, the Battle of the Arawes left 150 Japanese dead and over 120 wounded. Americans lost 118; there were 352 wounded, and four missing. The diversion was successful as it kept about 1,000 Japanese soldiers from reinforcing the troops at Cape Gloucester. There were also 89 Japanese aircraft reportedly shot down by American pilots.[36]

For the reader's interest (which you may want to skip and come back to read later), the remainder of this chapter is the full, original and unedited account of the battle at Arawe titled: *Campaign on New Britain,* Chapter 9, Flashback: "Action at Arawe: Concept of Mission" from the Historical Section – Division of Public Information – Headquarters U.S. Marine Corps by Lt. Col. Frank O. Hough, USMCR and Major John A. Crown, USMCR pages 140 through 151:

> The Arawe operation began eleven days before the Marines' initial landing at Cape Gloucester, and lasted until long after the last Japanese had been cleared out of the

northern portion of western New Britain. It took place at all only as a sort of makeshift afterthought on the part of ALAMO Force planners; yet it was conceived as an integral part of the overall New Britain campaign and as such deserves treatment in these pages, even at risk of confusing the general chronology.

Because the operation did not add up to a great deal, strategically or tactically, and the scale of fighting was overshadowed by that which took place on the island's opposite shore, many observers tended to discount it as a sort of comic opera interlude wherein a Japanese force numbering few more than 1,000 at maximum strength check-mated more than 5,000 U.S. troops. The Japanese, on their part, regarded it as a victory; one of sufficient importance to earn their commander on the scene the signal honor of two commendations from the Emperor himself.

Both conceptions oversimplify. No operation is especially comical to the troops participating, and the Americans who fought at Arawe (more properly, Cape Merkus) performed successfully every task assigned them; indeed, everything that the very limited nature of their mission permitted them to attempt. Thus, the "victory" aspect existed only in the imagination of the Japanese, since in actuality they accomplished nothing of the slightest importance. As a diversionary action, the invasion implicated one Japanese battalion which otherwise could have fought at Cape Gloucester, and the Arawe landing's indirect contribution to the ultimate destruction of enemy air power in New Britain would be difficult to overestimate.

As brought out in discussion of planning for the New Britain operation, the Gasmata phase had been cancelled and the target shifted to Arawe as less formidable, yet possessing the sheltered waters that the Navy wanted for development of a PT boat base. That Arawe also boasted an airstrip of sorts was a coincidence destined to have some curious repercussions: making a Japanese hero of major Shinjiro Komori, and causing considerable embarrassment to General MacArthur's public relations staff. The mission assigned the task force (coded DIRECTOR) was merely to "seize and defend a suitable location for the establishment of light naval facilities;" that, and to reconnoiter westward to determine the feasibility of a supply route up the valley of the Itni River for possible use in operations against Cape Gloucester."

Arawe Z-Day:

Designated on 30th November to accomplish this simple mission was the 112th Cavalry RCT, reinforced, commanded by Brigadier General Julian W. Cunningham, USA, a unit inexperienced in combat and lacking amphibious training, with little chance for acquiring much now, Z-Day being set for 15th December. That a foul-up might occur appeared something more than a remote possibility.

Nature contributed a few additional difficulties. Although amphibious scouts had been ashore briefly a few days before, the off-lying waters had not been explored, and there was no certainty that landing craft could reach shore through the complex of uncharted reefs known to exist. The plan, therefore, called for two smaller groups to land on subsidiary beaches in rubber boats from APD's, while the main force came in on LVT's to the western shore of Cape Merkus. These amtracks included 10 Buffaloes and 29 Alligators, manned by Company A, 1st Amphibian Tractor Battalion, 1st Marine Division, and traveled to the scene aboard *USS Carter Hall*, one of the new LSD's (landing ship, dock).

To get the terribly vulnerable rubber boats ashore, General Cunningham, chose to rely on surprise rather than strength: landing under cover of darkness with no forewarning. "Although it was considered that the moonlight might prevent surprise, the Landing Force Commander desired to attempt it without any preliminary bombardment". The group designated for nearby Pilelo Island landed successfully unopposed and destroyed a small party of the enemy. But moonlight disclosed the boats of the other group about 100 yards short of the eastern beach, where the Japanese took them under heavy, partially enfilading machine-gun and what was estimated to be 37mm fire".

Destroyer *USS Shaw* lay some 3,000 yards offshore in this sector, prepared to deal with targets of opportunity, but in the uncertain light her gunners could not discern the boats against the dark jungle shore, nor immediately sport the source of enemy fire; hence, held their own fire for many agonizing minutes until sure of not hitting friendly troops". Once she opened, Shaw silenced the enemy with two salvos. By then, however, the soldiers had suffered many casualties, most of the boats had been sunk, and the survivors were intent only on

33

getting away from there. General Cunningham, understandably irked, had some bitter comments to make regarding *Shaw's* delay in opening fire, which he declared endured for 20 minutes".

He also had a few things to say about the delay in the main landing, evidently the result of a combination of factors. The amphibian tractors were launched so far from their target as to require one and a half hours for their approach, during which time the different speeds of the two types of vehicle caused the formation to become overextended and generally fouled-up". The landing was scheduled for after daybreak, to be preceded by 15 minutes of naval gunfire by the supporting destroyers. Brigadier General W.F. Heavy, commanding officer of 2nd Engineer Special Brigade, was observing the operation from aboard a submarine chaser and became concerned over the possibility of the faster Buffaloes reaching the beach simultaneously with the friendly preparatory fire, so intercepted the leaders and ordered them to halt". This relieved the confusion not at all, and further delays ensured for which General Cunningham, evidently unaware of General Heavey's action, blamed the Navy.

But for all this unpropitious beginning, the story had a happy ending. The fire of the destroyers, though postponed, was extended in duration and proved eminently satisfactory. Air strikes and rocket barrages from close in took up where the shelling left off; whatever Japanese might have been on hand betook themselves elsewhere, and the horseless cavalrymen landed unopposed.

They found themselves on a roughly crescent-shaped terrain feature terminating in Cape Merkus, which connected with the mainland via a narrow neck called Arawe Peninsula in most of the reports. The soldiers reached this readily defensible ground by mid-afternoon, capturing three unemplaced mountain guns and mopping up a few stragglers along the way, and set immediately about digging positions and clearing fields of fire. With capture of off-lying islands by patrol action, this completed their main mission, as the land thus secured afforded control of the area wanted by the Navy for PT boat facilities.

The First Twelve Days

But if the Japanese ground defense of Arawe appeared pretty feeble, the violence of their reaction by air exceeded all expectations. Daylight attacks on the beach head began within a few hours of the landings and persisted with little noticeable diminution for a week. As many as 100 planes of all types coming over in a single raid: far heavier opposition then the enemy had offered at Bougainville or the operations in northern New Guinea. This gave rise to some serious concern regarding their capabilities for opposing the Cape Gloucester invasion, if the seizure of a comparatively unimportant place like Arawe could rouse them to such frenzy.

Actually, considering the compact nature of the target, these attacks were almost grotesquely ineffective, the most serious loss occurring at the 29th Evacuation Hospital where two men were killed and four wounded on Z- plus 2 and 18 tons of medical supplies destroyed four days later. But their intensity and persistence worked serious nerve strain on the men on the ground, until, like troops under almost any conditions, they began to become acclimated. Then, as fighter cover and antiaircraft fire shot down the attacking planes, and South Pacific fliers increased the effectiveness of their attacks on Rabaul airfields from the new Bougainville bases, the raids on Arawe diminished until at length they petered out altogether.

In the meanwhile, patrols of the 112th Cavalry, sometimes accompanied by ANGAU officers, explored the country beyond the defense line in an effort to contact the enemy, locate trails and bring in friendly natives for rehabilitation. One such group, operating some four miles to the east, discovered the so- called Lupin Airdrome.

This was perhaps the most useless piece of real estate in the whole region. Constructed in 1937 as an emergency landing strip (600 x 60 yards) on the route between New Guinea and Rabaul, it had been used only once prior to the war, by a single light plane. When forced to evacuate New Britain, Australians had plowed deep furrows across the runway to make it unserviceable. Since it offered no possibilities for enlargement or improvement, the Japanese had not bothered to repair it, and now tall kunai grass over-grew furrows and all.

The patrol went on about its business, monumentally unimpressed with its find, but on its return the leader naturally reported where he had been and what he had seen. Nothing in DIRECTOR Task Force orders stipulated that the useless field should be seized; even if it had been good, the commanding general would not have wanted it at this time, owing to its distance from the beachhead and the impossibility of including it within a defensive perimeter with the number of troops available. However, seizure of enemy air facilities always has news value. So some zealous public relations officer at one of the higher echelons promoted that beat-up kunai patch to the rank of "airdrome" and released word of its "capture" to newspaper and radio correspondents.

During the first week or so following the landing, U.S. patrols roamed at will through the territory to the eastward, making only rare contact with occasional stragglers. On 24th December General Cunningham reported his casualties as 25 killed in action, 71 wounded and 27 missing. In return for these losses, Americans estimated 78 Japanese dead by the 22nd. These were identified as personnel of the 115th Infantry and 14th Field Artillery Regiments, which caused some confusion and difficulty in estimating enemy's total numbers, as Allied intelligence had previously identified both units as operating in northern New Guinea.

But signs began to occur indicating that this early quiet would be short-lived. Patrol contacts to the east became more frequent. During the night of 25-26 December, an enemy force estimated to number 100 made a determined assault on the main line of resistance across the neck of the peninsula and was repulsed with some difficulty, 12 infiltrators being killed within the U.S. positions. The same night an advance observation post at Mio, near the mouth of the Sigul River, reported itself surrounded, though men and equipment successfully evacuated by water the following day.

On 27th December the task force announced that the Japanese had seized the villages of Meselia and Umtingalu, west of the airstrip, and U.S. outposts and patrols were withdrawn within the MLR. Documents captured in a clash near the latter village identified the enemy elements participating as belonging to the 1st Battalion, 81st Infantry, and the 81st Naval Defense Unit. Since the main strength of these was believed to be at Gasmata, General Cunningham drew the not illogical deduction that reinforcements were being moved into the area from that point.

In the meanwhile, an unexpected contact had occurred many miles to the west. An amphibious patrol of 19 men, including an ANGAU officer and four natives, proceeding in two LCVP's toward the Itni River to carry out the task force's secondary mission, was attacked suddenly at dawn of 18th December near Cape Peiho by seven armed Japanese barges packed with troops. In attempting to fight their way through the enemy formation, both landing craft ran aground and were destroyed. Observation of continued barge activity along this stretch of coast led General Cunningham to report on 27 December that the enemy were probably pouring in fresh troops from the Itni region as well as Gasmata. He requested reinforcements at once, and Company G, 158th Infantry arrived on 27th December followed by the remainder of 2.158 on 5th January 1944.

Enter Tobuse and Komori:

As may be deduced from description of Japanese dispositions in Chapter IV, the force carried in the embattled enemy barges comprised the advance echelon of Major Asyuki Toubuse's 1st Battalion, 141st Infantry, hurrying from Cape Bushing to reinforce the Merkus garrison in accordance with General Matsuda's orders. And the unit operating east of the U.S. perimeter was the 1st Battalion, 81st Infantry under Major Shinjiro Komori which had moved overland via the rough and mountainous cross-island trail from Iboki on the north coast.

Komori had been en route since early in the month and arrived within earshot of the air and naval gunfire preparation for the landing on the 15th. Pressing on he reached the village of Didmop on the Pulie River some ten miles northeast of the perimeter, where he paused to recognize and to rally the retiring survivors of the original garrison. Delayed by difficult terrain and river crossings, he did not move into attacking position until the 25th, when he launched the abortive night assault previously mentioned. That a Japanese commander should not hesitate to hurl a single under strength battalion (less one company) against a reinforced RCT in prepared positions is in keeping with the tactical concepts of those people. That the attack "did not succeed" as Komori himself put it, is even less surprising.

This repulse made Komori sufficiently prudent to defer further attacks until the arrival of Major Tobuse's battalion, which had become lost cutting its way through trackless jungle from its landing place at Omoi, some eight miles to the northwest. The two units made contact on 28h December, and Komori as senior officer assumed command of the combined force. But conferences with his fellow major decided him against any further attacks on that strongly manned MLR across the peninsula's narrow neck. Perhaps they had heard the triumphant U.S. broadcast regarding the "capture" of the "airdrome" and concluded that if the Americans thought it that important, the principal mission of the Japanese force was to prevent their enemy from using it. With this end in view, they set about preparing to contain the invaders on the narrow peninsula.

Their tactical dispositions showed considerable ingenuity. In the high ground 600 to 700 yards from the U.S. main line of resistance they established, not a single consolidated position, but a series of alternate positions from which they could place harassing mortar and automatic weapons fire on the invaders, simply moving from one to another when spotted by the Americans. And so cleverly did they take advantage of terrain and concealment that spotting became very difficult. Some conception of what Cunningham was up against is conveyed by the commanding general's own words:

"This is not an organized position in the accepted sense of the word it consists apparently of shallow trenches and deep fox holes...." ground is covered with a thick green mat about 12 to 18 inches in depth which makes observation absolutely impossible.....Officers and men ..... report that they have not seen a single Japanese and that they are unable to locate machine guns firing on them from a distance of 10 to 20 yards"

For several days following Tobuse's arrival, contact was limited to random skirmishing. On 4th January Komori reported repulsing a strong attack and two days later received his first citation from the emperor for this achievement. On the 5th he set total Japanese losses to date as 65 killed, 57 wounded and 14 missing, in addition to 10 died of illness. Meanwhile the Americans continued to shell his positions so heavily and persistently that by the 9th he confessed himself "getting a little annoyed with it".

On the opposite side of the perimeter, General Cunningham, on his part, was getting more than a little annoyed with Komori. Understanding his mission to be essentially defensive now that its primary object had been achieved, it never occurred to him that he was facing a "victorious" opponent (by Imperial accolade). Instead, he regarded the Japanese as no more than an unmitigated nuisance so long as they remained within harassing range. To put an end to this state of affairs, he attempted "three distinct sorties", but "the mission of driving the enemy out of position has not been accomplished by ground troops as now organized without prohibitive cost". He requested tanks and increased air support for his next attempt.

The tank unit most readily available was Company B, 1st Tank Battalion, a component of the 1st Marine Division which had been left behind at Finschhafen because of transportation shortage and limited range for tank operations in the inhospitable terrain of the Cape Gloucester region. Accordingly, this organization was attached in total to DIRECTOR Task Force on 11th January and reached Arawe via LCT the following day.

Company B was equipped with light tanks: M3A's mounting 37mm guns. Preparatory to the attack, officers and men spent three days in active reconnaissance and drill in tank-infantry tactics with the army Unit assigned for the mission: 2nd Battalion, 158th Infantry. The plan called for two tank platoons in assault and one in reserve, each attached to one infantry company.

Following intensive air and artillery preparation, the attack jumped off at 0800 on 16th January with ten tanks in line across a 500-yard front, each supported by approximately one squad of foot soldiers. Difficult terrain and stubborn enemy resistance slowed the advance to a crawl. Tanks bogged down in soft ground and bomb craters, while jungle undergrowth impeded progress and heightened the difficulties of tank-infantry cooperation.

Two machines were hit but soon retrieved. A section of the reserve moved out to over-come a pocket of resistance some 500-yards beyond the line of departure, and the assault elements overran all opposition, destroying the enemy's prepared positions and crushing numerous automatic weapons and one 75mm mountain gun, to reach the predetermined objective at about 1600. Since no part of the plan called for holding this exposed position with the limited force available, the attackers withdrew at leisure to the MLR after destroying two or their own tanks which had become hopelessly bogged down, satisfied that their enemy had been dealt a staggering blow.

Komori Makes a Noble Resolve:

The following day the tanks of Company B's reserve platoon moved out with flame throwers to eliminate a small pocket of resistance which the enemy had reoccupied during the night, but encountered no other trace of the Japanese.

For Komori had withdrawn his remnants in fairly good order, determined, as he radioed brigade headquarters, to "fight till the glorious end to defend the airfield" Telegraphic orders the following day made this mission official, with the admonition: ".... Upset the enemy plan to construct an airfield".   Inasmuch as the "enemy" had no such plan, action that followed partook of the nature of shadowboxing. Nevertheless, Komori's dispatches to higher headquarters for the next three weeks continued to emphasize the fact that the airfield was still in Japanese hands.   In recognition of this notable achievement, he received a second Imperial citation, relayed by 17th Division headquarters, on 7th February.   The U.S. press and radio, having reported capture of the field back in December, grew more and more bewildered – and said so.

The tank-infantry attack that cleared out all the Japanese within harassing range cost General Cunningham's command 20 killed and 40 wounded.   He estimated enemy killed at 55 and took one prisoner of war.   Major Komori did not report his losses for this particular action but listed his total losses to date on 21st January as 116 killed and 117 wounded, which conveys some idea of the nature of the fighting here as compared with that taking place simultaneously at Cape Gloucester, where on several occasions twice that number of the enemy were killed in a single day's action.

How many men Komori commanded at any time remains problematical as no captured documents enumerated these, but it appears unlikely that their numbers ever greatly exceeded 1,000. With these he had to guard his approaches from several directions as well as handle the difficult distribution of supplies over an extensive area – when there were any supplies to distribute. Early in the operation, the force had been supplied by air drop, often in daylight within view of the Americans, and many barges had stolen in from Gasmata under cover of darkness with food and ammunition, evacuating wounded and sick on their return trip. But as Allied grip tightened on sea and air, Komori became increasingly dependent on the trickle which found its way over the tortuous trail from Iboki. Carrying and distributing these supplies imposed still more of a drain on his manpower, and he withdrew his headquarters to Didmop to give more attention to this phase, leaving direct defense of the airfield to Major Tobuse.

Disillusionment of a "Hero"

Fighting deteriorated into a matter of rare patrol contacts and random skirmishing; of ambush and counter ambush. A strong U.S. combat patrol drove Major Tobuse's "defenders" from the airfield to alternate covering positions 300 yards to the west and ranged on all the way to the Pulie River unmolested. But when the Americans displayed no slightest interest in the precious airfield itself, in defense of which the Japanese were prepared to "fight till the glorious end", it began to dawn belatedly on Komori that his mission might have certain quixotic aspects. Meanwhile his sick list mounted as the shortage of food and medical supplies became increasingly acute.

When arrival of fresh radio batteries on 5th February enabled him to resume interrupted communications with 17th Division headquarters, he concluded a gloomy situation report:

"At present, the airfield is covered with grass 4 to 5 (feet) high. The airfield, 200 m (sic) in width 800 m in length, will be serviceable only for small airplanes. However, it will take quite some time to develop it. Consequently, I believe that it will not be of great value".

He had received copy of orders governing withdrawal of General Matsuda's force from the Borgen Bay area to the Talasea-Gasmata line as early as 22nd January, and began casting envious eyes in the same direction. On 8th February he hinted more broadly to that effect:

41

"As has been reported, the value of Merkus airfield is so insignificant that it seems the enemy has no intention of using it…. Due to damage sustained by enemy bombardments and to the increased number of patients, it becomes more and more difficult to carry out the present mission…. It is my opinion that as the days pass, replenishment of supplies will become more and more difficult and fighting strength will be further diminished; our new line will be cut off and consequently leave us with no alternative but self-destruction".

Division headquarters, however, was not impressed, and a telegraphic response the following day ordered him curtly to continue his mission. "Wondered what to do about the order all night long", Komori recorded in his diary. "Could not sleep last night …. I felt dizzy all day today".

He was cheered briefly when some of Tobuse's people ambushed an American patrol, killing two, wounding two and capturing two "automatic rifles" (probably Tommy guns). But the inconsiderate enemy retaliated next day, killing a valued sergeant major, another sergeant and a runner, and chasing a supply detail so deep into the jungle that two days were required to extricate it. Some of his own men broke into a warehouse to loot the meager stores remaining.

Despairing of further succor by sea, on 18th February he began evacuation of his hospital patients overland via the difficult trail toward Iboki. At last, on 24th February, he received the overdue warning order to prepare for his own retirement and promptly alerted his units. This was implemented early the following morning by receipt of 17th Division Operation Order A Number 106 directing him to fall back and join Colonel Jiro Sato, then at Upmadung collecting supplies preparatory to covering the 65th Brigade's further withdrawal. At once Komori ordered in all detachments and had his forward echelon in motion within a few hours.

In the meanwhile, the Americans had been organizing for another attack designed to clear the whole area, once and for all. On 27th February two platoons of Company B, 1st (Marine) Tank Battalion, moved out in support of the 2nd Squadron, 112th Cavalry and reached the airfield, which Major Tobuse had quit by order the previous day, without encountering so much as an enemy straggler. However, a patrol pushing farther toward the Pulie River came up with the rear elements of Tobuse's force en route to join Komori at Didmop and wounded three Japanese in the last armed encounter to occur in the region. The Arawe operation was over.

Major Komori put his own headquarters on the trail at 0630 on 28th February, "leaving behind the graves of 150 men", as he recorded in writing finis to his futile, impossible mission. He was not sorry to leave; at least, not then.

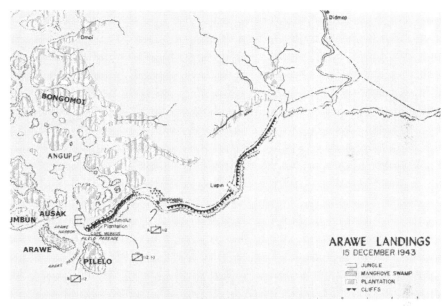

Map of Arawe Islands landing - December 15, 1943

Villagers from Amalut Village with WWII mortar rounds.

Micah with undetonated projectile at Amalut. WNBP, PNG

Abandoned USA M3A Stuart Tank at Demgalu Village. WNBP, PNG

Chapter 5

DISCOVERING A DIVE BOMBER – VAL #2

In the following month on April 19, 2003, we again loaded up the boat with fuel and the backpacks with biscuits, then headed toward Wako Village which was approximately 25 nautical miles (29 miles) west of Kandrian. We stopped at nearby Osol Village and picked up Patrick Alas as our guide, then proceeded on to a small inlet. After anchoring the boat in the shallow water, we were ferried to shore in a dugout canoe. We hiked through mangroves for a while then into the jungle, tripping on vines and stumbling over logs.

Within 45 minutes we came upon the crash site of another Val. (See page xii - NO. 5) The three-blade propeller was up on a hill with one blade broken off. The 14-cylinder Mitsubishi Kinsei engine was down in the valley about nine meters (30 feet) away. It was really corroded, and one of the cylinders had come off and was lying nearby. The tail stabilizer section was also found with the rear wheel, and the boys examined it thoroughly and tried to reconstruct it. Both of the stout landing gear, minus rubber tires (possibly burned off), were lying among the wreckage. We also found some instruments which were nearly unidentifiable because of the corrosion. The guide showed us two cylinders approximately 100 millimeters (four inches) in diameter and probably 76 centimeters (30 inches) tall; he thought they were possibly bombs. To us though, they appeared to be small oxygen tanks that we assumed were used for high-altitude flying. There was, however, a 15-centimeter (six-inch) long forward remnant of a 75-millimeter (three-inch) wing bomb lying among the wreckage. We also discovered other pieces of the wing's inner structure which were identifiable. We did not excavate too much in an attempt to find any identifying numbers. Since this was the first airplane crash site on land we had ever seen, we did not really know what we wanted to find. To have found a bullet to take home would have made our journey worthwhile.

Actually, the viewing of a crash site on land for the first time is rather unimpressive. There are too many little pieces scattered all over the place. We were hoping to see something that looked more like an airplane, such as the one we had found in the water. I had a deep somber thought that we were standing where a couple of airmen had lost their lives and that their remains were probably still there somewhere. We decided to conclude our search for the day and took a 30-minute hike back to the boat and made our way home before dark.

THE MURDER OF CAPTAIN GRAY

In August of 2003, the people from Pililo Island showed me some 50-millimeter (two-inch) shell casings they had been using as flower holders. One man told me that during the assault of Cape Merkus in the Arawes, a number of rubber boats had been sunk. I was certain that he was telling the truth since I had seen that historical assault in the movie *Attack! The Battle for New Britain.* The movie had depicted soldiers launching and embarking into those rubber boats as part of their training. Another man, John Kakiu, told me that he had gone to the Catholic school in Vunapope by Rabaul in 1937. He was there when the Japanese invaded Rabaul and "saw Captain Gray, an Australian officer who was captured at Wide Bay, after being forced to dig his own grave, was then beheaded by Dr. Chikami." John and two men from the island of New Ireland, which is east of Rabaul, buried his body on the mountain by Vunapope. After the war, he told this story to a man named Robinson who then returned to retrieve the remains for proper burial.

Research also verified this eyewitness account. According to Brother John Mahrhofer of Vunapope, he saw Captain John Robert Gray of the Royal Australian Engineers being marched between one armed party, followed by another party carrying shovels. Later, "boys" of the Vunapope School said that the Captain had been beheaded and buried in a grave. He died on February 20, 1942, and is now buried in the first row, grave AA1, at Bita Paka War Cemetery in Rabaul. Captain Gray was posthumously recommended for the Victoria Cross, the highest military honor available for Commonwealth Countries and very rarely awarded.[37]

There is another report of Captain Gray which, although recorded, does not correspond with the eyewitness account I uncovered. In the book, *The Darkest Hour* by Bruce Gamble, it was recorded that,

Captain Gray was subjected to some of the worst atrocities. He was the engineering officer captured at the Tol plantation and was the victim of a particularly heinous crime committed by members of the 3rd Battalion. He was taken to Vunapope rather than imprisoned at the Malaguna Road stockade; he was tied to a palm tree outside Lieutenant Colonel Kuwada's residence and questioned for hours in the blazing sun. Periodically, the Japanese slapped him with a length of rope, beat him with planking, and they sprinkled biting ants on his body. When they grew tired of the interrogation, they took Gray to a distant hill where missionary students witnessed his execution. First, a doctor named Chikumi, whose reputation for malevolence had earned him the ironic nickname, "Sunshine Sam," administered an injection that rendered Gray semi-conscious. Next, Chikumi performed a vivisection and removed Gray's still-beating heart, for no better reason than to study his reactions.

A statement made by Father Joseph Reischl of the Catholic Mission in Bitagalip, Kokopo, is similar to what Bruce Gamble had recorded. Father Reischl said a Japanese medical assistant named Takeuchi who seemed interested in Christianity often engaged him in conversation. Takeuchi was apparently being ridiculed by Japanese officers at the hospital for expressing his convictions that all the wrong they were doing would be paid back to them. The officers jeered him saying,

The missionaries were all in prison and couldn't do anything; the gods of the white people were of no help to them – the Japanese have superiority in the whole of the Pacific and the whites would never get it back." He countered by saying, "The God of the whites likes to punish them so He called the Japanese and gave them superiority to fulfill this punishment but because we are cruel and have no principles, He will take it back.

Takeuchi then told Father Reichl about Captain Gray and how he had been captured at Wide Bay where many Australians were killed. He was beaten on the barge while in transit back to Rabaul as he made Commander Kuwata very angry by repeatedly saying, "You have murdered my comrades – you are not gentlemen."

After they had arrived in Rabaul, Captain Gray was told he was to be killed. He asked for a piece of paper, which was given to him, on which he wrote a short message to his wife that said he was going to be killed and she was not to be sad, they would meet again in Heaven. He then knelt down and prayed. Afterwards, he was made to lie on his back, and Doctor Chikami injected both of his arms with an unknown drug that made him become unconscious. Dr. Chikami then "Cut open the breast and carefully lifted out the heart and timed its beating with a watch. After a short while, Captain Gray died." Captain Gray could be considered a martyr as he lived and died by his principles.[38]

THE EXECUTION OF JOSEPH

Another story I heard from the villagers at Kumbun was of seven or eight "white skins" that were brought through the area by the Aliwo plantation manager, Harold Koch, whose grave is now in Kandrian. Koch guided the men to Kumbun Island in the Arawes. An Anglican mission station there was staffed by Father Bernard Moore who had a schooner named *Sailwind*. He agreed to take them to Finschhaven. This boat, with a crewman from Utkumbun named Daniel Matavi, left at 6 P.M. and took the "white skins" to Finschhaven then returned in the morning. This story is interestingly similar, although the number of "white skins" is different, to John Lerew's account. Father Moore was later mysteriously found lying dead in his bed, fully dressed in his Priestly robe. His body was found by Nikodimas Somai from Kumbun. His grave marker at Kumbun village reads: "Being Station Priest in 1933 to 1942 and died on the 28-2-42. The course [sic] of his death was not known." This again raises the question, "Why did he not go with Lerew and the two planters a couple weeks earlier?"

There is another interesting story that I chose to share here in hopes that somehow, someday, someone will read it and gain closure over a lost relative. It is about a man named Joseph. Joseph was nicknamed "Kirani." He was reported to possibly have been from Samoa or Tahiti. He worked for the London Missionary Society in Rabaul and married a lady from Kumbun Island named, "Kuskus." They adopted a hapkas (child born from interracial parents) Chinese girl named Margarita. Later, Joseph worked at the Aliwo plantation, and they returned to Kumbun after Father Bernard Moore had mysteriously died there in the village. Upon their return, the Japanese infiltrated the area and, thinking he was a spy, executed him.

The story is that he stood next to a hole as a Samurai sword was laid on his shoulder. The Japanese soldier called out "Nippon Razor" and sliced his head off. An Anglican Priest from Kumbun, known as Father Vincent, says his biological father buried the body.

There is another account of the same incident as told by Anut from Pililo, who claimed to be an eyewitness to the murder at the age of eight years old. He said he held the basket (purses) of the three natives – Lewale, Dagadan, and Laudik – who dug the grave. Afterwards, Joseph was given a cigarette. He was then blindfolded and shot in the forehead with a rifle that blew the back of his head off. His body staggered, and he was bayoneted in the chest and pushed into the grave. Joe Kamano (possibly the officer who was once in charge of soldiers at Kandrian) was also there with four or five Japanese soldiers who may have been officers. I was told by Anut that "the grave is at the top of the mountain where the stream comes out on the beach on the east side of the peninsula at a place called, 'Mapatlo.'" I asked him if he would take me there but he replied that he was "too old and frail and unable to climb the mountain."

After the war, Joseph's wife Kuskus took their adopted daughter, Margarita, back to Rabaul and the Catholic Mission took care of her. She later married a policeman and bore two sons, Peter Arul and Andrew Posai, who now live near Gasmata. I met Margarita in Kimbe on the north side of the island. She said that she and her parents lived on the coast at Amalut (known by the Japanese as Cape Merkus and the location of the Arawe invasion). One day, the Japanese came by and told her father to come up to the top of the mountain. He held her in his arms and said good-bye but he would not let her go with him. She unwillingly let him go, deeply hurt and sobbing vigorously as he climbed the path up the side of the mountain. She later heard that he had been killed.

That is all I know of this story, but I thought that Joseph's story needed to be told. If anyone who reads this knows someone who left Samoa or Tahiti and served with the London Missionary Society in Papua New Guinea before WWII, it would be informative to pass this story on to any known relatives he may have who are still living.

Mariko with *Val* propeller by Wako Village. WNBP, PNG

Grave of Captain Gray at Bita Paka War Cemetery. Rabaul, ENBP, PNG

Chapter 6

THE WINDING PULIE

Here is a dilemma which I have faced for a long time: when the local people tell a story, they tend to exaggerate it a bit at first. Some have told me they do it to impress the hearers so they, in turn, will brag about who had told them the best story. Well, it gets one's attention; I can say that! What would anyone do if they heard of an airplane in the jungle that was "hanging in the tree vines and the oil was still dripping from the engine?" If people were like us, they would grab their hiking shoes and start running to find it! That is what happened on November 1, 2003. After having heard this story, we took off as soon as we could and sailed up the Pulie River. About one hour from the coast, we passed an area where a Japanese barge base had once been located and where a U.S. PT (Patrol Torpedo) boat had strafed during the war, but we did not stop to search for artifacts. It was interesting to consider how risky that attack would have been at night without the ability to see the river banks.

The story from the book, *Devil boats: The PT War Against Japan* by William B. Bruer was that when the PT boat idled up the river, someone stood on the bow sounding for water depth. There was also a Japanese interpreter on board, and when they arrived at the barge base, the man yelled out to those on shore. The Japanese thought it was one of their barges so they turned on the lights, and when they did, they were strafed. The approximately 24-meter (80-foot) long PT boat somehow turned around in the narrow river and gunned it to get away.[39] It is difficult to figure out how they could have done that as the river is meandering, and speeding in the dark would have been crazy. Having read that story, we sailed up the river assuming that if a PT boat had made it in these waters, we did not have to worry about water depth. The Pulie is a beautiful, winding river, and there are "spot tail bass" in there, but we were not there to catch fish – on that occasion.

TREKKING THROUGH THE JUNGLE

– VALS #3 & #4

We met Joe Warku from Urin who first showed us a four-foot-long, one-foot-diameter unexploded bomb lying alongside a tree. Of course, I had to take pictures of our kids around the bomb. It was probably good that Joan had not joined us on that day. After a short planning session, we eagerly headed west through the jungle at a rapid pace. We ran all the way, leaving no time to tighten a shoe lace for fear of being left behind and getting lost on the trail. After 45 minutes, we arrived at the airplane crash site, (See page xii - NO. 4) but it was not hanging in the trees. Like the other airplane we had seen, it was scattered all around. That was somewhat of a disappointment. In the midst of the wreckage this time, though, we found three oxygen cylinders. The engine, along with some fuselage pieces and a round bullet canister for the machine gun, was also found.

We were accompanied by a Japanese fisherman, Toshi. He had come to Kandrian to catch a world-record yellow fin tuna and was interested in accompanying us. He was quite helpful when we found a piece of the fuselage that had a stencil painted on it; Toshi was able to translate for us. That stencil information helped us to identify the airplane as indeed another Val, manufacturer number 3487. This airplane was most likely lost during Japanese air raids against the Arawe beachhead from December 17-26, 1943.[40] Again, sensing we were at a grave site, I asked our Japanese friend what would be a respectful, cultural thing to do in this situation, to which he replied, "Bring flowers." We returned to the boat, hiking at what seemed like lightning speed, which left us all strewed out along the trail with Toshi heading up the rear, exhausted. I do not know why our guide had walked so rapidly; perhaps that was his normal pace but it nearly killed us. I have found if one walks down a gravel road, most local people will lag behind. Reportedly, the little rocks hurt their calloused feet. On a soft jungle trail, however, they can leave us in their dust.

There was an old man by the name of Lukas Sulu at the hamlet of Moyioko, which was close to the bomb we had seen earlier in the day. He told us of a fuselage deeper in the jungle on the other side of the Pulie River. That was quite a hike away, so we said that someday we would return and he could show it to us then.

After the New Year, on January 30, 2004, we again set sail to find an airplane. A teenage girl, Thompson Makawong's daughter, guided us on a 25-minute hike north between Naverau and Magap River through a garden to the crash site. (See page xii - NO. 6) There, we found only small pieces of the tail section and a landing strut which looked like another Val. There was half a data plate on the tail with Japanese writing; it had instructions on how to lower the landing gear. There was no information about the type of aircraft it represented. Some other aluminum pieces had been heaped up alongside a tree, and more pieces were in the water at the mouth of the river on the east side; it appeared to indicate someone's intentions to sell these items later. We did not see the engine nor did we find a stencil with the manufacturer's number. This was probably the least impressive site we had seen to date, so we returned home somewhat disappointed.

March 26, 2004, found us making a hurried voyage to Wako again after we heard rumors from there. It was reported that someone had found an airplane that still had the machine gun on the back. In addition, a medallion the size of a PNG Kina coin (approximately 37 millimeter or one-and-a-half inches in diameter) had been found in the cockpit. That was all it took, so off we went to Wako village to search for Pita Lekung. After we had found him, he and Rafail guided us into the jungle where we all became lost (and it is not a good thing when even the guides get lost) but eventually arrived at the same airplane wreckage we had seen about a year earlier, in April of 2003. (See page xii - NO. 5) That was quite another disappointment, and after excavating a short while, we returned by a more direct trail to the river bank. This time, there was no dugout canoe to ferry us to the boat. We waded through the waist-high water and muck while trying to keep our cameras dry and our shoes on our feet.

Upon returning our two guides to Wako, we met John Tukai who told us of an airplane he had found one day while he was chasing a wild pig with his dogs in hot pursuit. He said that the airplane was complete, but that the front glass was broken. He walked around to the side and looked into the side door area. Naturally, I was greatly interested and asked if he could make a sketch of the aircraft; he drew a two-engine model. The only problem was that he could not remember where it was, as he was running wild himself when he found the airplane and he has not been able to find it since; this was another dead end. We left him with the challenge to find the airplane and we told him that we would return someday with a reward if he found it and could show it to us.

Val undercarriage. WNBP, PNG

Val date plate manufacturer number 3487. WNBP, PNG

Val engine. WNBP,PNG

Val oxygen tanks. WNBP, PNG

Val tail wheel. WNBP, PNG

Val stencil Aichi D3A2 type 99 model 22 MN 3487. WNBP, PNG

Chapter 7

THE LOST FLEET

On April 2, 2004, we made our second trip to Gasmata. A Korean man named "Iljae," a member of SIL (Summer Institute of Linguistics/Wycliffe Bible Translators), chartered my boat. The Gasmata airstrip (See page xiii – NO. 13) had been closed, and Kandrian where I resided was the closest he could get by air. The seas were fairly calm, so we enjoyed the two-and-a-half-hour boat ride. Having been to Gasmata only twice before in 15 years, it was still quite interesting, and I was again going to be able to see the remains of the Japanese airplanes at the Gasmata airstrip.

Once we arrived at Gasmata and Iljae had disembarked, I explored a bunker along the shoreline. Some of the local people told me of a Japanese ship that was sunk in the passageway. Being curious, I drove the boat back and forth in the passageway, and each time I passed over "something," my depth finder would show shallow sections then drop off quickly again to indicate deeper sections. I made six passes marking what I assumed to be the sunken ship, so I knew fairly well where it was and could now locate it on a future dive.

Ten days later, we returned to Gasmata to pick up Iljae; we decided to go a day early and do some more trekking and some diving research. On April 12, 2004, we dived on the location that I had previously detected with my depth sounder. (See page xiii - NO. 19) The water was fairly murky with visibility of only about 6 meters (20 feet). As we nervously descended, not knowing what we would find, a large ship came into view. This ship was different from the *Taka Saka Maru* in that it had two cargo holds in front of the conning tower and the bow was more rounded. The steel plating was starting to separate like a banana peel from the sides of the boat. It was sitting flat in 33 meters (110 feet) of water; therefore, we had plenty of time to explore this great site. The low visibility did take some of the excitement out of the discovery, and we only have some blurry pictures for that memory.

During that time, we also met a younger man named Pius who told us of an airplane he had seen in the water alongside a reef. We asked him to guide us to the location, and we eagerly put on our diving gear and jumped into the water, excitedly anticipating the finding of another warplane in the water. Pius had said that it was not too deep; he had seen it while free diving for pislama (sea cucumbers used for soap, medicine and consumption in China and Malaysia). Micah and I went back and forth at different depths, but we never found the reportedly intact airplane with its wings outstretched. Pius suggested we go to Akur village to find another person who could give clearer instructions as to where the airplane was located. This time the female informant said that it was on the back side of the reef, so we started the routine again. To our disappointment, we never found an airplane. We kept that story in the back of our minds to consider it for another day of plane-searching in the future.

In August of 2004, my oldest son Micah, having completed his high school courses, was ready to leave our tropical paradise. It was difficult to believe that almost 19 years had passed since we first arrived in PNG and Micah was only five months old. He had been with us from the beginning so all of our memories of PNG included him. My wife Joan taught him to read and write, then home-schooled him all of his educational years. For at least one month prior to his departure date, I contemplated his leaving; I often would have to fight back tears as the emotions were so strong. I did not know what I would do without him nearby. I was sure going to miss him. Joan had a stronger upper lip and felt that it was time for him to get on with his life. I accompanied him back to the United States and got him settled into a nine-month course of study in California at Hume Lake Christian Camp. Although transitioning missionary kids was not the exact purpose for the school, we knew the course would be beneficial in preparing him for a new life in America.

As I returned to Papua New Guinea and passed through Port Moresby, I was unable to catch my connecting flight to Hoskins, so I spent the night in POM (Port Moresby) at the Holiday Inn. Browsing around the gift shop, I noticed a book that grabbed my attention. The title was *Hostages to Freedom-The Fall of Rabaul* written by Peter Stone. It was an account of the Japanese invasion of Rabaul and subsequent activities of WWII on the island of New Britain. I am not much of a reader and frequently even have a difficult time reading my Bible, but I could not resist that book despite its huge price tag. I knew my wife would fall over when she heard what I had paid for it. Once I started reading it, I could not put it down. It is a large book for me, but I devoured its contents from cover to cover including every footnote. I have since recommended it to every WWII enthusiast I meet. I should get a portion of the royalty from the author for all that advertising.

On December 1, 2004, we took our dive buddies Dave and Joy Mueller with us again to see the Gasmata ship. They were only in the water five minutes, since the visibility was less than three feet; they became so discouraged that they aborted the dive. The locals were really curious and, in no time, we had attracted at least five dugout canoes full of suspicious eyes. It became pretty annoying, so we headed home without following up on the "plane on the reef" story. On the way home, our Volva Penta diesel engine in the boat broke some valve springs. Fortunately we had our auxiliary 15-horsepower outboard motor which was painfully slow going, but it was still better than paddling! Moving that slowly left little else to do, so to pass the time, we put the fishing lines out with hopes of catching some dinner. We did not catch any fish, though, and unfortunately the lures dragging behind the boat actually made us move even slower. As the sun set, the slow rocking of the boat made us sleepy, and we were glad to get home before dark.

THE LOST LURE

We had found that fishing lures were difficult to obtain and expensive. On one late afternoon, I was trolling with a visitor, Danny Mixter, when my precious *Rapala* lure became stuck on the reef. Because of the lateness of the hour, we decided to call it a day, so I cut my fishing line and tied a plastic bottle to the end of it to mark the location. That would enable me to be able to find it again to recover the lure. I also knew that the nationals would want to salvage that lure if they could, so early the next morning, I grabbed my mask, fins and a small dive tank and then jumped into the dinghy and returned to the reef with Danny. When we arrived at the reef, I was glad to see that the plastic bottle was still attached to the fishing line. I dropped the anchor and entered the water. The current was quite strong, so I held onto the anchor line and descended to the bottom (which turned out to be only about six feet). I was able to see the lure, but it was out of reach, so I braced my feet against some brain coral. Just as I was about to release the anchor line, I realized that the small air tank had run out of air.

Thinking that it was going to be a quick operation, I let go of the anchor line and reached for the lure which had lodged itself with both of the hooks and began to tug at it. The rear hook loosened, but the front hook remained attached to the reef. When the rear hook released, my hand slid back, and the hook caught my hand and punctured my palm. There I was – attached to the reef, with a punctured hand on a hook, holding onto an empty air tank.

For a brief moment, I foresaw my wife, Joan, and how upset she would have been had I drowned while trying to retrieve a lure. I quickly reached over with my other hand and yanked at the lure again – thankfully, it came loose. For some reason, I had held on to the dive tank during all of that time, and once I was freed, I shot up like a Poseidon Missile to the surface to get air. I tossed the tank into the boat as Danny looked on in disbelief at the lure which had pierced my hand. We attempted to remove it, but the barb would not allow it to release.

We drove to the house and when we arrived, I called out to Joan and the children to come out and see the huge fish we had caught – it was me! After they had seen that and expressed their disgust, they returned to the house – to get bandages and disinfectant, I was hoping, but they never came back. I took the opportunity to snap a couple photos for memory's sake, as this was surely one of those "Kodak moments." Danny and I went to my workshop since we realized that the only way that hook was going to be removed was to cut the barb off. First, we removed the lure body from the hook so I would not get stuck with the other treble hook. I then held onto the hook with my pliers while Danny pushed my palm with his thumbs on each side where the hook was to protrude through the skin. I held my breath and pushed until I could not stand it any longer but was unable to have the hook protrude through the skin. After a short breather, I took another deep breath and pushed again, and this time, the hook tip began to protrude through the skin to about 3.2 millimeters (one eighth of an inch). I needed another break, but then I took one last breath and pushed until the tip of the hook *and the barb* broke through the skin. Did I say it hurt? Well, the pain was excruciating. I then took another photo.

I gave Danny a pair of side-cutters and asked him to snip off the hook, but he was unable to do so – the hook was still in my hand. I reached for a hacksaw, installed a new blade and placed the hook in a vise. To my surprise, we were unable to cut through it. We could not comprehend what that hook had been made of, but it was definitely not about to surrender to our efforts. Next, we decided to try my 100-millimeter (four-inch) electric grinder. It seemed to work at first, but the hook began to heat up due to the friction; it felt as if I had held a lighted match in my hand. I yelled to Danny to back off, then the hook cooled and we were able to grind at it again; after a few more gentle touches (with rests in between), the barb was gone and I was finally able to remove the hook from my palm. Surprisingly, it did not pull out easily. That was quite an ordeal and I have retained tiny scars of that encounter on my hand.

April of 2005 found us again diving on the *Taka Saka Maru* in the Arawes. Since I had already taken my son, Micah, back to the States, my second son, Jared, accompanied me this time. Jared was now 15 years old and was also a certified diver. He had always been a faithful gopher (assistant that would "go for" tools needed) for Micah as they had worked side by side. With Micah gone now, it was his turn to step up to the plate. To my surprise, Jared took over right where Micah had left off. He became immensely proficient in everything as well. We did not think alike, but I merely had to give him a list of things to accomplish and, in the blink of an eye, the jobs were completed. What a production machine, a father's – and mother's dream! No arguing, no debating, he just did whatever he was asked without delay. He also had a heart of gold and watched over his two sisters like a hawk, as he still does to this day. And, he watches over me, too. I admiringly say, "He is *one* of my most favorite sons."

When we went to the dive site, we were accompanied by a fellow from South Africa named Dylan. Dylan was in his mid-twenties and was a deck hand on a 26-meter (85 foot) sailboat named *Firebird* out of the Virgin Islands. An older couple and he were circumnavigating the globe and had stopped in Kandrian. He was bored after having spent two-and-a-half years on the ship so we invited him to come along on a dive.

Actually, we went up to the Arawes to look for an anchor that had been lost by a Lutheran Shipping barge when its hydraulic system failed. The crew had let out all the anchor chain then tied a 30-meter (100-foot) rope to the chain and a buoy at the other end of the rope. The water was deeper than expected, and the chain pulled the buoy under the water so they could not find it, so they asked me if I would dive in an attempt to locate it. The water was crystal blue with visibility at or above 46 meters (150 feet). There were a few large jellyfish floating around beneath us that appeared to glow. Other than that, it was just dark blue everywhere we looked. The three of us aligned ourselves 8 meters (25 feet) apart and made a grid pattern at a depth of nine meters (30 feet) in the area pointed out by the barge captain. Surprisingly, on only our second pass, Dylan spotted the buoy at 20 meters (65 feet). We rescued the anchor, and the barge captain gave us a two-liter tub of ice cream. He was very happy and so were we! Postscript: two years later the company reimbursed me for the salvage dive.

Later that day, we conducted another dive on the *Taka Saka Maru*, and just as in the two previous dives, the water was clear and the *Taka Saka Maru* was just as exciting as ever to see. This was Jared's first time to see the ship, and we found him uncharacteristically talkative when we surfaced.

THE LOST PEOPLE – CARGO CULTS

Diving or hiking in these areas can sometimes be a challenge, since the locals are always suspicious. There are many stories of gold or treasure having been found here and there, and, true to such rumors, Papua New Guinea has many areas that have gold. In addition, gold bullion had been flown out of the country during the war. In a previous chapter, I told the story of the pilot, John Lerew, who did not make the second attack against Gasmata on February 10 as he was on a "mission to pick up gold bullion." Wouldn't it be nice to find a crashed airplane full of gold bullion? That is what the people think, too, so whenever we arrive on the scene looking for an airplane or a sunken ship, they assume that we are searching for gold. It has even been rumored that I have found gold in the stomachs of fish and diamonds in eels' mouths while diving. To a PNG local, why else would anyone want to dive deep into the unknown sea or hike into the remote jungles? Surely, not just to take pictures! Even when we explain that that is all we are doing and we show them the pictures, they then want to know what we are going to do with the pictures.

The nationals have this same suspicion towards missionaries. They cannot fathom why someone would leave their family, home and land, then bring his family, often times including little children, to a foreign land. In their reasoning, "there must be some underlying purpose," and the only thing they can construe is that they have come to find prosperity. They too have similar thoughts, and sometimes that consideration is the impetus for them to allow foreigners to come and live in their villages or trek around inside their land areas. They anticipate that by observing and befriending such strangers, they will discover or be told the secrets of how to accumulate material goods, or "cargo." I am sure that I have disappointed many a national since I do not know the secret if one even exists.

Before World War II, the people who lived in the interior had an understandably limited worldview. They had no concept of factories that built ships, airplanes and trucks. Even the making of clothing was a mystery because the women wore grass skirts and the men would wear bark-wrap clothing. It was no wonder that when the war reached them and they saw airplanes flying overhead dropping crates of supplies, the only way they could explain these phenomena was that their dead ancestors had sent the cargo. After the war when the supplies stopped coming, "cargo cults" of all shapes and sizes arose to try to coax the ancestors to send the cargo again. None of the cults were effective in that quest, so they presumed that there must be another way.

There possibly was some consideration that if the country could be independent and have its own government, the cargo would come. That partly became a reality in 1975 when the country did get its independence and the cargo did start to flow for some. The campaigning politicians promised to give their constituents boats, outboard motors and even trucks, among other things, if they were elected. Surprisingly, once elected, some politicians actually did send the gifts with hopes of their re-election. I know of one case where a satellite dish was given and wire joined throughout the town so the people could watch TV. For those who did not receive any gifts, they continued to search for the secret to getting cargo (or wait until the next election and vote someone from their clan into office).

In PNG culture, most everyone is socially equal. Almost all of the people have gardens, and they live the same way, aside from those who live in the cities. Ambitious people are put down, and life is made miserable for anyone who tries to get ahead in life. The culture of "sharing what you have" (Wantok system = One language system) also hinders people from being motivated to work for pay, as they would be obligated to share what they earned. On the other hand, they did want money; but jobs were scarce and many did not want to be confined to a daily work schedule if they could figure out some other way to get cash. Therefore, many hours were spent sitting around strategizing on how they would acquire wealth. The one way that seemed to work for many of them was to get money from any foreigners who crossed their paths. Foreigners were represented in the form of tourists who fished or dived or even those who came merely to look at the beauty of the country. Other foreigners were timber company employees who may have accidentally desecrated burial grounds or run over their dogs or pigs with their vehicles. Even a missionary looking for World War II relics could be considered a foreigner and an avenue to get rich quick!

Thus, whenever we planned a dive or hiked here or there, there was always a meeting with the locals in the area to inform them of our plans. At times, a hot head would begin yelling and demanding that we leave the area, or a bigman (chief) would want compensation for whatever we were planning to do. We always had to explain our motivations and our intentions in order to earn their trust, as well as to show them respect. This is understandable as it was their land we were on. When my children were with me, for some reason, it seemed to help ease the tension and the young men always warmed up to them. I am not sure I would want to search for aircraft and ship wrecks without them.

Money is always involved, and we usually paid a fee to the bigman or some local level government official. I likened it to buying a ticket to a movie show or purchasing a hunting license. Guides were also paid – as were others who went along for the adventure – and they were fed. We tried to get the people excited about our purpose, and they usually helped us. Gaining their trust was hugely important, and on many occasions, the villagers themselves have found the "pieces of aluminum" with the Japanese writing or the data plate with identifying information. It is worth noting that it is always a hassle when dealing with the locals, and at times, one must fight the urge to give up and walk away.

One thing I found was that if I sat and talked with them and explained that these airmen or seaman had given their lives so that the people of PNG could be free, they then seemed to understand. I also asked them if their sons had gone away to battle somewhere and they never heard from them again, how they would feel? What if they heard that their remains were found, would they want them returned home? In every instance, the reply was "Yes." I also explained that, if we found remains, I would report them to the respective Embassy in the capital city of Port Moresby. After that, a team would come and get the remains, identify them and coordinate the return of them to their families. This explanation, although almost inconceivable, always softened their hearts, and they then allowed us freedom to pursue our search with their assistance. It amazed me that even in these remote areas amid people of another culture, there was a commonality and understanding of the importance of the lost being found.

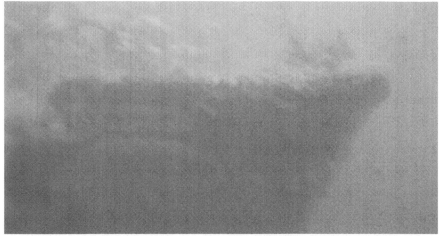

Bow of Sunken Japanese Merchant Ship, Gasmata. WNBP, PNG

"Singsing" (Spirit appeasement) at Yumielo Village. WNBP, PNG

Diving for fishing lure.

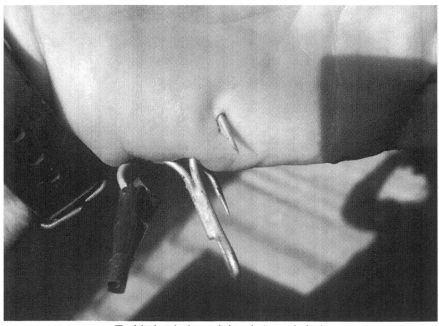

Treble hook through hand. (actual size)

Chapter 8

PANCAKED – P-38 LIGHTNING

We spent a year in the USA, and a while after returning to PNG, my interest in finding new WWII aircraft and ship wreckage was rekindled in March of 2007. On the front page of *The Post Courier*, a national newspaper, a report of eleven WWII U.S. airmen's remains that had been recovered was featured. They were found in the highlands area of PNG and were being transported back to the United States for identification. The picture on the front page was of a casket draped with an American flag and carried by U.S. military men. This was interesting to me since, a few years earlier, I had met some short-haired Americans at a restaurant in Lae, the second largest city in PNG, who told me they had come to PNG to search for remains in one of the provinces in the highlands. One plain-clothed soldier told me how gasoline may have been absorbed as preservative, and they had found a hand still holding the control stick of a military aircraft. This sounded like one of the stories we had heard from the local people. That seemed plausible though since the fuel which could have been used in the aircraft may have simulated a form of formaldehyde which has a systemic name of methanol. Most likely, however, the tissues were probably preserved in deicing fluid, which all the aircraft carried (due to high altitude flying). More research would be required before a determined conclusion could be made. I was not certain whether what I had read in the paper referred to the same wreckage site that had already been excavated, but it was interesting to learn that, after all these years, human remains were still being found and recovered.

After reading that article and my kids getting on my case about a "spare tire" I was lugging around, I felt that a hike through the jungle with them might help to relieve me of some excess weight. Most importantly, it was a time for Dad to get out with his teenage youngsters, especially since one day they may not want me to be so nearby. In this case, they actually really *wanted* me around; these were always treasured moments – not ones to be missed.

Back on the trail – I had recalled the story of the two-engine plane with the broken glass that we had heard about from John Tukai from Wako. He had sketched a rough drawing in my notebook earlier in March of 2004. So, on April 21, 2007, having not done any WWII relic hunting for three years, being recharged, we loaded up the boat and headed out. We picked up Asap from Yumielo Village on the way; he served as our guardian of the boat while we hiked the interior. The seas were flat and the skies blue as we set out that morning and the new 250-hp Suzuki four-stroke outboard motor pushed us effortlessly at a cheek-flapping twenty-eight kts (32 mph) over the glassy waters (we had changed the diesel engine after repeated failed attempts to keep the old one running). It was a beautiful day to be alive for this venture. We arrived at Wako village in an hour and we were greeted by one of our past guides, Rafail. Unfortunately, the man who we were seeking had already gone to his garden (being subsistence farmers, the locals have three to four gardens in rotation to provide food for their families). With that, we opted for Plan B and headed to the Pulie River looking for Lukas Sulu, the man who had told us, in November of 2003, about the warplane fuselage he had seen.

As we glided up the Pulie River, swerving and listing port and starboard on the snaky river, we found a man at the junction in a dugout canoe who gave us directions to find Lucas. Turning to the right at a junction in the river, we continued up the Iliak River and picked up Andrew Duwin who knew of an airplane farther up the river. We stopped at Urin village where we also picked up Andrew Nawa, who was the land owner of the ground upon which the plane sat. Three additional villagers joined us for the ride; a ride on a larger boat like ours was quite a novel experience for them.

The instructions from Andrew Duwin were that we were to go up the river until we came to a timber company log bridge. We were then to park the boat and walk on the timber company road one kilometer or so to where the airplane was located alongside the road. As we sailed onward, the water became quite shallow, and we were pleased that we could tilt the outboard up enough to clear the bottom. My concern was that the tide might go out and trap us up the river, forcing us to spend the night there.

Proceeding on through shallow then deep waters, zigzagging from one side of the river to the other, trying to stay in the channel, we eventually tied up to a fallen tree leaning over the river. I was wondering about the log bridge and curious as to its location. While sitting on the bow, I pulled on my golf shoes that Mr. Bill Butler from Hawaii had given me which are excellent for hiking over logs; the steel spikes provided excellent "bite" and gave me sure footing. I scooted along on my hind parts, not wanting to walk on the fiberglass boat deck with spikes. I then slid off the bow onto the fallen tree and made my way up to the river bank. The villagers, who do not wear any shoes, waited patiently for me and, I am certain, they were glad when I finally reached the shore. We soon vanished into the jungle; I brought up the rear following my daughter, Mariko.

Mariko was 15 years old then and still happy as ever and adventurous, so she enjoyed accompanying us on these excursions. Mariko is unlike her younger sister, Mieko, who even at 11 years of age, would prefer to stay at home with Joan and paint her fingernails. Mieko was our last bundle of joy. She was a "girlie girl" who enjoyed wearing fairy dresses and putting on makeup. Although initially not outspoken, she became the "clown in the family." That clown instinct became useful when fingernails needed polishing or faces needed to be painted. She only came on one of our adventures but that was enough for her. Possibly her age at the time deterred her interest.

Mariko, on the other hand, was the very talkative one, so as we hiked, she talked and talked – and talked. This was one of those precious moments, because it provided an opportunity for me to talk, and listen to my daughter, so I was enjoying this time with her. As I stumbled along, the thought came to me, "I hate hiking." Think about it! Leaves and branches smack you in the face while vines are tugging at your legs trying to trip you and at the same time small thorns are scratching your shins leaving small bleeding lines like cat scratches. I noticed this time that I seemed to be the only one having trouble hiking. Was I getting old? Or perhaps it was that spare tire the children had dutifully pointed out.

Hiking on numbly, thinking we were taking a short cut to the timber company road and wondering how far it would be, I was relieved when after only 25 minutes I heard the youngsters call out saying that we had reached the crash site. (See page xii - NO. 9) I immediately knew it was not another Val. I stood there, somewhat bewildered; my mind was stunned with awe and elation as it tried to compute the meaning of what was directly before my eyes. I could almost hear the hard drive in my brain spinning. Jared, Mariko and their friend Seth, a lanky teenager who lived close to us in Kandrian, ran all around as they looked at the engines, the wings, the landing gear and the guns. The airplane was mostly intact, not like the other planes we had seen that were scattered around in little pieces over a 15-meter (50-foot) radius. This one was just lying there as if it had fallen from the sky and impacted the ground in a flat position. Aviators refer to this as a "pancake" landing. The engines, although detached, were found where they were supposed to be at the forward edge of the wings. They were hidden under the cowlings so the two long V-12 Alison V1710s were not immediately visible. Both three-bladed propellers were visible with blades bent forward, which indicated that the engines had been running when they crashed through the trees prior to the final impact. The port (left) propeller was enmeshed in a tree which had grown around one of the blades. Where was the main cockpit where the pilot sat? There were two fuselages immediately behind the engines. Then it hit me, I was looking at a P-38! Man, what a find! I yelled out, "Jared, it's a P-38," to which he replied something to the effect of, "No kiddin,' Dad." He was more attuned to how the different models looked, and he had a sense of comparison from his many hours of flying Flight Simulator on the computer. Surprisingly, he actually learned *something* playing those games.

In order to positively identify this aircraft and crew, we would need to find some numbers or names that could be traced to official records. I dug my camera from my backpack and took a close look at the starboard engine, taking pictures and looking for anything with writing on it. I found the tag on the starter motor that had broken off. I snapped some pictures of the casting numbers on the manifolds; even this might provide some help in the overall identification of this aircraft. We tried to open the engine cowlings to see if we could locate more data plates, but we were unable to loosen all the clips. What we could see, though, was that the grey paint on the top surface of the engine-intake manifolds looked surprisingly new, and the shiny safety wires were still holding their bolts in a locked position. I was totally focused on my picture-taking while the kids made the rounds looking at everything in the area and alerted me to anything they had found that might have some importance. As I closely examined one of the engines, they completed their scouting around, and they resorted to making fun of my tunnel vision and only seeing the engine when there were so many other things to see.

The cockpit area was inexplicably missing for some reason; perhaps there had been a fire, but the cross support was there and intact. I told Mariko to start digging around in that area to see what she could find – remains perhaps. As she meticulously scratched the ground, I was busy taking pictures of the four 50-caliber Browning machine guns and the 20-mm cannon that were lying around the main wreckage.

The villagers were busy scouting for bullets and had even located some live ammunition. They also found a piece of thick canopy plastic. The right landing gear in the up position was clearly visible as the back section of the fuselage had torn off and was lying about 6 meters (20 feet) away. Inside the wheel well, I could see what was left of the tire and the wide rim. I can still remember thinking that the wheel was pretty stylish. Then on the inside of the wheel well, I noticed a data plate. It was a Lockheed Aircraft Corporation Burbank California tag with the serial and model number stamped into it. I was happy as I hoped that this would identify the airplane and pilot.

By now, Mariko had unearthed the dual control lever and a fuel and oil gauge face plate. We knew she was digging in the right area where the cockpit had been, so I instructed her to "Keep digging!" Jared had found a rusted 20-mm M1 cannon-feed mechanism with a tag on it showing that it had been inspected in 1942. The strange thing was that the tail section was not in the immediate area. I told the villagers to look around for the tail section because we still had not found any identifying painted numbers which the tail section would likely have. They went into the bush as I continued to inspect each and every square inch of the wreckage, taking pictures as I moved along.

Eventually, after a couple hours of inspecting and after the locals had not found the tail section, I finally made my way to the back fuselage section. Lying there also was a rounded part that had five round openings in it and some 75-millimeter (three-inch) flex tubing attached to it. I thought it might have been a part of the underside of the engine and the holes might have been the exhaust ports. I moved on and took a picture of the radiator in the fuselage (the P-38s were water - cooled). Jared walked over and we talked about heading back to the boat as we had concluded that we had seen everything there was to see. There was one section we did not investigate because it was covered with red ants. I believe now that that was the cockpit. I mentioned the section with the exhaust ports to Jared, and he quickly set me straight and identified it as the nose cone, and the five ports were where the machine guns were designed to go through it. That made sense, and so I told him to hold it straight and I took his photograph with Seth as they held it. As I sighted them through the view finder, something else caught my eye!

After I snapped the photo, I quickly went to the nose cone and turned it on its side. There it was! It was what we needed to identify the airplane. A name had been painted on the side of the nose as had been done on many of the planes from that era. We were not able to discern any detail at first because some of the paint had worn off and the nose had been bent in the crash, so it was difficult to read. Then too, it was dirty, so we used our canteen and poured some *precious* drinking water on it, wiped the mud off of it with our fingers then tried to dry it with leaves. We learned that leaves do not work well as rags. Mariko joined us, and we all tried to decipher the imprinted lettering. The first letter "R" was clear; the second letter was not so clear; the third was "g;" fourth was an "i." We could not define the fifth letter, but the sixth letter was definitely an "a." What did it spell? R?gi?a. Was the second letter an "o" making it read, Rogi?a? We excitedly deliberated over that name for quite some time but finally agreed that probably it said "Regina" and the second name seemed to be "Coeli." Whose name was that? Perhaps it was the pilot's girlfriend or his mother? We realized that we might never know what this represented, but we did know that the name would be a big help to authorities who would complete a detailed identification of the plane we had found.

It was getting late and we had collected something concrete to identify the wreckage, so we decided to terminate our adventure. As we packed up to leave the site, I wanted to take a small aluminum tag that had been riveted to the starter motor, but the land owner would not let me take anything from the airplane. He probably thought that all of it was valuable and since it was on his land, he took possession of everything. I later heard that the engines were possibly worth a million dollars apiece, so there is a great deal of value lying out there in the jungle. Just before we started the return hike, I noticed, on the outside of the starboard wheel well, a faint outline of the USAAF insignia which was covered by moss. The insignia was the white star in the middle, but the blue outline had faded away. We snapped a couple additional photographs then hiked back to the boat.

While continuing downstream, one of the guys who had come along for the ride nonchalantly mentioned that, years ago when he was operating a bulldozer for the timber company, he had come across an airplane not far away from where we had been searching all day. I exclaimed, "What?" and then anxiously inquired for more details. He said that he had lifted the wing with the blade of the bulldozer. It was not far away from this crash site; it was farther up the Pulie River. We made certain to get his name and his village location for future contact. We dropped all the villagers off at their village of Urin then proceeded to navigate toward Kandrian.

As we sailed downstream, we could tell that the tide had indeed receded. Our VHF radio did not have the range to enable me to contact my wife, Joan, in the event we would have to sleep on the river and wait for the tide to rise. We had another SSB radio but the on/off knob was frozen from salt corrosion. I had been expecting the worst, especially since Joan would worry about us – it would of course be worrisome for a parent to realize that her children were late from a "jungle trip" and were staying out *at night*! So imagine my relief when we launched the boat and glided over shallow areas that appeared to be only a foot deep with the sandy bottom clearly visible. By this time it was around 4 P.M. with only a couple hours of daylight left and a long ways to go.

The winds had increased, so the seas were not as flat as when we started this trip; this made for much slower going. We talked about the find and could not wait to get home to get on the internet and tell someone, anyone who would listen. About a half hour out of the mouth of the Pulie River, we saw a splash approximately 61 meters (200 feet) in front of our boat. We kept our eyes glued to that area and, to our surprise, a six-foot marlin again jumped all the way out of the water with a fish in its mouth. Wow, you do not see something like that very often. It truly had been quite an amazing day.

When we arrived home, the routine with the boat required us to get it out of the water. I backed the trailer down, winched the boat up onto it then slowly pulled the boat out of the water. Because the boat was so heavy I could only get it out with the assistance of a winch pulling from a one-meter (approx. three-foot) iron I-beam buried in the ground. Afterwards my children began their two hour routine of washing it down and vacuuming the carpet floor while I refueled the tanks. In this way, the boat would be ready to go in the event we had some emergency that demanded us to get underway fast.

The refueling process was actually quite an ordeal since there were no gas stations in the town where we lived. All the fuels for trucks, airplanes, generators, boats, and even refrigerators (refrigerators used kerosene and some models used LP gas) came from the mainland town of Lae on a barge. Lae was the second largest city in PNG and as stated previously, famous for being the last place that Amelia Earhart had taken off from before she went missing. The barges would take four to eight weeks to arrive so we had to maintain a large stock of fuel. We usually ordered 30 to 40 drums at a time, each of which held 44 gallons. When the barge arrived, it would take the better part of a day to shuttle the drums from the wharf to a back section on our property. We often hired local men to assist us with the loading and unloading of the drums, which involved rolling them on and off the truck using two 50 X 100 millimeter (two x four inch) timbers. They weighed 170 kilograms (375 pounds) each so it took three men to roll them onto the truck. To get the fuel out of the drums, we used a hand pump to fill five-gallon containers. It took 25 revolutions to pump one gallon. Then, one by one, those containers would be siphoned or poured into the fuel tanks. We refueled trucks and boats that way for 23 years.

After cleaning and refueling, we then pulled the boat into the shed and after locking her up, I hurried into my office. I did not know who to write to inform them of the find so I wrote the US embassy in Port Moresby. I then remembered a co-worker who had mentioned a website he had found called *Pacific Wrecks,* so I did a Google search and found it. I logged onto the site for the first time; it was quite informative and there was a category for MIAs with the aircraft listed. I searched through the P-38s, but did not see any with the name "Regina Coeli" or anything similar. I then found a list of individuals who had contributed to the site, and I wrote John Douglas, who resided in Port Moresby. By e-mail correspondence, I met Gail Parker, whose husband was the editor for *After the Battle* magazine. I had been in contact with Gail previously as she had written an article regarding the Val we had found in the water by the Arawes. Since this sort of thing was within her area of interest, I thought she might find our information appealing so I wrote her too. I also wrote to the *Pacific Wrecks* webmaster, Justin Taylan, and someone from the 475th Squadron. I told them all about the find and hoped someone would respond.

Lockheed P-38 *Lightning*. WNBP, PNG

Jared with P-38 propeller. WNBP, PNG

P-38 machine gun. WNBP, PNG

P-38 oil/fuel gauge face plate. WNBP, PNG

Chapter 9

QUEEN OF THE HEAVENS

Up to this point, our adventures had brought little excitement to anyone. Even my wife only looked at our pictures out of politeness. When visitors would come to our home, I felt that I had to twist their arms to show them my box of "souvenirs" consisting of bottles, bullets, an engine valve from a Val, some 1943 Australian pennies and the projectile detonating fuze from the *Taka Saka Maru*. It was understandable; this was our hobby and there just are not that many people interested in such things – so we thought.

The next morning I checked my e-mail and to my surprise, people *were* interested and had responded! John Douglas wrote:

Dear Mark,

Thank you for passing me the information, which to me is very interesting. You and your family must have had a very good adventure. I would love to see the plane one day. I think this plane is 42-66856, a P38H from the 433rd Fighter Squadron, 475th Fighter Group. It was in a collision with another P-38 flown by a Lt. Neely on the 18th DEC 1943. The pilot of your plane was 1st Lt. William Jeakle. This aircraft lost its entire tail assembly in the collision. It was last seen spiraling at 9,000 feet, 15 miles north of Arawe, near the Pulie River. Lt. Neely made a safe landing at Dobuduru, despite a damaged wing and prop and had to be treated for shock. Lt. Jeakle returned to duty on 6th January 1944. He must have had his own small adventure as well, taking nearly three weeks to return. If he is still alive we should be able to track him down thru some of my American fellow enthusiasts. There might be also a bit more info in the 475th FG book which I don't have at this time.

Cheers,

John Douglas

He later wrote:

> William (Jake) Jeakle returned to the Squadron camp on 28th December 1943. "Nobody was happier than the distraught Neely to see Jeakle back after 11 days in the jungle."

> No parachute had been seen to blossom from the tailless P38. One of the few flying boats then on rescue service had picked up the fortunate Jeakle and taken him back to safety.

> In September 1944, nearly a year later; William Jeakle returned to America after 160 missions (and I don't know what happened to him after that).

> Austin Neely died when his plane flew into the sea in bad weather on 16th April 1944. There was a lot of air activity (and plane losses) around Arawe, in mid December 1943. A regiment of the 1st U.S. Cavalry had landed there on the 15th and there were a lot of battles (on a relatively small scale).

This battle in mid-December was shown in the video I had seen, *Attack, The Battle of New Britain*. Things were coming together. I was skeptical at first with this report because the airplane looked as if it had just dropped out of the sky from where the report said it was "last seen spiraling at 2,743 meters (9,000 feet)." How could it have landed itself so perfectly? One of my editors, Dr. Richard Perez, suggested it must have "pancaked." So, the "spiraling" description meant falling like a Frisbee to land in a rather flat position. In most cases, spiraling refers to a spinning motion either vertically or horizontally – horizontally spinning then came to be called pancaking.

AIR BATTLE OVER THE ARAWES

John Douglas also sent me this report from John Stanaway's book, *Possum, Clover & Hades: The 475th Fighter Group in World War II*[41] which described the air battle on December 16, 1943, just two days prior to when "Regina Coeli" crashed.

> For several weeks the missions were routine and uneventful in the cleanup of Finschhafen and Wewak. The first

real action since Alexishafen came on December 16 during a patrol of the Arawe sector of Southwest New Britain.

Tom McGuire was back on flying status and was scheduled for this mission. There was certainly no more controversial pilot in V Fighter command; his absence since October was a breath of relief to many who despised his constant voice over the radio in combat and his return was also cheering to some who believed that, for all his faults, he was an omen of good luck with his utter fearlessness and skill in battle.

Lieutenant David Allen was leading the 431st when it took off for the patrol around 11:30 in the morning. As soon as he got the Hades Squadron on course his compass went out and he relinquished the lead to Don Bellows and took over Hades Green Flight. Within a short time Bellows had to abort the mission and Tom McGuire took the lead.

Hades Squadron was reduced from sixteen to nine P-38s when it arrived over the target area. At 45 minutes past one in the afternoon the controller gave McGuire a plot of enemy aircraft coming in his direction from the northwest. Seven Betty bombers and swarms of zeros were sighted just above Cape Bushing to the north of Arawe.

The calls were coming in from various members of the Hades flights, but for some reason McGuire was unable to locate the enemy. His frustration at not finding the Japanese aircraft was increased when other P-38s took the initiative to attack.

Lieutenant Carl Houseworth led his own Hades White Flight down from about 19,000 feet with David Allen and Frank Lent of Hades Green Flight following him. Lent came down hard at the third Betty on the right side of the formation and saw pieces of canopy come off in the head on pass. Frank Monk and Lieutenant Chris Herman saw the Betty begin to break up and trail smoke.

Allen with John Tilley on his wing made a pass from the same angle as Lent. The Betty that Allen fired upon started to smoke and turn fiercely, but the American pilot was too busy dodging the line of tracers coming from the bomber's waist position to see what was happening to his target. Lieutenant Bill O'Brien, who was coming in to attack right behind Allen's lead element watched the Betty burst into bright flames and fall like a blazing rag.

John Tilley shot at another Betty and stayed on Allen's wing until he cleared the defensive fire zones of the Japanese bomber formation. Somewhere below the now disorganized bombers the two P-38s ran into large numbers of Zeros, and Tilley tucked in close on his leader's wing until the enemy fighters were left behind.

When they were in the clear Allen and Tilley scooted back up to 20,000 feet and resumed the attack on the Bettys. One Zero passed between the two P-38s and the startled Americans broke off their attack to once again shake off the enemy which was now coming down from above.

Once again the pair climbed for position above the bombers which by this time were flying raggedly in a nondescript formation. One of the Bettys was chosen for a stern attack and obviously became alerted when it raced for a cloudbank. Tilley started firing at about 500 yards and ran right up the tail of his target when he noticed that all the gunners had stopped firing. The Betty's left engine burst into flames and Tilley dived away when it was certain that the bomber was doomed.

Tom McGuire had sighted the enemy in time to follow Lent and witness his bomber kill go down. However, he was much too late to get to the surviving Bettys before they escaped into cloud. Even when he did manage to engage a straggling Zero the best he could do was inflict some damage on it.

Possum Squadron was having better luck when Warren Lewis led it to the retreating bombers. The sixteen P-38s of the squadron were at 13,000 feet when a Zero was sighted in a hole in the overcast above. As he was climbing Lewis spotted two Bettys flying side by side toward Talasea on the north coast. He picked the one on the left and closed in to fire a burst that turned the bomber into a ball of flame.

Lieutenant Charles Grice was leading the last Possum Flight and saw Lewis down his Betty and a moment later saw John Babel follow him in and shoot down the second in virtually a mirror image. Grice followed the lead flight up through the clouds and ran directly into Zeros above.

There was only one thing to do and Grice went back into the milky grey mass. When he emerged below he saw another Betty being attacked by a P-38. The apparently undamaged Betty made a slight right turn in his direction and Grice was able to send his cannon shells and tracers into the rear gunner's opening. Unhindered by the danger of the rear cannon the P-38 was able to spray its tracers into the left wing root, sending the bomber down in flames.

Meanwhile, Lewis had remained above the cloud layer and latched onto another Betty. Three enemy fighters in the air failed to deter Lewis when he shot a good rear quarter shot and tore his second kill to pieces. Williaml Jeakle claimed one of the Zeros and Clarence Rieman dispatched a Tony that he found somewhere to give Possum six kills for no losses in the first engagement led by its new commander.

Translated Japanese documents claim a somewhat differing view of the engagement for Imperial Naval Air forces. The nearby landings of December 15 had aroused heavy Japanese attention and thirty fighters covering eight bombers had numbered six invasion ships sunk as well as five American aircraft shot down." The translation also admits the loss of two bombers and four fighters.

This next section of a report was most interesting and shed some light on our find.

On December 28, 1943, a haggard and worn William Jeakle was returned to the 433rd Squadron camp. The tail of his P-38 had been chewed off by his squadron mate, Lieutenant Austin Neely, during the battle around Arawe on December 18. Nobody was happier than the distraught Neely to see Jeakle back after eleven days in the jungle.

John Babel was also happily surprised to see Jeakle come back relatively unharmed since no parachute was seen to blossom from the tailless P-38. One of the few flying boats then on rescue service had picked up the fortunate Jeakle and taken him back to safety.

The last entry in John Babel's diary for 1943 waxes a bit laconic after the whirlwind days that preceded New Year's eve. Babel was overjoyed not just at Jeakle's lucky return, but at the sure prospect of ending his combat tour and returning home after many months in New Guinea. "Dec 31 '43 Flew bomber escort to Alexishafen; no enemy activity. Red alert in PM ... Started celebrating New Year in our tent & ended up at Group club.

Richard Dunn wrote of the Japanese side of the battle:

" 248th Hiko Sentai: A Japanese "Hard luck" Fighter Unit, part 3

On the 18th of December four Hayabusas of the 248th joined with the 59th Sentai and flew a fighter sweep to Arawe, New Britain along with Type 3 fighters. The U.S. Army Air Force reference history described the combat: "[E]nemy pilots displayed considerable skill and aggressiveness. This was especially true on 18 December when 16 P-38s, 433 rd Fighter Sq., jumped 10 to 15 ZEKES, OSCARS, and TONYS at midday. The P-38s dove through the enemy fighters and were in turn jumped by about 15 fighters, which had been hiding in cumulous clouds. Definitely on the defensive and outmaneuvered, the P-38s destroyed only three of the enemy while losing two P-38s..." The 248th. claimed one P-38 without loss. The Japanese lost a single Type 3 fighter.[42]

As you can see from the reports, each side has their own slant to the air battles, and it makes you wonder who if any was telling the truth? Some may think the differences in the reports were due to exhaustion while the reports were written or they were written quickly to get the reports in, therefore they suffered some in accuracy. My personal opinion as to the differences is that each side wanted to look good to their commanding officers, for the media, and possibly for the morale of the men.

Justin Taylan, the webmaster for *Pacific Wrecks*, and Rod Pearce had also written, and their assessment was similar to that of John Douglas. There was only one P-38 in the South Pacific with the nickname, "Regina Coeli," so they were pretty certain that we had found 1st Lt. William Jeakle's lost P-38 airplane. The fact that it had had a mid-air collision which ripped off its tail explained why we were unable to locate the tail section. Further, since the pilot had reportedly survived, that explained why my daughter Mariko never found any remains as she excavated the cockpit area. And, since the pilot had survived, that explained why I did not see the P-38 listed in the MIA section of the *Pacific Wrecks* site. The question now became, was the pilot still alive to tell his story?

P-38 USAAF insignia. WNBP, PNG

P-38 20- mm-mechanism feed data tag. WNBP, PNG

Jared and Seth with P-38 nose cone. WNBP, PNG

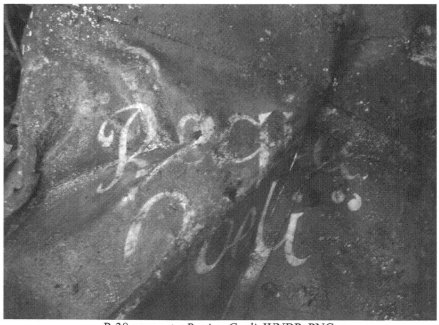

P-38 nose art - *Regina Coeli*. WNBP, PNG

Chapter 10

PILOT – 1st. LT. WILLIAM JEAKLE'S STORY

The week that followed was full of e-mails both coming and going. John Douglas was sending me reports of the battle in the Arawes. Justin Taylan was hard at work searching for information on the pilot to determine if he was still alive, where he was located, and how we could contact him. John Stanaway, a P-38 National Association historian wrote and said the name *Regina Coeli* is Latin for Queen of the Skies. I had originally thought it was a reference to the pilot's wife or girlfriend. It appears that a previous pilot, Captain Joe McKeon, who had four kills with the airplane, is the one who named it. I found the name to be the title of a twelfth-century Catholic prayer. It is a Latin hymn sung or recited during the Easter season from Saturday to Sunday.[43]

My long lost buddy, Rod Pearce, sent a message congratulating me on the find. It was an exciting week; each morning, I rushed to my office. I held my breath in hopes that the telephone would be working so I could get online to check my e-mail to see if any new news had been received.

Speaking of the telephone not working – when we had initially moved into the village, there were no telephone lines that reached so far out of town. After a couple of years of walking or riding over three kilometers (two miles) to town to see if someone would let me use their telephone, I was able to convince the telephone company, Telikom, to install a phone jack on the telephone pole nearest me at the edge of the town. I then mounted a lockable metal box on the pole that had a telephone jack inside. This was not an ideal situation, but it was closer to my residence and it relieved me of the need to plead with someone to let me use their telephone. Surprisingly, no one ever broke the little lock I had installed on the box.

Years later when facsimile machines were invented, my parents in Illinois mailed me one, so I pulled up to the pole, opened the box, plugged my fax machine into the telephone jack then connected an inverter into the cigarette lighter in the truck. I then sat there in 90%

humidity sweating profusely while I sent a fax. I was kidded by my sister-in-law, Teresa, about the need to climb a pole to make a telephone call as was done on the TV series, *Green Acres*. It was not the most comfortable way to make a call, but I was thankful to have established the ability to communicate outside of my home area.

When we eventually moved into town, the telephone line was connected to my office, and one would think that all was blissful, but there were now a dozen or so connections between my house and the telephone pole. This meant that any time it rained (and we got 3.6 – 4.5 meters or 12 – 15 feet of rain a year), or one of the connections corroded, or when the locals cut a section out of the line so they could braid the different colored wires together, the telephone of course did not operate. One never knew from one day to the next whether the telephone would work. When something went wrong (which was often) it would take a few months to get a linesman from Telikom to come from the north side of the island and repair the lines. When Wimpar would finally come, I provided transportation for him to make certain he would repair my telephone. I also observed him closely as he repaired the lines so that I could then repair them myself which I often did in between his visits.

Once the lines were all repaired and reconnected, there was the constant problem with the system itself which was operated with the use of batteries. One example is that the telephone only worked during the day when the sun was hitting the solar panels that, in turn, charged the batteries. After sunset, only about one hour would pass before the telephone died. In addition, rainy or cloudy days denied the solar panels the ability to get any sunlight, and therefore, the system did not work then either. Beyond that, there were times when the system itself did not operate for one reason or another not related to the batteries. Actually, it was a miracle that the telephones operated at all, but it was most frustrating when they became inoperative for *months or years* at a time. What was even more frustrating was when my telephone would die, but my friend's telephone continued to operate. That was infuriating not only because I was jealous, but also because I was the guy who was providing transportation for the linesman to go out to repair it. So if anyone's phone worked, it should have been mine!

On this memorable day, the telephone did work. I was able to receive e-mail messages and saw that Justin had written to say that he had found that the pilot was born March 31, 1920, in Detroit, Michigan. Later, a disappointing message from John Stanaway reported that "William Jeakle had passed away in October of 2004." We were all disappointed to say the least. But, per John's encouragement, Justin made one telephone call; he had found Jeakle's relatives! He learned that there are only 47 people with that uncommon surname in the USA. He also learned that there was a granddaughter who had posted a nine-minute video on YouTube of an interview where "Glen," (the name 1st. Lt. Jeakle used after the war) described the incident. In it he said:

My worst day was December the 18th 1943. About this time I peeled right off behind a Zero. Got him...he was going to be deader than hell. I looked back to see if my guys were with me. Yeah, the boys were still behind me. Yeah, Pete is back there, the boys were back there. I looked to the side, and 'oh my god' there is a P-38 staring me right in the face - right there. Staring me right in the face. And I shoved everything forward and just dumped everything. And I was hit. It felt like a Mac Truck. As soon as I was hit, I lost all control. Broke...what he did, the wing of his plane cut through the right boom, and cut everything off, all my controls. I had no pedals, nothing at all. So the next thing I said was 'get outta that thing. I pulled the canopy, tripped the canopy. Which pulls pins back here to release the canopy, and it went back alright.

Someone had put a copper wire in the canopy back to hold the canopy from falling all the way back. But when I pulled the pins, I released the canopy all right, but now it was flailing back and forth because it was hooked on the front, flailing back and forth across the top of the cockpit. So, I had to unstrap the seat belt, and work to try and break that copper wire...to get the canopy out of the way.

Meantime, the plane is all over the sky with no control to it at all. And, I tried to get out, and the oxygen mask is still hooked up to me, I have to get that off. Then I realize the ear gadgets are still hooked up to me. So, the law was if you gotta get out of that thing [the P-38] don't just bail out because if you do that boom is going to hit you and break your back. So I scootched down on the side of the canopy, down on the wing. I looked back, and the whole thing is gone. The other part [boom] had broken off too, there were just two stubs back there. So, I did not have to worry about the booms at all, so I let go.

I no sooner got floating down, and here come two Nips after me. And they went sailing ass by me - with their tracers and stuff whipping by me. How they missed me, I don't know. And they whipped out there and were coming around to get me again. I thought: "This is no good. This is crazy!" To realize that at one moment you're alive and the next moment you know you're going to be dead...you just know your going to be dead.

So, I pulled the shroud lines down, just dumping the shrouds down, just to get the hell down out of that area. Now I am free falling. Down I go. After I got down so far, I looked down and hell, I am almost on top of the trees! So, I let go of the chute. About that time it popped open, just as I hit the trees. I'm looking down and falling face forward, and I realize I still have about three floors to go. Three stories to go [approx 30']. So I try to get my feet underneath me, kick my feet underneath me. Just about then I hit the ground. This knee went the wrong way, so that took care of that knee.

I was told if you get shot down on New Britain, head towards Rabaul, because possibly Aussie scouts or natives would help you. But I knew previously that the Marines are going to land at Cape Glouster on Christmas Day. So I thought, the hell with that, I'm not going to go way up towards Rabaul, I will go towards Glouster. And I tried to walk, but I could not walk very well. I was in bad, bad shape. So I thought the first thing I better do is hide my path, and walk down a stream...to get away from where I landed. So I started down this stream, the next thing I discovered this orange-yellow color dye that you had...that you broke so that if you went into the ocean...that's trailing behind me. So I had to get rid of that damn stuff!

I was in sago swamps is what I was in. That first night I remember trying to make a nest in the water with sago palms, a big nest so I could sleep up on it, on top of the water.[44]

That was a interesting piece of information regarding 1st. Lt. Jeakle and his ordeal. Also during the research, it was learned that the other pilot, Lt. Neely, who had had the mid-air collision with 1st Lt. Jeakle, had passed away. Sadly, Neely himself was classified as MIA (and has never been found). He was a victim of "Black Sunday," April 16, 1944, when the 5th Air Force lost seven airplanes due to bad weather.[45]

All together, it was quite an experience, to say the least. It was a real life adventure. I had heard Jeakle's grandson wanted to visit and see the wreckage site but he never came to PNG. And the adventures did not stop there – it had only just begun. In a week after we had found the *Regina Coeli*, I was full of excitement as e-mails were received, and more and more information on the airplane was revealed. We were all reenergized and eagerly anticipated the next weekend when we could launch out again in search of the other airplane that the bulldozer operator who had accompanied us on our previous trip had nonchalantly mentioned. He said that he had "lifted the wing of a plane with the blade on his dozer" as he was a member of a construction crew which was building roads for the timber company.

1st. Lt. William "Jake" Jeakle

P-38 throttle control levers.

P-38 *Regina Coeli* throttle control levers. WNBP, PNG

Chapter 11

THE GOLDEN GRAIL – SAN ANTONIO ROSE

During that same week, after we had found the P-38, I received a message from a co-worker, Craig Lowell, who was teaching the Bible to the Kol people in the middle of a dormant volcano in East New Britain. He had heard of our find from Douglas Walker, who had been communicating with him about his attempt to find a B-17 in which his father was lost on January 5, 1943. His father, Brigadier General Kenneth Walker, one of the highest-ranking military officers to die in combat during WWII, was flying as an observer on a mid-day low-altitude bombing run on Rabaul. After the B-17s dropped their bombs and were forming up again, the crew of another B-17 noticed one of their comrades "falling behind, smoking, and 15 to 20 Japanese fighters all around him. He went into the clouds and the airplane, the *San Antonio Rose*, was never seen again."[46] Douglas had seen our find of the P-38 Lightning on *Pacific Wrecks* and was hoping we would be able to find his father's missing B-17 Flying Fortress. This was the first time I had heard about this aircraft so I started to research it.

I also had asked Lenore Tillitson, who had translated the New Testament of the Bible into the Myu language, to help me investigate this. She was living in California, so she visited the University of California, San Diego library as it had postwar records of the Australian patrols in PNG. Her goal was to find any information regarding two crewmen who had parachuted from the airplane and who were eventually captured.

One of them was the co-pilot of *San Antonio Rose*, Captain Benton Daniels. He was captured in Tol Plantation on the coast of Wide Bay and taken to Rabaul on January 12, 1943. That would have been one week after the airplane was reported missing. Tol Plantation, is where approximately 158 Australian soldiers were bayoneted or shot to death after they had fled Rabaul from the Japanese invasion of January 23, 1942.

The other survivor was an observer on the airplane, Major Jack Bleasdale. After parachuting, he had spent 20 days in the jungle with a native family. Later, he was also captured and taken to Rabaul. There is information that he had made it to Rabaul, but by July of 1943, no POWs who had survived the war had ever heard of him. Therefore, it can be assumed that he had been executed or he had died by some other means within a couple months of his capture.[47]

I had asked Lenore to check on any known information regarding the patrol reports around a village called Lemingi. This village is centrally located on the Gazelle Peninsula, and the Japanese had established a small base camp there. My thinking was that if the airplane had gone down in that area, it was possible that there would be something in the patrol reports about it.

As per her nature, Lenore did extensive research, but she did not find anything that mentioned the two pilots, or even the patrol officers having seen any airplane wreckage. She did, however, find claims for compensation by the locals whose relatives had been executed by the Japanese; they had been charged with assisting downed airmen. She also confided with me that her search through the reports was difficult because of the atrocities that had occurred and about which she was forced to read.

At first, I thought it might have been possible that the villagers who had been executed for assisting downed airmen may have assisted Daniels or Bleasdale. I contacted some friends who resided in that area. They poked around a little bit but did not hear of anything in relation to those two airmen or an airplane having been found in the vicinity.

There is a trail that extends from Rabaul to Lemingi Village to Tol Plantation, and there have been reports of a crashed airplane along that trail, but it was not the *San Antonio Rose*. That was the same trail that the members of Lark Force had used as they escaped from Rabaul after the Japanese invasion. So, because my friends near Lemingi had not heard anything and Lenore did not find anything in the archives, I do not believe the airplane is in that area.

So, where is that airplane and the other crewmen? There have been some who think that the airplane flew past Wide Bay and crashed into the Kol mountains interior of Milim Village – unpiloted. That theory was based upon a number of factors such as weather and time of day. The phenomenon of airplanes flying by themselves has been verified. But based upon information I had garnered and research data I had gathered, I became skeptical of that theory. My information has led me to believe that the airplane is located in the southwest quadrant of the Gazelle Peninsula near the top of the mountain range.

Here is the basis for my assumption. The estimated altitude is mere speculation; I have seen a report of a Japanese pilot who had drawn a map of the air battle that day showing how the bombers had regrouped after they had dropped their bombs. The pilot drew a diagram that showed his five attacks on a B-17 and the location of the aircraft at the time of the attacks. He had probably been attacking B-17 Serial Number 24538 (not *San Antonio Rose*)! According to his diagram, the bombers were near to the coast of the Gazelle Peninsula which was south southwest of Rabaul. The report about *San Antonio Rose* was that it was lagging behind at 1,524 meters (5,000 feet). One engine had failed or had been strafed and was probably smoking; therefore, I do not believe it could have made it over the 2,134-meters (7,000-foot) mountain range that is north of Wide Bay. I believe that as the pilot saw the mountain range coming near, he realized that he could not ascend to clear it, but he wanted to get as far away from Rabaul and as close to the coast as he could before giving the order to bail out. If the pilot had already been killed in the earlier attacks, the surviving crewmen may have bailed out as they realized the airplane was descending. It has been said that people do not jump from good airplanes. As long as they are flying, aircrew will stay with the airplane until they are certain it is hopeless. Remember Lerew of A16-91? He jumped out at 122 meters (400 feet). So, I believe, as do others, that they stayed with the airplane as long as they could.

Once on the ground, one of the crew, Daniels, was soon found by natives and taken to the coast where he was captured and taken to Rabaul seven days later. That is not a lot of time for someone to hike to the coast, get captured and wait for a boat and ride it to Rabaul. Bleasdale may have been injured and may have stayed with some villagers for 20 days then made his way to the coast where he too was captured and taken to Rabaul. So, it appears to me that they parachuted not too far from the coast; otherwise, they would have been taken to Lemingi Village. This should provide a clue as to the whereabouts of the B-17.

Another bit of information revealed that there is currently a timber company cutting trees in that area, but they are on the coastal side of the mountain range. They probably only go about three to five kilometers (two to three miles) into the interior then stop, as the mountain range becomes steep and treacherous, especially for the company's bulldozers. My theory is that, if someone were to go up there and make inquiries with the local villagers starting at Tol, stories of two airmen being captured in that area would be heard. If the villagers at Tol had no information, possibly the timber surveyors may have heard or seen some wreckage. This is an extremely rugged area, and it would be virtually impossible to find a wreck site without a guide, so one cannot *just* go and start hiking around.

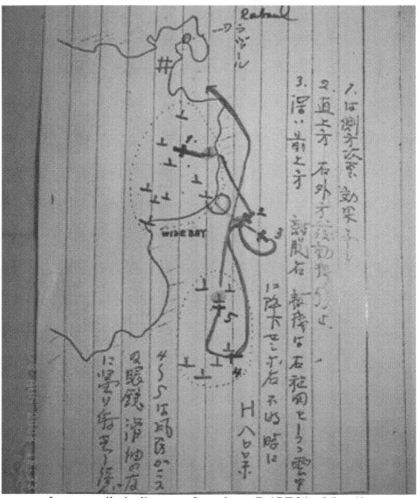

Japanese pilot's diagram of attacks on B-17/B24s. 5 Jan 43.
Source: National Institute of Defense Studies. Tokyo, Japan

Chapter 12

THE RISING SUN – VAL #5

Continuing the chronology of our adventures, Saturday morning dawned not a minute too soon and, like the previous Saturday, we loaded the boat again with crackers and rice to give to our guides and workers. We also packed hiking shoes, drinking water, insect repellent and a camera. We always took medical supplies including anti-malarial and antibiotics as with the high humidity, even a small scratch could become quickly infected and left untreated would develop into a tropical ulcer. I even took a little 23-centimeter (nine-inch) diagonal screen, 12-volt operated TV/VCR so that I could show the villagers at Urin the movie of *Attack, The Battle for New Britain*.

We picked up a couple of local men at Yumielo; we needed them to watch the boat as we hiked the area. One was an old man from Gasmata who wore thick glasses so he was commonly known as "Eyeglass," but his baptized name was Paul. Paul was visiting his son-in-law, Mambel.

"Mambel" may seem like a strange name to an English speaker. When we first arrived in the country we went through a six-month orientation period. Papua New Guinea has been known as a unique country in that it has over 820-distinct languages and, thankfully, we did not have to learn them all. Fortunately, about 100 years ago, a Pidgin English came into existence and is known by most of the population. That language has become known as "Melanesian Tok Pisin." It was that language that I used to communicate with the people of all the various language groups.

Another culture shock we experienced involved the cultural norms. One of the features had to do with names. Traditionally, it was not uncommon for people to have names that related to things in their worldview. One example was a man I came to know named "Asap;" this was the word for "wave" (as on the ocean) in his clan language. Another man was named "Balus," (the word for airplane). There was also a woman who was named "Mumiangru," (the word for "reef" in her language). Another man was named "Baret." It translated to

"Ditch." While we had no understanding as to how he had come to receive that name, we assumed that he had been born in a ditch alongside the road.

When the Catholics arrived, they gave everyone a baptismal name which had been taken from the Bible. The most popular names were James and John. In addition to that, the people also had nicknames that reflected something about them. That explained how Paul was also called "Eyeglass." I also met a man named "Big Head." One can guess how that name was derived. So, everyone had three or four names, and it was not uncommon for a person to be known by one name to one person or group, and yet by another name to another person or group. There were other people who did not want you to know any of their names and, when asked, would use another person's name. Because of such idiosyncrasies within the various cultures, one can begin to recognize that cultural differences provide special problems in communicating with the local people. We had a real educational experience as we worked to understand the local culture.

We began our trek headed toward the Pulie River. In our effort to get Paul and Mambel interested in what we were doing, I showed them the movie. Their eyes were glued to the screen; for one thing, they have little opportunity to view movies and they never had seen actual footage from the war that had threatened to disrupt and, even, destroy their lifestyles through a take-over of their island paradise.

After we had reached the mouth of the river, we raced up the river to Urin village. Having secured the boat to some overhanging tree branches, I set foot ashore and asked for Pita (Peter).

The villagers were curious about a couple of things. One was regarding the airplane we had found, and I was eager to show them a map of its location and explain to them how it ended up lying in the middle of the jungle near their village. They were also a bit suspicious as to why we were searching for airplanes. We understood their concerns because of a well-known myth common throughout this area and most likely all of PNG. Everywhere I had traveled on the island, I had met people who wanted to know about a warplane loaded with gold that had crashed in their back yard. So when I returned looking for another airplane, they could only deduce that I was looking for the gold. I told them that I did not believe that legend, but if it were true, I merely wanted to find the airplane and they could have any gold that was found (although they would no doubt have had to discuss its ownership with the PNG government) and that all I wanted to do was shoot photographs! That seemed to pacify their suspicions. I also explained to them the importance of human remains to our culture and the possibility that if there were any to be found, that the American, Australian or Japanese governments would probably send someone to retrieve the bones.

That was good news to them as they would, no doubt, be hired by the military to help find the remains, although that would not be as profitable as finding an airplane full of gold! I also showed them the movie we had brought with us. I set the TV on an empty 44-gallon drum and plugged it into an inverter attached to a 12-volt battery. They too were mesmerized as they watched battleships shelling the shorelines and bombers dropping bombs on coconut plantations which were not that far from where we were, so the terrain in the movie was somewhat familiar to them. Over the years, they had grown up hearing stories from the old men concerning what they had seen during the war years. This was the first time that these villagers had been given the unique opportunity to see the story of the battle, and they could even hear the explosions and rat-a-tat-tat of machine gun fire.

After the battery had been depleted, the TV stopped; we re-boarded the boat and headed out to go find the airplane. This time, no less than 20 villagers had joined us. I was a bit disturbed because the boat was so loaded, and embarrassed because I had not taken enough food for that many people. It is a culturally acceptable motivator to feed your workers so I always brought food along. I probably could have asked them to limit the number of guides who wanted to join us, but I believed that the boat could handle all of them, so I did not want it to become a contentious issue. Now, I was saddled with a boat which was so heavy that it became frustratingly difficult to generate any speed. It did plow through the water for what seemed like forever, but eventually (and to my surprise), we were skimming along on the glassy river. After only eight minutes, we were back to the junction of the two rivers and then turned sharply 90 degrees to the right as the boat rolled way over on its side then headed up into the interior by the Pulie River for another 17 minutes. The "crew" was truly impressed with the speed, agility and size of the big boat.

We pulled up to the bank of the river on the starboard side under an overhanging branch and tied the line to the tree. I again donned my spiked golf shoes and scooted off the bow onto the shore; we unloaded the boat and set off, in a line, into the jungle. We had only hiked for five minutes when we came to a deserted timber company road. We crossed over a log bridge and I thought; at last, this must be the log bridge about which I had heard. On the other side of the road, we broke bush again – but only for a short distance when we came upon an airplane wing which was almost completely covered with vines. (See page xii – NO. 3) This was the wing that the dozer operator reported that he had lifted; he had actually moved it about 15 meters (50 feet). I was disappointed again at not finding an airplane that was intact (like the previous P-38). While our party cut and removed all the vines and tried to identify the airplane from the wing structure, the youngsters and several of the locals roamed around the area searching for more parts. By that time, we had become quasi-experts on identifying various airplane types, and we soon noticed the speed brakes on the underside of the wing; that indicated it was another Japanese Val! The familiar large landing gear with no tire was lying there next to one of the bomb holders that attached the bomb to the underside of the wing.

When I lifted another smaller piece of the wing, it revealed the Japanese roundel, the "Rising Sun," (Hinomaru) which was the big red national disk insignia used by the Japanese. The "Rising Sun" is derived from the Japanese word, "Nippon." Broken down, "Ni" means sun and "Pon" means origin. It also refers to the country of Japan in that language. The Japanese believed that their country was the land of the Rising Sun and that the sun rose every day *for them*! They also believed that Japan provided the rest of the world with light and, therefore, it was a divine appointment that they should rule the world.[48]

As I examined and took photographs of the wing, I could hear the youngsters saying: "Here's some over here!" "I found the engine!" "There's more over here!" They have always been quick to venture around while I spent more time examining certain pieces in an attempt to find identification numbers. After I had completed my investigation of the wing, I broke bush and caught up with the youngsters. There it was – the big 14-cylinder engine complete with propeller blades still attached. That was the first time we had ever found one this intact; in all the other wrecks we had seen, the propeller was detached from the engine, and it made me wonder at what angle it hit the ground? When propellers of a crashed airplane are bent, they reveal the angle of the crash and the speed at which the engine was turning at the time of impact. One might also locate gouges in the ground which would have been made by the propellers. Obviously, because of the elapsed time and the effects of the bulldozer, no gouges were found.

As we continued to investigate the site, I explained to our helpers that we were looking for any writing or number on the airplane pieces. With that, they began a serious search to cover the entire wreckage site. The dozer had done more damage than the operator wanted to admit, as it was evident that he had driven over the airplane. We knew that because we found the tail hook, which was used for carrier landings, along with other parts buried in the mud. That was a bit discouraging as the airplane may have been in fairly good condition prior to the bulldozer having pushed it and buried it.

Despite my reluctance to bringing so many villagers, they proved to be an invaluable asset. After I had told them our goals for the search, they all proceeded to cut into the brush and trees in the area and made a 50-foot radius clearing. They stabbed the ground with their machetes and listened for the sound of metal as their blades sunk into the soil. For the next four hours, we searched that entire area. I took a central position and they brought me piece after piece; I then examined each piece in search of some writing or a number. It was great to have all of them there even though they had been up all night celebrating with a ceremonial dance called a "Singsing." Some of them were quite tired and rested on the ground sleeping while the others carried on the search with interest.

After a couple of hours, a familiar piece was brought to me; I had seen it on a previous search. It had been painted with a stencil which identified the airplane model and manufacturer number. That is what we needed to positively identify the airplane. Unfortunately, the four-digit manufacturer number was not clear since two of the digits were indistinguishable.

We continued to examine each and every piece of aluminum, large and small. At the rear of the engine, on what was remaining of the fuselage, on the right side of the airplane, just behind the firewall, there was a four-digit number, 3450. Two of the numbers matched with the stencil we had found earlier; the first number 3 and the last number 0 were prominent and legible. On the lower portion of the third number on the stencil was a rounded part that suggested the possibility of the number 5. Through an amazing coincidence, we had found the manufacturer number! From the writing on the stencil and that number, we would be able to confirm the type of airplane it was and what month and year the airplane was built. Unfortunately, the information we had found would not be adequate to reveal the airplane's mission when it crashed; nor could it tell us the name of the pilot and crew member. Those details required the complete number that would have been painted on the tail of the airplane.

By this time, our goal had switched from finding bullets to identifying the airplane, with hopes of determining whether the pilot (and/or crew) had survived the crash. If they had not, it was possible that the remains were still in the area. If we could find them, perhaps we could be instrumental in those remains being returned to their families. I heard that when the Japanese soldiers went to battle, they left cuttings of their hair and fingernails with the family. In the event they did not return, the family would mourn over these.[49] That kind of information could have also been useful in the postmortem identification process.

As we continued to scour the area, we found plastic pieces of the canopy and several aluminum framing pieces, so we spent some extra time in that area with hopes that we could find human remains. We also searched extensively behind the engine where the cockpit would have been. Unfortunately, after the bulldozer had run over the airplane and pushed it around, it was difficult to say that anything that may have been there originally was still there. Some other pieces of aluminum with Japanese writing on them were found, and one was probably from the wing tank filler area, as it was labeled in English and read "Fuel." My son Jared found the tail wheel, and attached to the strut was an aluminum tag with Japanese writing on it. I had hoped that the tag would give us some more information about the airplane.

By the time we left the area, we had unearthed five mounds of airplane pieces that we had stacked up, but we did not find even one of the three guns with which that airplane would have been outfitted. My guess was that we were not the first to dig at this crash site and that those guns had probably been taken. Because of all the small pieces that were found, I also wondered whether this airplane had crashed with its bomb and exploded. After four hours of poking, digging and examining, everyone seemed to be tired – except me. Even the youngsters had had enough, and so, satisfied with having found the aircraft and identifying numbers, we headed back to the boat. I apologetically gave our helpers the little bit of rice and tin fish we had brought along as payment for their help in clearing and searching the site, and I explained that I had not anticipated so large a group. I thought that the next time I go up there, I would take more food. We returned home without incident.

On that following week, I sent e-mails to Justin Taylan of *Pacific Wrecks* and to my Japanese fishing friend in Japan. Toshi wrote back and told me about the stencil lettering; he confirmed it was an Aichi D3A2 dive bomber, in other words, a Val. Justin also wrote to say the manufacturer number confirmed that the airplane was built by Aichi in October of 1943 and was probably lost in the December 17-27th raids on the Arawe landing. This was one of the 815 D3A2 models built from August of 1942, through June of 1944.[50] Toshi said the aluminum tag off the rear strut read:

> Factory kayaba
> Use machine 99 dive bomber type 2
> Part number? 190050?
> Serial number kayaba 451
> Weight (K) 252
> Oil quality type1 hydraulic fluid

Val rear strut data tag. WNBP, PNG

Val wing with roundle. WNBP, PNG

Boat *Sirocco* on Pulie River, Urin village. WNBP, PNG

Chapter 13

CANNIBALS AND HUDSON A16-165

After those two wreckage finds, we had reached an adrenaline high. The following weekend, we had cargo to take to our Akolet team in Gasmata, so we decided to spend the night and have the next full day to look around. Once the 1,400 kilograms (1.5 tons) of cargo was unloaded in Gasmata, we set off to see what we could find. I was determined to find that airplane in the water that we had always heard was there. Ironically, it seemed that everybody knew where it was located, but no one had actually seen it. I asked people in the area, and as we followed the various stories we found an old man who said he had seen it. He claimed that he was in his canoe and had speared a turtle. The turtle escaped with the man's spear, so he jumped into the water to chase it. As he swam after his spear, he had seen a two-engine airplane. After we heard that, we asked him to take us to the location where that had occurred. He agreed, and when we reached the scene, we realized that it was the same place we had checked out two years previously. I had him re-enact his story, as I silenced others from chirping in (as it is customary to support someone even when you do not know if they are telling the truth or not). As the old man, Pius, told his story, I told him to direct the boat to the spot of this incident with the turtle. When he said that we had arrived, we dropped anchor. I again asked him to have a good look around and make certain this was the spot. He confirmed it. "It was right here," he said.

Jared and I dressed in our dive gear and pessimistically jumped into the water. We were not excessively excited because Micah and I had searched this same reef earlier without any success. Even so, we dived in, full of hope. We searched in a grid pattern at different depths all the way to the bottom at 24 meters (80 feet). I doubted that Pius had chased the turtle that deep, but we had not seen any evidence of an airplane in the shallower depths, so I thought it might have slid down the side of the reef during a land shift (or an earthquake). At that depth, the water was so cloudy, Jared and I almost had to hold hands to keep from losing track of each other. We were just inches from the bottom and continued on course, but to our dismay again, the mysterious airplane eluded us. After we surfaced, we took Pius home to his village and encouraged him to really review his story again and try to remember exactly where he had seen the airplane.

From there, we continued onward to investigate another airplane that we had seen on a nearby island. (See page xiii – NO. 14) It had a pair of nine-cylinder Cyclone engines. One was stuck straight into the ground, so it looked as if it had crashed pretty severely. Some of the village people had tried to dig up the propeller to sell it, but it was buried too deeply into the ground. There was only a wing and the engines; there seemed to be no further remnants of the aircraft. We did see the engine tag and photographed it with the hope that it would help us to identify the airplane.

When one locates a crash site, it is always baffling as to why so much of the aircraft is missing. One wonders whether it had blown apart because of the ordnance it carried, or perhaps upon a high speed impact it merely broke apart and parts were scattered all over the crash site with little of it left to be seen. In many cases, the engines have survived the impact – probably because of their density. Another thought was that we were not the first ones to scan that particular site. Many scavengers (cannibals) could have been responsible for much of the missing proof of aircraft identification.

As we traveled around the Gasmata harbor, we wanted to connect with another old man who had some knowledge of aircraft wrecks. As we pulled up to the shore, we could not believe our eyes. There was a dilapidated aluminum boat on the bank, and it was full of scrap aluminum airplane pieces! We went ashore and met the owner of the boat, and he was really proud of his fortune. He was waiting for the day when he could sell all that scrap aluminum to someone for a good price. That was his retirement fund! He told us how he had shuttled it over from the airplane we had just examined. So at last, we had one answer as to why we were only finding engines and landing gears. Anything that could have been physically ripped off and carried away had already been taken; that left only the heavier parts where the airplanes had crashed.

With his permission, we sifted through the scrap in the boat in an attempt to find some kind of identification mark. We found a tailfin with some painting on it. There was a design indicating three rectangles. One was in red, but we could not discern what the other colors might have been. At that time it did not mean anything to us but it looked important enough to report, so I snapped a photograph of it.

B-25 ENGINE

That same day, late in the afternoon, I heard of one other aircraft wreckage on the island called Avirin. It was getting late, but I began hiking around the island with a few other men and boys. It was a lot farther than I had anticipated, and after walking along a sandy beach, wading over a reef and stumbling through some mangroves we found an aircraft engine on the south side of the island. (See page xiii – NO. 15) It was larger than any others I had seen, but there was no data tag on it. It did have some English writing, so I knew it was not a Japanese engine.

After we returned home I researched this engine and found that the *Pacific Wrecks* website had some information about this crash site: (http://www.pacificwrecks.com/aircraft/b-25/42-64846.html)

B-25G-5 Mitchell Serial Number 42-64846
USAAF, 5th AF, 38th BG, 822nd BS
Pilot 1st Lt. Clifford A. Jaebker, O-795399 (KIA)
Co-Pilot 2/Lt Noel F. Learned, O-795778 (KIA)
Navigator 2/Lt Marek G. Pzegeo, O-672973 (KIA)
Radio S/Sgt Henry B. Lang, 37373993 (KIA)
Gunner S/Sgt Charles L. Hinsch, 32246203 (KIA)
Crashed November 22, 1943
MACR 1171

Aircraft Engines: R-2600-13 AAF Serial Numbers: 43-24227, 43-24228.

Mission History

Mission 325-H; This bomber took off from Durand Field (17-Mile Drome) for a bombing mission against Gasmata Airfield and Lindenhaven Plantation. Hit by anti-aircraft fire in the right engine; that caused it to spiral into the ground. It crashed in flames on Arwin Island.

1st Lt. C. S. Fuller reports in MACR 1171:

"Lt. Jaebker was flying on my right wing constituting a two plane formation. We were at about 600 feet altitude getting our spacing for our first run on the target and in order to fall in behind the lead formation I had to make a 90° turn to the right. As I banked I looked over at Lt. Jaebker to see his position and I saw him shake his head and then slide under my plane and up in position on my left wing. Shortly after a slight turn to the left was necessary so once again I looked over at him. His plane was in a steep bank to the right and going down. The top hatch over the pilot's compartment was gone and the cockpit looked as if it had been burned out. In the split second that I saw the plane before it passed under me the cockpit looked empty and the right engine was on fire. The plane then passed under me preventing further observation. I later saw a column of smoke about 500 ft. high coming from Arwin Island in the vicinity of where the ship went in a bank. Previous to my run on the target I noticed several bursts of ack, ack coming from Gasmata airdome but did not notice any bursts near our formation."

Wreckage

After the Gasmata area was occupied by the Australian Army, a report by natives stated: two bombers came over Gasmata low. This bomber dropped its bomb, and was hit by enemy shore guns and caught fire, lost height and crashed into the mangroves of Awrin Island. No airmen were seen to jump from the plane. The other plane flew over the ship and was set on fire and crashed into Gasmata Harbor. [Note: this reference to a second crash was not the same day].

Lt. W. A. J. Saville, AIF patrol officer visited the crash site on Arwin Island. Lt. Saville located '264846' (USAAF Serial Number) on the cockpit dash board and reported the wreckage as mostly burned but two main wheels were intact. These remains were recovered September 22, 1944.

The bones were burned and recovered and turned over to the US Army HQ at Arawe, who assigned them unknown identities: X-22, X-23, X-24, X-25, X-26. It was deemed "the condition of the remains does not warrant identification." These remains were sent to Finschafen cemetery in AGRS custody.

It appeared that we had, indeed, located the aircraft that was described in this report.

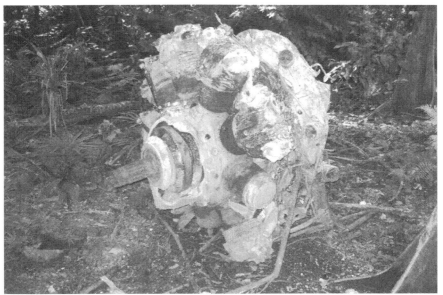

Lockheed Hudson A16-165 Cyclone engine, Angap Island. WNBP, PNG

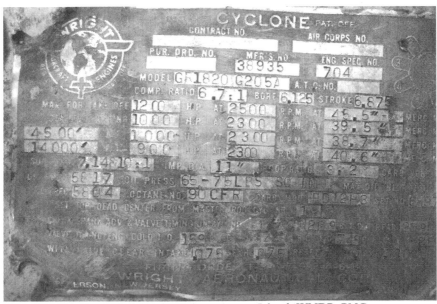

Cyclone engine data plate, Angap Island. WNBP, PNG

Lockheed Hudson A16-165 vertical stabilizer, Gasmata. WNBP, PNG

Chapter 14

THOSE BLASTED MANGROVES

– BEAUFORT A9-204

As we hiked back to the boat, a younger fellow in his late teens began to walk with us, and he said that he had seen a two-engine airplane in another mangrove area. I continued to question him more about it, and he said it was still complete. With high interest, I asked him more specific questions about the wreckage. By the time we returned to the boat, it was almost dark so we continued our conversation and made plans to go see this airplane in the morning.

I did not sleep well that night since I was so excited to see this complete two-engine airplane. We camped on the boat tied up to the wharf that Jared and I had built at the old Gasmata government post. Morning dawned and not a minute too soon; we did not wait around, but ventured off to get our guide for the trip. After a bit of haggling, a price of PNG K20 (US $6.50) was paid for the services to be rendered.

We drove to the north side of the Gasmata airstrip and pulled up next to some thick mangroves. I knew from the day before that I did not do well while walking on mangroves, but we proceeded deeper and deeper into this swamp area. (See page xiii – NO. 16) I had never seen mangroves so thick, but we continued onward with excitement, waiting for the moment someone would say, "It's over there." Instead of hearing, "it's over there," someone picked up a piece of aluminum about 15-centimeters (six-inches) long. As we scrounged around, more little pieces were found including the piston head of an engine. As it turned out, that was it! Only a bunch of small pieces here and there were found stuck in the muddy muck and mire. I went to the guide and confronted him face to face and asked, "Where is the twin-engine *complete* airplane?" He did not look at me nor did he reply. I could not believe he would make such a bold statement then accompany us to a site knowing full well that he had lied. Where was his integrity? How could he have even shown his face? What audacity! Where was my 20 kina?! But it is pretty well known that, in this culture, deception is what they have been taught, not integrity. The culture was not based on

Biblical or any other moral principles so there were no constraints about lying or telling the truth. Actually, it had been my experience that the first response to a question asked was to reply with an untruth. That young man could possibly have been a hero to his peers since he had pulled the wool over my eyes and escaped with my cash. Or, culturally, he may have merely said what he thought I wanted to hear.

From what we saw and later heard, the airplane may have been an Australian Beaufort that had crashed with its bombs attached and exploded upon impact, scattering airplane fragments in all directions. To investigate this site thoroughly would have taken a long period of time and a great deal of dedication. I wondered if anyone has exerted a great deal of energy in such searches, since WWII veterans have been dying and the families of the lost crew have lost touch with their history and hope of finding them.

The Bristol Beaufort was a British twin-engine torpedo bomber designed by the Bristol Aeroplane Company. Beauforts were most widely used, until the end of the Second World War, by the Royal Australian Air Force in the Pacific theatre. Although designed as a torpedo-bomber, the Beaufort more often flew as a level-bomber. The Beaufort also flew more hours in training than on operational missions, and more were lost through accidents and mechanical failures than were lost to enemy fire.[51]

As we left the mangroves, we proceeded to another reef; we still wanted to find that elusive airplane in the water. We tried our tested and true procedure of dragging two swimmers with mask and snorkel behind the boat. We boated back and forth along the edge of a reef. We found no hints, nothing. We spoke with another old man who "knew" where the airplane was located and returned to the same reef; this time, we searched the back side. On this occasion, we suited up with dive gear and swam back and forth, up and down, but still the airplane eluded discovery.

Somehow in the conversation, someone mentioned an engine on the reef which was nearby to where we had already searched, so we went back there to get a closer look. It was a 14-cylinder engine which Jared immediately suggested might be Japanese. From our previous experience, we knew how the Val engines looked and could identify them, and this one looked similar. (See page xiii – NO. 14)

After we had anchored the boat in the area, we found the tail section of an airplane following a short period of snorkeling. We could not discern whether the engine and the airplane were from two separate wrecks or one, but we did discern one thing: it was definitely not a Japanese Val such as we had seen at the other crash sites. We were able to determine that it was a twin-tailed airplane since one of the rudders was still identifiable, and it was lying to the outside of the rear stabilizer. To our amazement, we also found a box of bullets that had been lying on the reef in three feet of water for 65 years.

Ryan Coleman was with us, and he spotted what appeared to be a large wing in about 6 meters (20 feet) of water. I swam over to have a look at it, and I free-dived down to it and realized that, sure enough, it was a wing. It was one that required further investigation! Unfortunately, due to our time constraints, it would have to wait. We left Gasmata somewhat discouraged having not found anything definite we could identify, but it was a good adventure and it gave us a lot of homework to research.

During that trip, we had also heard about a three-masted German ship that had been burnt and sunk by the natives. The report was that this happened prior to WWI, so that would have made this incident occur around the turn of the 20th century.

Many local people knew of the story, and a few men guided us to the location. It was supposedly inside a secluded bay among the islands. Jared and Mariko donned their dive gear while I piloted the boat. We lowered the boat anchor, and they held on to it as it dangled at a depth of 12 meters (40 feet). I dragged them along a grid pattern of the area but they did not see the ship. Actually, they did not see anything as the water was so cloudy.

Hudson rudder, Gasmata. WNBP, PNG

111

Australian Bristol Beaufort.

Gasmata guides. WNBP, PNG

Chapter 15

THE BIBLE TEACHER – VAL #6

We had not forgotten about that twin-engine airplane that John Tukai had drawn in my notebook, so the following weekend, we set off to find him. We collected our boat security men at Yumielo village (which was a couple miles to the west of Kandrian), and we headed out once again for Wako. This time, the seas were a bit rough, and I had a notion to turn around, knowing that if they were rough that early in the day, no doubt it would become even rougher later in the day when we were going to return against the waves. But my courage kicked in and I asked myself, "How can I turn back now?"

By the time we neared Wako village, which was located on the coast, the seas were irritatingly rough. After we idled through a small channel which led us right to the front of the village, we were unable to anchor since the rough water jostled us severely. It took all of Jared's skills as a captain to keep the boat away from the reefs on both sides and in front of us as we bobbed up and down and back and forth. Nobody on the beach was eager to push a dugout canoe out into the surf to come to greet us but finally, an older man waded into the water and swam out to us through three-foot waves. After he swam approximately 200 feet, he reached the boat and pulled himself up onto the fore deck; understandably, he looked rather tired. We told him why we had come, and after he spent some time yelling back and forth to the people on the shore, another man swam out. That man was one of our old guides from years ago and the brother of John Tukai. Once again, John was not there. I had begun to think that John was avoiding us, which was what he would more than likely do if he really had not seen the reported airplane. Another older man had told me that, even if he was chasing a pig with his dogs when he came upon the airplane, he still would have remembered where it was. So I had the feeling that John's story may have been fabricated.

After a short conversation, he and the other man jumped back into the water and headed for shore. We proceeded to navigate our way back out through the reefs and through the small channel. The seas were not looking good, and we knew we were in for a bumpy ride when we returned to the house later in the day; we would have to forge our way while heading straight into the waves. That did not bother us for now, though, as we were soon to reach the calm waters of the Pulie River.

When the ocean waves meet the water flowing out of the mouths of the rivers, they swell; they were especially large there since the water is shallow where it exits the river to the ocean. Sometimes, while maneuvering in to some rivers, the bottom of the boat scrapes the river bed and the propeller then hits the bottom causing the engine to stop, only to be swamped by the next wave which hits the stern. Fortunately, the mouth of the Pulie was four-and-a-half meters (15 feet) deep, so although the swells were huge, there was little chance of hitting bottom. Navigating was still a challenge as it was similar to surfing in on the swells, except with a boat instead of a surf board. The calm, flat waters of a river were always a welcome site after having been on the open seas where the waves were merciless.

Once inside the river, we passed a wharf made by a timber company where they loaded logs onto a pontoon which was then towed out to an overseas vessel. A little further up the river on the opposite shore, they had constructed another wharf for loading logs. That was the side of the river where we had heard about another crash site, so we pulled up to that wharf. We left our security guards with the boat, and then hiked up to the timber company base camp which was only a half mile away. We spoke there with the camp supervisor and some workers about our search mission. There was some confusion about who had knowledge about the location of the crash site. Finally, a younger man spoke up and said that he had heard about it. To our delight, the supervisor was headed up to that area, so he gave us a much appreciated lift in his Toyota Land Cruiser.

We rode for at least one hour on winding gravel roads with me sitting up front with the driver and no seat belt while my children stood in the back of the Toyota pickup truck. Occasionally, we encountered a section in the road that had become a mud bog, and the truck slipped and slid in and out of the ruts, but eventually we arrived at the village of Sabdidi. The supervisor told us that he would go further into the interior and then return in three hours to pick us up. We thought that was plenty of time to find the crash site.

We talked with the people at Sabdidi about our reasons for this trip; initially, they did not seem to be overly cooperative. Finally, a younger man named Francis approached us and after he had heard our mission purpose, he said he knew the location of the crash site and would take us to it. We headed out of the village following an old timber company road which made it easy to hike. It seemed as if we had walked a long distance, but in actuality, it was only a one-hour jaunt. At least there were no vines to trip me or tree branches to slap me in the face. We arrived at a small hamlet, but as I looked at my watch, I realized we did not have much time to continue on since we had to get back to meet our ride back to the boat. Assured the site was "klostu" (close to), we proceeded onward. Some smaller children escorted us through a garden site and onto the side of a hill. (See page xii – NO. 2)

To our disappointment, there were hardly any recognizable parts there. We did find the tail wheel, and, just as with the last airplane we had found, the tail wheel had an aluminum tag strapped to it. That tag identified the company that had manufactured it and some other particulars about the strut, such as how much oil it held. From our previous experiences, though, and the design of the tail wheel, we were reasonably certain that the airplane was yet another Val.

As I walked past a section of the wing structure, I noticed a data plate that was attached to the inside hinge area. That was the first time we had ever seen the hinged area opened, since on the other occasions, they had been in a closed position which concealed that data plate. It had become green from moss, and I tried to clean it with a leaf. One of our guides handed me the husk from a beetle nut (they used them to brush their teeth). I scrubbed on the data plate, and surprisingly, the makeshift cleanser worked really well! To my delight, I was able to make out some of the Japanese characters which resembled the characters on previous stencils we had found. I was unable to resist prying the data plate off to take with me for further investigation.

We had only searched for approximately 15 minutes, but sadly, it was time to start our return trip. I wished that we had had more time to look around the area. Perhaps, there were more parts of the airplane, but it was time to curtail this trip and return. I was unable to get a GPS reading at that time due to the thickness of the tree canopy. As we hiked back out through the garden into an opening where there were no trees, I paused and was then able to get a satellite signal. I made a waypoint of the location of the crash site on the GPS as I had done with all the other sites. After we shared some biscuits and we paid our guides for their assistance, I pressed onward at what I thought was a fast pace. Jared and Mariko stayed at the hamlet since they wanted to get some "kulau" (half-ripe coconuts) to drink. We had usually bought kulaus for a dime here, but in Hawaii, I had once paid five dollars for one. Imported foods in PNG were relatively expensive. I then found myself racing as I tried to get back to our drop off point. When I had almost reached it, there, to my surprise, Mariko had caught up with me.

One may question my sanity in leaving my children behind as I continued to the next village. This may seem irresponsible to some, but one thing we had learned was that the village people, in their own areas, actually looked after us and our children. One can relate it to assisting a tourist to find their way around your neighborhood. In the major towns though, we always kept a short leash and would not let our children out of our sights.

We walked and talked along the way of our "rugged hike" (almost paved-road condition) and came upon stacks of firewood that were gathered so that they could later be carried by some local women or girls on their heads back to the village. We had always thought that we had been roughing it, but this was representation of an even rougher life for the villagers. Although cute to see, even little five-year-old girls carried firewood on their heads, and the loads became larger and larger as the children grew older. As we walked a bit further, we met a couple of youths who were perspiring profusely after hiking up a hill from the stream where they had gone to fill some five-gallon jugs with water. Again, it was a reminder of the effort of daily life for these people in the middle of a jungle.

We finally arrived at the pickup point right on time, after I had run almost the entire trail, it seemed. Picture my surprise when Jared arrived at the same time! I never knew how he had gotten there so fast. I thought to myself, "I must be getting old." All of that surprise and elation dissipated almost immediately when we found that our ride was not there. We sat there for one hour (an hour I wish we could have spent back at the crash site) and waited for a truck to pick us up. We were happy when, at 4:00 P.M., we did hitch a ride on another timber company vehicle. We all stood in the back of the truck this time and held on for dear life as we raced back to the base camp. Incidentally, we stood the entire trip since there was no space to sit down – the bed was full of people. There were men, women and children, along with woven palms made into baskets which they used for carrying taro, bananas and spinach like greens from their gardens to their huts. That was another example of the rugged life these isolated people lived. I was greatly relieved when we arrived back at the boat, although it was much later than I had hoped and dusk was soon to be upon us.

Leaving the timber company wharf and heading towards the mouth of the river, we could see that our fears about the seas getting rougher had come to reality. The swells at the mouth of the river were probably two to three meters (six to nine feet) high. We slowly proceeded through the passageway, but once on the open seas, the big swells were so close together, pushed by a strong headwind, that it created a chop making it impossible for us to go fast. So we backed down on the throttle – and put out some fishing lines.

It was a slow ride bobbing back and forth, up and down, and after about an hour, we heard one of our fishing reels sing out! I quickly jumped down, in the dark, from the flybridge to grab the rod and worked to get the catch under control. Afterwards, I handed it to Pasio (our boat security), to reel in our catch. He cranked and cranked until his arm was sore and tired. In the end, he said that it had been worth the pain as he had brought up a huge yellow fin tuna. We gaffed it and it went wild! We then brought it inside the boat and threw it in the four-foot cooler, but it was too large for the cooler and did not fit! We had to leave the lid open on the cooler as the tail stuck out. Wow, what a catch! It was, surely, the biggest yellow fin we had ever caught. For some reason I do not remember weighing it, so I am unable to precisely comment on how heavy it was. I have seen larger fish, but any angler would have been proud of that catch.

It was about 9:00 P.M. when we finally arrived at home. My wife, Joan, did not seem worried since we had been able to call her on the radio, in advance, and let her know where we were and that we would be late. There were other times when we had been unable to contact her, but even at those times, she was not overly concerned. I asked her why she never seemed alarmed, even when I had the children along and she said that because over all the years and times we had been away, we had always returned, so she was able to rest in that fact and wait patiently. I am sure, however, had we not returned, her ability to rest would have been comparable to the misery of those who are still waiting for their loved ones to return.

One of the most encouraging things regarding that adventure, even though we did not find many pieces of the airplane, was that we had met Francis. He was the guide who had taken us directly to the crash site. During our time together, Francis and I walked along the trail and talked; I soon discovered that he was a Bible teacher. He was not just any Bible teacher, but he was a man who had heard the good news of Jesus Christ who had died on the cross for his (and everyone's) sins, and he (Francis) first believed that message 17 years earlier. He had heard that story after I had brought a fellow missionary, Mike Micholavich, to his village of Gergering to teach them the Bible. Francis was just a young man then, but he had heard and understood the message of the Bible, that the lost may be found. He turned from his sins, he believed in God's provision of Jesus who had come and paid the penalty for sins, and then chose to proclaim that message to others. He was making monthly trips from his village to Sabdidi to check up on the Church there. He was a modern day evangelist. It was a genuine joy to have boated, driven and hiked so far *and* to find, what is actually more important than WWII wrecks, someone who had come to know Jesus as his Savior and walked in obedience to His Word.

After I returned home, I sent the pictures of the data plates to my fishing buddy, Toshi, in Japan. I should have sent him a picture of the tuna as he had once caught a world-record-sized tuna in our area, using only a six-pound test line; he would have appreciated the huge tuna we had snagged that night. My friend translated the data plates which confirmed that this section of the wing was made by Aichi, weighed 162.2 kgs (357 lbs) and was to be fitted on a Model D3A2 airplane and was model 1520. That confirmed to us that we had positively identified the aircraft! That was a real victory for this line of work; an even more desirable find would have been the serial number on the tail or fuselage of an aircraft. That type of information would have enabled us to trace back to the mission of the airplane, the crew and their fate. Justin Taylan later wrote:

[TOP TAG]

Place of Manufacture – Aichi Aircraft Company, Ltd.
Airframe Use – Type 99 Carrier-Based Bomber Model 22

Manufacture Number – Aichi No. 9501
Weight – 162.2 kilograms
Inspection Stamp – Navy symbol (a flower); Aichi Co. symbol (an A and a C in a circle); individual symbol (a 2 in a circle)
Inspection date – blank year; blank month; blank day

[LOWER TAG]

Airframe Number – Aichi No. 1520

The number on the smaller tag was the aircraft manufacturer's number. That meant that a part which weighed 162.2 kilograms, having Manufacture Number Aichi No. 9501 and true serial number 501 had been installed on a Type 99 Carrier-Based Bomber Model 22 with Manufacture Number Aichi No. 1520 and true serial number 520. The part was the 501st of its kind to have been manufactured, and the aircraft was the 520th Val Model 22 that Aichi built. The number would have been found painted on the fuselage stencil, and on the stencils painted on the various components would have appeared as follows: 愛知第１５２０号 .

The airplane was assembled during November 1943; it was one of 52 Vals Aichi assembled that month, Manufacture Numbers ranged from 1479 through 1530. Those MNs were made by adding a base number selected according to the last digit of the true serial number of the individual aircraft. Since the digit in this case is zero, then the base number was 1000. The same system was applied to the component numbers. The MN for the 501st part was made by adding 9000 to the true serial number. All of the MNs had to exhibit the same characteristics. The sum of the first digit and the last digit of the MN had to be 1 or 10.

Children in dugout canoe. WNBP, PNG

Girls carrying water. WNBP, PNG

Val data plate, MN 1520.

Chapter 16

THE MISSING LINK – A-1?

While we had become excited about every opportunity to continue our searches, we realized that each adventure had two possibilities – success or failure. There were many occasions when we had launched out excitedly only to be disappointed and disheartened by our finding. Our zeal to locate crash sites and the opportunity to locate human remains for return to families had now become paramount in our minds.

On May 26, 2007, we returned to Gasmata. I had heard of an airplane farther up in the jungle from a friendly man named Alfi from Ais village. He had married a girl from Zebu Village in the interior of Gasmata. Alfi informed me of an airplane his in-laws had told him about, so we decided to go find it. We also decided that since we were going so far inland, that we would spend two days and also explore another lead we had found from a map obtained from Justin Taylan that identified approximate locations of other crash sites.

We boated up the coast just past Gasmata and stopped at the mouth of the Ringring River. I asked some of the locals if the river was navigable for our boat, and I was assured that it was. I had heard of a Japanese barge having been sunk on the river, so we asked them about that too. They said that it was nearby and kindly jumped on the bow of the boat and guided us a short distance up the river. As we sailed to the other side into a small tributary, we found a half-sunken small barge. It was pretty rusty but quite interesting to see and a visual reminder that the war had been fought in this area.

We continued to sail up the Ringring River and finally pulled over and tied up to a fallen tree. When we went ashore and walked up the hill, we discovered a village, and to my surprise, we also came upon a road. As we walked along the road, I saw remnants of a truck from the glory days when the timber company had operated in this region. I had seen sights like this many times before of new but bashed-up trucks rusting away in villages.

In the early 1990s, Malaysian timber companies came into the south coast areas to harvest the big trees. They caused quite a controversy as no one had ever before witnessed such radical changes so quickly to their land. Bulldozers cut roads to the interior where few villagers had ever ventured. Truckload after truckload of large trees was taken to the coast for shipment to buyers from Japan and China. There were many occasions when the tree-cutting was halted by angry villagers who claimed that a company bulldozer had run over or destroyed a traditional burial ground or that they had driven on and destroyed a garden. There were constant road blocks and protests and arguments among the people themselves regarding land boundaries.

The work somehow continued to move forward (likely after tiring negotiations), and the village leaders received large checks for government approved royalty payments in exchange for the trees that were cut out from their land. They said that the royalty payments were in exchange for the bark only from the trees. The buyers, and eventually the villagers, too, knew that these trees could sell for many times more than what they had been paid. Often, the checks were divided up among the clan members, and the wise ones bought such things as corrugated iron for roofing their homes. That roofing would save them a lot of work, as thatch roofs deteriorated in just a couple of years causing them to have to rebuild the entire house. The unwise ones bought cases and cases of beer to get drunk. They then beat their wives and fought with their fellow brothers, or else, they harassed the Malaysians. Crime escalated and even payroll trucks were held up by armed, masked rascals who used homemade shotguns. Police "riot squads" were then called in from Rabaul to attempt to catch the culprits. Because the government was consistently short of funds, calling in a riot squad required they be flown in – at the victim's expense! So, not only would one be robbed, but if they wanted justice, they would then have to pay airfares, provide housing and food as well as transportation for the police. The Kandrian police force consisted of *one* full-time and *one* reservist crime-fighter; unfortunately, those two were unable to handle the increasingly difficult situation. Perhaps, had they had a vehicle they could have been more effective.

There were times village leaders did not divide the royalty payments, they preferred to send a delegation to a town to purchase a truck for the entire village. So, here was a situation where people who had never seen a $100 in their lives, yet they found themselves involved with the purchase of a brand new Toyota pickup. That was somewhat disconcerting to me since I was driving around in an old "rust-bucket." The day of delivery was a special day when the shiny new trucks arrived by barge. Someone would jump behind the wheel and drive away from the wharf overloaded with no standing room left in the back as they rocked the truck and sang gleefully.

For a while, one could see the new trucks parked near the streams, being washed and pampered. The newness of these trucks was short-lived though, and soon there were shattered windshields. That usually occurred as a result of an angry drunk who, in his stupor, had smashed the windshield with a rock. If that was not the case, the truck may have been beaten-up from rolling into a ditch – while driven by a drunk. It was not uncommon for people to have been killed after having been propelled from the back bed of a truck that was operated by a drunk and driven off the road. So the occasional heap of metal alongside the road was actually a rather common sight.

It also reminded me of the truck I had sold to a local man. I had repainted the truck so it looked like new. While I was on furlough for a year, a fellow bought it from my co-worker Dan Rempel. By the time I returned, the truck was not running. First, he had overheated the engine and had to constantly add water to the radiator. Then, when it was low on oil, someone had filled it with hydraulic fluid and that caused the engine to seize. So, there it sat for a couple of years as people "borrowed" parts from it. I even bought some leaf springs myself. Then one day, three years after the truck had been sold, I received a dirty, handwritten letter from the buyer who wanted half his money back because he did not get the use out of the truck that he had expected.

Of course, I was shocked and I told him to meet me at the police station so that we could discuss it. At the negotiation site, I was met by him and five of his relatives; I was there alone. The policeman had joined us to oversee the discussion; he merely wanted us to settle the matter amicably. He did not favor either side. After much discussion, wherein they had no legal support, I had to remain calm in order to protect myself against future rock-throwing or the possibility of having nails buried in the road to sabotage me every time I traveled through their village. Therefore, I then agreed to pay the guy PNG K600. (Approx. US $250). We shook hands and parted as friends and, although he was smiling, for some reason, I was not happy. I wonder why?

As we hiked onward, we eventually arrived at the village of Zebu. The village looked similar to a long airstrip with houses on each side. At first it appeared there were very few people in the area, but I was glad Alfi was with us. He communicated with the few locals who were there and told them that we had come to see the crashed airplane. They had no problem with that and agreed to escort us through the jungle, along with over a dozen young people and children. In all, there were 21 in our party; it ended up being quite a large group that included young and old who had joined to tag along. As one can see, our visits to the villages would often cause quite a commotion as we would be the center of attraction.

Young boys were called, "Mankies." I had always assumed they had been given that name as they climbed trees as avid as monkeys. The older boys and men often sent them up the trees to fetch beetle nut or kulau (half-ripe coconuts). The kulaus were a delightfully refreshing drink and often squirted like a soft drink when the shell was cracked. After drinking the liquid, one could eat the soft white coconut "meat" inside. Coconut meat and a beef cracker was a good meal, especially if one was hungry.

We had hiked for only a short distance, perhaps 20 minutes, when we arrived at a dry stream bed. (See page x - NO. 17) We found small pieces of airplane wreckage strewn over a large area. There was something sticking from the ground, and the people said that it was an aircraft engine. It looked as if the only thing left was the muffler with a 75-millimeter (three-inch) pipe jutting out from the middle. I did not believe that the engine was buried under this site, but about seven-and-a-half meters (25 feet) away from this artifact was an actual engine! It was clear because the people had dug down into the ground about five feet which exposed it. The cylinder heads were broken apart, and the exhaust collector was severely damaged. The people wanted the propeller so they could sell it for scrap metal. They had already dug one-and-a-half meters (five feet) into the ground and had exposed two of the propeller blades, but the third blade was aligned and buried straight down another five feet or so into the ground. They finally realized that it was futile, so they abandoned the endeavor. That airplane must have impacted almost vertically and fallen into the soft streambed, burying the engines upon impact. That seemed unbelievable since, for some reason, I had thought that when airplanes crashed, they either glided into the surface or, in some cases, pancaked onto the ground. That was not the case for this one. It appeared to have flown straight down into the ground.

There was a section of the wing lying on the ground, but it was pretty bashed up. It had an accordion-like look to it. There was no fuselage present. It had probably already been found previously and chopped up for scrap. Approximately 40 feet away from the other engine was another inner wing section. It had the letter, "A" then a dash "-" and the number, "1." So it looked like: A-1. There was another number, but it was in a section that had been ripped through the middle. I examined it from different angles as I attempted to discern the number – and that was difficult, since only half of it was intact. I took photographs from all angles for later study and for referring to other entities. It was rather exciting as we all tried to guess what number or letter it could have been. My best guess was that it could have been a "G."

We turned the wing over in an attempt to see if there were any numbers on the bottom side. All the boys lined up on one side and lifted the wing and stood it on end. There were no numbers, but it had the British roundel. It was a big round circle, perhaps one meter (three feet) in diameter and had been painted on bare metal. The paint had worn off, but in the middle of the circle was a red circle. It was, perhaps, 46 centimeters (18 inches) in diameter. Later, research revealed that in June of 1942, the red circle was painted over so as to not be confused for a Japanese aircraft. I snapped a few photos of the helpers as they held the wing upright. They always liked to have their pictures taken, then crowd around the camera afterwards to see themselves on the tiny digital screen. That had always engendered a lot of laughs, as they called off the names of the ones they recognized in the photograph.

From the limited information we had found, we could determine that it was an Australian or a British airplane, but not the type or model. I studied that number frontwards and backwards and tried to identify that partial number or letter. Later, one of the helpers had searched in the bush and found a piece of metal that had black paint on it. We tried to make it fit on the wing, turning it every conceivable way; it was like fitting a piece into a puzzle, and eventually, we found it! It fit exactly and it revealed the number "6." So, at this point, what we had so far was, "A-16." It would have been great if we could have only found additional identification numbers. I encouraged our helpers to search around for more scrap aluminum. After they had searched further, they finally brought me a piece of metal that looked as if it could fit into our puzzle. Unfortunately, it was extremely mangled and had an accordion-like appearance. If we could have straightened that piece out and made it flat, we could probably have read more numbers. Unfortunately, we had nothing like a hammer with which to flatten it. There was little remaining to examine, so we decided to conclude our search and return home, and we took that piece of accordion-shaped aluminum with us with hopes of reshaping it.

We walked along the trail back to the village as one of the young men told me about the timber company that had been cutting trees in the area. He then mentioned that this airplane which we had just searched had damaged the trees, and he felt that his people should be compensated for the damage. Once I heard that, I stopped quickly in my tracks. As we stood there, I explained to him that we had been walking on a grown-over path that a bulldozer had made while going into the jungle as it knocked down trees left and right. If he had wanted to talk about damage to the rain forest, I think a good place to start would have been with the dozer operator and ultimately the timber company, which I am sure had already paid royalties and had probably paid for environmental damages.

I then looked him in the eyes with a perplexed face indicating that I was somewhat annoyed and asked, "Do you know that several men had probably died here?" I told him that those men had come from another country to fight for his grandparents because they could not defend themselves. If it had not been for men such as these, this land would not be his and he would not have been able to ask for compensation. I went on to say, "If we can track down this serial number and find out who had lost their lives here, you would not be asking for compensation, you should be writing the families of the lost soldiers and telling them "Thank You" for sending their young sons and fathers to make you free." With that, I began to hike again, still in an upset mood. This young man seemed like a nice guy as he did not argue with me. Perhaps, he just needed his head adjusted to realize who was owed what; that little history lesson certainly gave him something to ponder. Compensation? – give me a break! Where in the world did he come up with that thinking?

GOING HOME IN A BARREL

When we returned to the village, we found an older man sitting by a fire. He was the village chief, or Bigman. That title reflected an honorific for men in his position. I introduced myself, and we sat down together. I politely explained my mission and my intentions regarding why I had come to his village. Then I showed him the piece of bent aluminum and explained that if we could straighten it, it was possible that we could learn a great deal about this airplane and figure out what airplane it was, what happened to it, its origin and, ultimately, the fate of the crew and whether human remains could be found. He then asked me who was paying me for my patrol. I told him I was not being paid, and that I was also following a godly or spiritual influence to help my fellow man, as I attempt to locate, identify and return human remains to survivors of these aircraft crewmen. I told him that I was also involved in this as a personal quest. I assured him that I represented no foreign government. I explained that some people might have preferred to play rugby or other sports, but that I enjoyed searching for crashed airplanes from the war that was fought in this area. He again asked me who was funding my operation and added that the airplane had broken the trees in his jungle and also had ruined the ground where it had buried itself. He too expected compensation!

I quickly realized where the other fellow had obtained his faulty "compensation thinking." The village chief, Steven, continued to press me for compensation and wanted to know who was funding my "walk about" (patrol). I continued to attempt to inform him that I had merely come to locate and examine the airplane wreckage. His primary purpose for grilling me was that he wanted money. That incident reminded me of when Ben wanted payment for the dive I had made on the sunken Japanese ship. I did not know where Alfi and Jared had gone, and I needed their moral support for this discussion with the Bigman. As I sat there, I held onto my wallet while being shaken down for PNG K500 (US $200). I did not have that amount of money on me, and even if I had, I was not about to give it to him. I tried to give him a history lesson as I had done with the other villager on the trail, but he was not buying the story. He had dollar signs in his eyes. I am not certain how long we jockeyed back and forth, but eventually (seemingly hours), I rose to my feet to leave. I asked him if I could take the bent aluminum airplane part with me to try to straighten it out – to which he said, "No." He did, however, want copies of any correspondence I had had with whoever was paying me to come search out the crash site. I informed him that unless I could figure out the airplane's identity by using the wing part, there would be no minutes or any compensation. Since he would not allow me to take the piece to straighten it out, then he needed to do it and send me a message regarding what he had found. We parted peacefully, and I left with hope that he would, in fact, contact me regarding his findings.

As I left, Jared emerged from the "haus boi" (house boy = place where the boys and men slept), and we left together walking through the village. As we walked, he told me that he and the other men and boys in the house were eating, and he had asked them about their belief in God and how they thought they planned to enter into heaven. They felt that as long as they were good, were baptized as babies and confessed their sins to a priest that the imagined heavenly scales would tilt in their favor and God would let them into heaven. That sounded feasible; however, that is not what the Bible teaches. He told them that the Bible teaches that God required a blood sacrifice to take away sin and that the sacrifice had to be perfect. In addition, the blood of goats and rams did not help one to make the grade. So, God sent *Himself*, in the form of a man named Jesus Christ, to live a perfect life and die on the cross, shedding His blood to cover our sins. Whoever believes that Jesus died for their sins would be saved from hell. He told them that that was what the Bible teaches. So Jared had had a good time eating and then Bible-quizzing, while I was sweating out a difficult discussion with the village head wondering whether I was going to get out of the village with my shorts and shirt intact!

As we walked out of the village, he also told me that one of the people in the haus boi had told him the story of the airplane and how one of the crewmen had survived the crash. He had met another white person who had been hiding in a cave; they then made their way to the coast. I was not in the mood to hear the story as Steven was following us down the trail; I was still engrossed in the discussion I had had with the Bigman. When we finally parted, I (reluctantly, but as a gesture of friendship) photographed him for memory sake – perhaps it was merely a bad memory and one which provided me a target for dart-throwing.

This incident typified one of the potential hazards of conducting this kind of research on an individual basis.

As I reviewed my photos of the wreckage later on, with a more experienced eye, I saw where the cockpit of that aircraft would have been. At that time though, I was still pretty much a novice at this entire procedure. I have realized that the people had obviously scoured the area and taken the aluminum for scrap. Since the ground at the site was so soft, it probably allowed for the engines to be buried. After that experience, I began to wonder whether remains could have been found with more effort to search between the two engines.

I contacted my researchers, Justin Taylan, Daniel Leahy and John Douglas and told them of the aircraft and its location. Daniel replied and told me that the "A-16" designation meant the airplane was an Australian Lockheed Hudson. Later it was determined that this airplane was A16-91, flown by Wing Commander John Lerew. This was one of the aircraft that had been shot down that was mentioned in chapter 1. The wreckage had first been found after the war by Sqn. Ldr. Keith Rundle. Remains of the three crew members F/O Willian Albert James, Sgt. Kenneth Duirs McDonald and Sgt. Raymond Cherrington Henry were recovered at that time. Surprisingly, Lerew did hook up with another man (actually two) that he had met hiding in a cave, and they eventually made their way back to Port Moresby and ultimately to Australia. I wondered how that villager had known that information. I had never sent my "minutes" to Steven nor did he send me a message indicating what numbers had been found on that piece of bent wreckage.

Hudson propeller by Zebu Village. WNBP, PNG

Hudson A16-91 wing. WNBP, PNG

Hudson serial number A-16. WNBP, PNG

Chapter 17

STUCK ON A REEF

We entered the rainy season and were cooped up for the next three months; we must have received four-and-a-half meters (15 feet of rain). Our rainy season was also the time when we would get malaria more often. On the average, we probably had malaria attacks every few months. Malaria was like the flu that passed from one family member to the next. At first, one of us would get the symptoms of high fever, headaches and general feeling of exhaustion. Then, someone else would come down with the symptoms. It was as if the same mosquito flew around the house and stung all of us. We treated ourselves using chloroquine, and as long as we started the medicine at the first signs of the attack, by the third day we were about 90 percent back to normal. However, if we waited a day to take the medication, the symptoms became more severe and lasted longer. Untreated malaria can evolve into cerebral malaria and even death.

It was great to see the sun again and to be able to get out and continue searching for aircraft wreckages. I had been itching for a chance to chase down some rumors I had heard. On October 10, 2007, I was asked to pick up a family that was 105 nautical miles (121 miles) west and we knew that we would pass through the Arawes on the way. We went one day early to take some time to hunt for an airplane which had been seen in the water, and from its description, it was close to the Val that we had previously seen in those waters years ago. Our trip started out as an uneventful excursion, and with calm seas, we approached the island of Pililo. We slowly pulled up to the beach and rested the nose of the boat on the sand as I disembarked. I had not been there long before I encountered a group of people who had gathered around me curious to hear why I had come to their island. I had packed pictures of the *Taka Saka Maru*, the sunken Japanese cargo ship that lay just in front of their village at 142 feet under water. I also took along a wartime photo of the ship as it was being bombed. And, compliments of John Douglas, I also showed them the four reports I had from men who had actually fought during the battle of the Arawes. I distributed them to an eager crowd, all of whom wanted some piece of the paper to hold. I told them that I wanted them to return the reports and that I would stop by again in a couple of days to retrieve them. As it turned out, they requested I leave the reports with them for further reference to which we agreed. Once I had built their trust, I asked for Rafael who had told me about the airplane he had seen in the water. Rafael was not there, but he was not far away, so I took a couple of village men with me and proceeded by boat in search of Rafael.

We went to one village and received word that he had left and was fishing on the outside of the island in deep water so we continued to seek him out. While cruising, we finally saw his boat – he was headed back to Pililo. We chased him and finally caught up with him in front of Pililo Island – where we had started our search. What a waste of gas and, at over US $6.50 a gallon, one did not want to waste a drop! After a short greeting and envying the four freshly caught tuna lying in the bottom of his boat, we asked about the airplane. He knew why we had come back there, but gave me an excuse about some ceremony for which he had to prepare. That should have been my first clue. I asked him to come aboard for a short while and merely show us the spot and we would take him wherever he wanted to go. With that, he, along with four other men, came aboard with us, and we headed toward the mouth of a river. He said that we had come too soon and the water was not clear; he recommended that we should return in a couple of months. Once we arrived at the location, he pointed to an area about four acres in dimension and he said, "It's in there somewhere." That should have been my second clue.

We trolled around and continually checked our depth sounder which was showing the water to be 18 meters (60 feet) deep. He indicated that the wreckage was close to a black rock. The water was cloudy, and we could not see anything. We did find a reef which indicated six meters (20 feet) on the depth sounder, but we were unable to locate either the black rock or the airplane. I wanted to give him the benefit of the doubt, but I finally concluded that he never had seen an airplane. After that, I said, "I'll show you an airplane in the water." We were actually quite close to the Val we had found in 2001, so Jared drove over there with his eye on the GPS for the location, and when he yelled out that he had found the position, I dropped anchor. I told the five men on the boat if they wanted to see an airplane in the water, they needed to follow the anchor line. No one moved. I removed my shirt and grabbed my mask then jumped into the water.

I had not been in the water too long when I saw the Val; it was still there – upside down. I yelled to the five men standing on the bow to come and see it; no one moved. Finally, Paul Wolff's younger son, Josh, jumped in and we free-dived down to the wreck. When I returned and reentered the boat, I questioned them as to why they had not come to see the airplane. They said that it was because they were wearing long pants. That was not true at all, they were wearing shorts! Actually, I think that they were afraid. Culturally, they have had a fear of spirits and believed that they would be surrounded by the spirits of the dead crew from that airplane and, as such, did not want to get near it. That was good, in a way, as that fear has probably kept some of these wrecks safe from vandals over the years.

We then proceeded to take the village men back to their village. Incidentally, I have not seen my Leatherman knife/pliers since, and I suspect that someone had "borrowed" it while I was in the water. When we returned to the village of Kurumalak (where Paul Wolff lived), we refueled the boat for our trip to Sagsag the next day for the pick-up of a family. I was shocked to see that we had used 29 out of 105 gallons of fuel during the jaunts in this area, running here and there with no accomplishments. The engine burned two gallons for every mile we traveled, so we had covered approximately 97 kilometers (60 miles)! I was a bit discouraged, to say the least.

I saw some locals sitting and sharing, "talking story," so I went over to greet them. One man told me about an airplane he had seen with a cousin in Wako. I was tired by then, but I listened to his story anyway. I could only think, "Wako, yah, I know about that one. I have tried to find it four times now." He was pretty convincing; he said that he had seen it and that it had two drop tanks on each wing. He could not tell me how many engines it had, which was strange, because engines and propellers are usually pretty noticeable. I never did follow up on that lead as we had grown weary of searching in the Wako area.

Soft-spoken Thomas then told me of a story he had heard recently of an airplane that had been seen out on a reef. I trusted him, and Rod Pearce had told me about an elusive twin-engine airplane he had been trying to find so I was interested. As he talked though, he understood that I was tired, so he encouraged me to go lie down and we could talk about the airplane later. He was right, I was tired, so I left him and had something to eat at Paul's house, took a shower, then returned to the boat and fell fast asleep.

I awakened right at daybreak and began to ready the boat for our trip to Sagsag. Josh Wolff was to accompany us, so I called him on the radio as he was still at the house. Surprisingly, he was already up and ready and, in a short time, appeared at the boat. I had established a GPS route to Sagsag, but it did not start until we had left the Arawe Islands. By 6:30 A.M., we were on our way. It was a calm morning with flat seas and we cruised along at 28 knots (32 mph). We checked our chart to establish our exact location, so I slowed the boat to 22 knots (25 mph). Josh and I talked as we looked at the chart, when suddenly, there was a loud bang and the boat was tossed back and forth. I quickly grabbed the throttle and pulled it back, but in my haste, passed neutral and hit reverse. As we were literally "clam banging" along, I realized that we had hit a reef and were still bouncing along on top of it. By the time I realized it, had shifted into neutral, and started to tilt the engine up, we had stopped!

Coming down from the flybridge, I could only image the damage we had received to our new motor and wondered if we were taking on water. Jared climbed into the water and checked the propeller first. Surprisingly, the stainless steel propeller was still in good shape. We had sustained only a couple of minor bends in the blades. I climbed into the water and stood on the reef in knee-high water to double-check the motor as well. I found that the side mount had cracked, and Jared noticed that the trim tab had broken off. We took a hammer from the tool box and beat on the propeller to repair the dings. Thankfully, the boat did not appear to be sinking so we pushed it over the reef. There were four of us, and one local man who, apparently, did not have a change of pants, so he removed his shorts and sheepishly entered the water – naked, and covering his privates with his cupped hands. The sun had not yet risen, so we could not see the extent of the reef other than what we could see nearest to us, so we just started to push the boat back in the direction from where we had come. We bumped into brain corals and changed course several times. We then walked around to determine where the water was deepest, and we tried to pull the boat in those directions. We had barely moved, maybe 30 meters (100 feet), when we became hung up firmly and could not move at all.

I called Paul on the radio to tell him of our predicament since we had not traveled far away from his location. He offered to help push us out of this dilemma, but I told him that what we needed was to have water under the boat, to which he replied that the tide would be in by the afternoon. The Matt Hall family we were to pick up had already left their house; they had to hike to the coast to meet us and expected us to be there by 10:00 A.M. Unfortunately, there was no way to contact them and let them know that we might be a bit late.

An older man paddled by in a dugout canoe and showed us the nearest edge to the reef. It was only about 15 meters (50 feet) away, but the outer edge of the reef had the highest standing corals, so even if we could have reached it, the water would have been even shallower. Jared checked out the coral and said, "Hey dad, these are brain corals and we can move them." I was skeptical of this enterprise, but we started rocking the brain corals and, to my surprise, we could move them! With that, we started to make a narrow path for the boat to reach the edge of the reef and to deeper water. Within 20 minutes or so, we were clear of the reef. The sun had risen by then, and we could see that the reef was huge! Fortunately, we were able to release our boat from that reef that stood in the "middle of the road" and we were once again underway. With the sun up now, all the other reefs shone with a bright aqua color, so we had no problem navigating through them. We carefully marked them on our GPS in the event we had to return this way in the dark. We then ran for two hours at 28 knots (32 mph) and pulled in to Sagsag at precisely10:00 A.M. – right on schedule!

Men in dugout canoe, Arawe Islands. WNBP, PNG

Greeting by villagers. WNBP, PNG

Boat on reef, Arawe Islands. WNBP, PNG

Chapter 18

MACHINE GUN – VAL #7

After I returned back to Kurumalak to spend the night, I went to converse with Thomas about his friend who had seen the airplane on the reef. We made plans to embark the next morning and to try and locate it. On this trip, we planned to use a little dinghy with a 25-horsepower motor in order to conserve gasoline.

When the next morning arrived, in spite of rising at daybreak again, (which is not like me, as I generally am a late-night person), Thomas had already used coconut palm branches to slide the dinghy off the sandy beach and into the water. After hanging the motor on the transom of the boat, we departed to find his friend. We made our way around to the island of Kumbun and passed over some reefs where we had to pull ourselves along with a long pole. When we pulled up to Kumbun Village, a middle-aged man greeted us. His name was Allan; he was the one we had come to see. He said that when he saw the boat coming with us in it, he knew the reason for our visit. Without any delay, he boarded the boat and we launched out, stopping at Kurumalak again to pick up another younger passenger and a diving mask.

I thought we would stay close to the islands, but we had headed out to sea. We kept going and we felt that we were in route to Lae – 225 kilometers (140 miles) away. I began to worry whether we would have enough gas to complete both legs of the trip. I was also concerned that we did not have any life jackets in the boat. As we continued, we could see a rain cloud to the south and joked about having the power to stop the rain. Some people in PNG believed they could make it rain or that they could even stop the rain but – none of *us* had that "gift." The rain cloud closed in on us and grew larger, until finally we felt the cool breeze and the cold drops began to fall on our heads. It was not long before it was pouring like cats and dogs, with a high wind pushing it. It seemed to have reached freezing level. We were not acclimated to such weather (I hate being cold), so I curled up on the bottom of the boat in a fetal position so that the side of the boat would block me from the wind. Jared had taken an old piece of plywood from the floor and sat in the bow hiding under it.

As I lay there, I reflected in my mind about the tarp I kept in my big boat that was back at the village. I could visualize exactly where it was stowed and wished I had grabbed it for this trip. I was also thinking how miserable I was and asked myself whether I was having fun yet. We floated along and were pelted for what seemed like forever. Thomas and Allan sat hunched over with their heads bowed, and they said that I looked like a "manki" (pre-teen boy) curled up on the floor. These people have lived a harsh, difficult life and have learned to endure many hardships without the comforts of modern civilization. To even sit in a chair with a pad on it was a rarity for them. You can surmise how hard it would be to give them a shot in the posterior. So, in this situation, where they had to sit in the cold rain they easily adapted; they had learned to grit their teeth and suck it up. Modern Americans have become spoiled and soft by comparison. No wonder they said that I looked like a little boy when I had crouched in the boat. The wind slowly ceased and the rain stopped. We were all drenched and removed our shirts to wring them out.

As we pressed onward, our guide directed us to the west side of the reef where he remembered having seen the two-engine airplane in about 12 meters (40 feet) of water with the pilot's door open. He and three other companions had seen it years ago and then again the previous year as they were diving for sea cucumbers. We anchored the boat for a reference point, then four of us entered the water and formed a line. We were about seven-and-a-half meters (25 feet) apart from each other then started swimming away from the boat. We had swum for a mile or two, not actually, but it was quite a distance before we moved over and came back around passing the boat again. We turned 90 degrees again and returned to the boat. After all that, we were not able to find either an airplane or any indication of one having been there. We did see some big fish, and I was afraid my guide and his friend would abandon the search to go spear fishing for breakfast.

After we returned to the boat, we rested awhile and ate some salted crackers. We then decided to institute our tried and true method of pulling snorkelers behind the boat using a GPS to mark our trek. With that, Jared and Thomas reentered the water and held onto the ropes we had tied to the transom of the boat. We began to search with our normal grid technique. We searched the grid in a back and forth pattern and moved out and away from the reef a little farther with each pass. We made five passes covering half of the reef, but still no airplane. Our guide was beginning to doubt whether this was the right reef, or if it might be another one further away. I was, of course, a bit dismayed. I did not want to search anymore, so we decided to return home.

As we began our return trip, the men were talking while I calculated how much gas we had burned and wondering whether I should tell my wife about it. Suddenly, the men raised my attention and said that Allan knew of another airplane on another island. I had heard of it before, but had never seen it, so I agreed to let him show us where it was and how to get there. In my mind, I was already having doubts about our guide, but I did not want to reveal my true feelings and spoil the fun, so we proceeded to the island of Angap.

We pulled into the mangroves and everyone debarked; we left Thomas to secure and watch the boat, then we trekked up the hill. When we reached the top of the hill and walked a bit further, the hill began to slope downward. Once we reached the bottom of the hill, we found ourselves back in mangroves again. I had grown to hate walking on mangroves. I am not certain why that is the case; it may have arisen as a result of my glasses or my balance or whatever else, but I have developed a very difficult time walking on those nubs and winding roots. We searched for a while, and then I heard the familiar message, "wait here and we'll go find it." It was just as I had thought – another dead end. I sat down to change into my golf shoes hoping they would grip better on the mangroves and on the slippery slope. Jared continued to walk ahead, but I did not want to be left alone so I hurried with putting on my shoes. As I sat there, though, I stopped to consider what it might have been like to sit on the middle of this island with enemy forces all around. After I broke out of my stupor, I rose to my feet and followed the group racing to catch up to them. When I drew near to Jared, I realized that he had reached the crash site and was looking at an airplane engine! (See page xii - NO. 8)

Jared had always wondered how 14 cylinders could be connected to a crankshaft for the short distance an aircraft engine allowed. Normally, with a four-cylinder engine or even an eight-cylinder engine, the length of the engine can accommodate all those connecting rods as they are attached to the crankshaft. The problem is that an airplane engine is not that long. Finally, his mystery was solved as this engine was cracked open and we could see inside at just how the engineers had designed it to solve that problem. It would have been nice to share that information with the reader; but it would have used far too much space. I am not certain I could have explained that engineering feat adequately, so with apologies to the reader that information will, of necessity and for our purposes, remain a mystery!

As I approached Jared, he immediately told me that it was another Val. We had learned that the Japanese had made a total of ten raids in the Arawes from December 15, 1943, thru December 29, 1943, and had lost 13 Vals; this was the seventh one we had found.[52] I found the framing from the belly section and it still had the bomb-hanging mechanism attached to it. This was the first time we had seen that section intact. I snapped a photo of it and continued to search. We found two huge wheel struts lying alongside the engine. The rubber wheels were missing, possibly as a result of a fire, as in other sites we had seen. Our guide, Allan, told us that originally this airplane was hanging in the vines and the locals had come and cut it down, hacked it into little pieces and sold the aluminum. I am not certain about the "hanging in the vines" (we had heard that story before), but there was definitely no aluminum remaining. There were no wings, no fuselage and no propeller. Apparently, the locals must not have been afraid of the spirits around *that* crash site!

As I continued to photograph the engine, I heard someone call out, "Here is a machine gun." What? This was our seventh Val crash site, and it was a surprise to make such a find, as we had only once previously seen guns that were mounted on an airplane. This crash site had the least number of airplane pieces, but there was a machine gun lying nine meters (30 feet) away; it was all rusted and corroded. The barrel was so corroded that it was extremely fragile, and I was afraid it would break off if I had tried to hold it. But Jared wanted a picture of it so he picked it up and surprisingly, it did not break apart. We also found three small oxygen tank cylinders which are used for high altitude flying; we have witnessed items like these at other Val crash sites. The locals probably left these alone, thinking they were bombs.

Our guides were digging up little pieces of wire and various artifacts in the area. They hiked up the hill a bit but did not see anything there. I could have spent the entire day there digging around. We wanted to have a better look at the landing struts, so we stood them up and cleaned them off a bit. Once they were in a vertical position, one could see that the Val would have stood a good five feet from ground to the bottom of the wings. Since we had never seen a complete Val before, we were forced to imagine how big they actually were. Up to this time, we had only a couple photographs to indicate how they actually looked.

As previously mentioned, I could have spent an entire day at that site even though we had not discovered any data plates, but we necessarily had to return to Kandrian which was a few hours away, so we reluctantly vacated the site. Before we left, I mentioned to the team that this was not just another Val crash site, this was, possibly, a burial site of some unknown soldiers, as a total of 26 airmen had been killed in action in the attacks on the Arawes. It was a somber thought and a memorable moment, as well.

As we prepared to depart, Allan asked if I wanted to take the machine gun. I replied that Jared would love to have it, but we wanted to avoid any accusations from other clan members about missing artifacts or scavenging to be directed at us, so we left it. Allan said, "Don't worry, if anyone were to say anything about it, I would tell them, 'I said you could have it.'" I graciously declined. I have heard such encouraging words before, but when the accusations arose, the encourager was usually nowhere to be found and one would be left to defend himself, alone. In response, he said that he would take it, so his friend picked it up and carried it to the dinghy. On the way, he rested and commented that it was "not a field gun – it was very heavy." As we boated back to Kurumalak, I asked him what he had planned to do with the machine gun. He kind of shrugged and answered, "I don't know." I then asked if he wanted to sell it ….

Using the little boat proved to be economical, and I was glad we had not run out of gas as I had feared. We left the Arawes on our bigger boat named *Sirocco*, and we encountered choppy seas which were not comfortable for our passengers. We made it home safely before dark and unloaded the Hall family, whom we had picked up at Sagsag, with all their cargo – including a washing machine and an exercise bike. When we pulled the boat out, we inspected the bottom and found some new gouges from our temporary grounding on the reef, but thankfully, we found no serious damage. While the youngsters began to give it a bath, I filled the fuel tanks in preparation for our next run. The engine had burned approximately 135 gallons of gasoline which calculated out to about US $877.00.

Val engine, Angap Island. WNBP, PNG

Jared with *Val* machine gun. WNBP, PNG

Chapter 19

A WING AND A MOUNTAIN

During the last five months I had heard two reports of airplane wreckages a long distance up the coast and east of us. Both reports were from credible timber company workers. One report by Mr. Mok was of a large wing 20 kilometers (12 miles) to the interior, and the other report was of a fuselage containing bullets 8 kilometers (4.8 miles) to the interior. I relayed those reports to a co-worker and fellow WWII enthusiast, Craig Lowell, who was working in East New Britain. His location was actually closer to the source of these reports. We had previously discussed making such a trek together thinking (hoping) that perhaps it was the B-17 named *San Antonio Rose*. (Does that name sound familiar?) Later, Craig contacted me about him having made a low key trip with only a couple of nationals from his home village. In September, a helicopter ("low key") had flown him and his two village friends to a timber company called Matong, on the south coast of the island. The Malaysian camp personnel were warmly accommodating and gave the three-man team a ride to the wing's location, only a 45-minute drive from the base camp. As it grew late, they returned to the timber camp, and the camp personnel graciously fed and housed them. On the following day, they returned to the wing-site and spent the entire day in that area. In one of Craig's photographs, the wing showed signs of internal burning close to where it had been ripped away from the rest of the wing.

The timber company logging road passed just nine meters (30 feet) from the wing, so it was pretty easy to locate – if someone were to show another person how to find it. In the past, many times when the timber company bulldozers were cutting new roads, other workers or friends rode along and frequently ran into the bush to find beetle nuts. That is how they discovered the wing. The actual crash site was nearly at the top of a mountain at approximately 914 meters (3,000 feet).

At that site, Craig said to his crew, "Let's go down the hill and see what we can find." Craig and his crew trekked down the mountain and within an hour, had found other parts of the same airplane wreckage. They marked the spot with their GPS as they made a preliminary examination of the wreckage. They confirmed that it was a B-17 since they located the belly turret that housed a machine gun.

One could have only imagined their excitement as they expanded their search; they found a total of five guns, radio parts, oxygen tanks, a propeller with a yellow tip which protruded out of the ground, the rear landing gear and many other parts of the aircraft.

Craig was anxious to report his find, and I could not wait to hear all of the details. We talked for quite some time on the telephone, and later I was able to see the photos he had taken. What a find! But, he could not positively identify the airplane other than its type. *San Antonio Rose* was a B-17; that made this find that much more exciting. What airplane had he actually found? What was the squadron number? A hundred other questions flooded my mind and they all begged for answers.

THE TALE OF THE TAIL – TEXAS #6

After examining Craig's photos, I searched the internet and looked up photographs of B-17s. To my delight, I found a site that had actual wartime photographs of the guns and was able to match the gun located in the radio room to one of the photos Craig had taken.

Later, I took some of Craig's photos to the surveyor who had given me the report of a fuselage; he said that he was able to stand up in it and that he had found bullets of four different sizes in it. A close examination of Craig's photos confirmed that there was no area wherein a man could stand upright. In addition, the surveyor said that he did not see any guns or any oxygen tanks. I was able to plot the location I knew of from the GPS coordinates and I showed it to him on a map which indicated that this was *not* the same location where he had claimed to have seen the airplane. From our meeting, I left convinced there had to be two different airplanes on two different mountains.

Even with the information from Craig, he had not positively identified the wreckage he had discovered. I became highly motivated to go there to attempt to identify the airplane that Craig had seen and the one the surveyor had reported, so I quickly made plans to visit the site. It was apparent (to my family) that searching for and finding aircraft wreckage sites had become a hobby that had consumed my thoughts. I wondered if the government should have hired me to do it.

Our mission airplane was able to accommodate us the following week so we began to prepare for the trip. Prior to departure, I had sent messages to Brian Bennett and Justin Taylan asking for information. In addition, another event occurred prior to our departure – all of the telephones in the town of Kandrian had become inoperative. What utter frustration I experienced in not having communication, especially as the date of departure was nearing and I was waiting to determine whether I should confirm the trip or not. I was, however, able to use a satellite telephone and make contact with Justin and, despite much noise and static while walking around my yard trying to get a good signal, hear that he believed the crash site was that of "another B-17 called *Texas #6.*" After I had received that information, the connection was lost, and by then it was too late to abort the undertaking. The mission airplane was due the next morning, and my mental state of excitement was quite high. I was packed, ready to go – and understandably did not sleep well. The plan was to take food and water, sleep on the site and spend two full days searching for anything that might lead us to positive identification of the airplane. I still personally believed there were two airplanes up there, and that all the local stories and previous treks were only focused on one of them. I greatly wished to find them both and either confirm or eliminate my suspicions.

On the following day, my son Jared and two local friends from Yumielo village, Asap and Pasio, boarded our mission Cessna 206 piloted by Randy Smyth. Asap and Pasio had been good and faithful friends over the years, and I knew that they would be helpful. It was also exciting for them to get to fly up the coast and see another area that they had never before seen; it made them all the more eager to join in on the expedition. The flight to Manguna airstrip by Matong timber camp from Kandrian lasted 75 minutes – approximately 241 kilometers (150 miles) away. After we landed, we made our way by hiking, canoeing and trucking to the camp where we were shown the same gracious hospitality by the camp personnel as Craig had received. When I arrived, I spoke with the surveyors and examined the maps they had which depicted the area. They had heard of the wing, but they had no information regarding another crash site, although now we were able to approximate the location of the second site which, as it turned out, was not that far away from the base camp. It was determined that the second site had not yet been harvested by the timber company, as the trees were not of a sufficient quantity nor quality to warrant the company going into the jungle to harvest. But the surveyors had been on that mountain and I hoped that they had, perhaps, seen a second crash site – but they had not.

That night, with at least 20 locals gathered around looking at the photographs that Craig had taken and, also, the photographs of a B-17 I had printed from the internet. Our quest was the main topic. We summoned the two locals who had gone to the site ten years previously with the surveyor I had met in Kandrian, and they agreed to come with us to confirm that what Craig reported is what they had seen. These two guides were now up in their years and were not really eager to trek, but they were comforted once they heard that the timber company had established a road that went to the site.

On the next morning we sat and stood in the bed of a new Toyota Land Cruiser and raced up the mountain to what we estimated to the 914 meter (3000 foot) elevation in less than 45 minutes. The camp manager himself was our chauffeur. When we arrived, he asked the old men to lead us to the airplane. Because the winding road and the bulldozed landscape had changed the way things looked, they had become disoriented and had lost any clues they may have had as to their location. The manager, though, then found and showed us the huge outer left wing lying on the uphill side not more than nine meters (30 feet) from the road. He left us to explore the area with our GPS coordinates, and I remembered Craig had told me that he trekked "downhill from the wing." The wing lay almost at the top of the hill so "downhill," based upon Craig's comment, could have been any of three directions. Fortunately (or so we thought), we had the GPS coordinates. We activated the hand-held contraption, fed in the coordinates and bingo, the arrow pointed to the direction we were to go. That was as easy as apple pie. With that information, my son and I headed into the jungle and left the two older men and the two locals who had accompanied us from Kandrian to follow once we had found the site. I confidently believed that with the GPS we could find the wreckage first and yell out for the other people to join us.

I had forgotten that once in the jungle, the hand-held GPS became almost useless due to the tree canopy and the systemic failure which occurs without a good signal from the satellites. I should have remembered that from a previous adventure when we found the Val tail wheel near Sabdidi Village. Now, even though the compass feature which indicated directionality was totally non-functional, the distance indicator did seem to work, and my trek was being recorded. With that, it was like playing a game of hot and cold. As I approached the waypoint, the distance indicator would read 76 meters then 73 meters (250 then 240 feet), so I knew that I was getting closer. Then suddenly it changed to read 76 or 79 meters (250 or 260 feet), indicating that I was moving further away from my goal. The readings were frustrated by the tree canopy as well as the fact that the GPS was slow to react. After one-and-a-half hours of stumbling through the jungle with vines cutting my shins and several incorrect indications from the GPS that read that I was within six meters (20 feet) of the waypoint, we headed back to the road. My recorded trek showed that we had hiked almost entirely around the wreckage, a couple of times, yet we did not see it.

After a short rest, we walked onto the cleared road until our GPS needle pointed perpendicular with the road, and five of us trekked down the hill using a compass to keep us on course. After a short while into that trek, the sole tore away from my left golf shoe; that left me to complete the hike in my sock and with the remnants of my shoe flopping atop my foot. My son was aware of my tender feet, so he asked me if I was OK. Surprisingly, hiking in my sock was somewhat like walking on a soggy shag carpet. The heavy rains in the area had softened and rotted everything in the jungle. There were no small trees to hang onto for balance except for the ones that crumbled in the hand or the ones that would fall over with your weight, and even when the larger trees had fallen, the trees were not hard enough to stand upon. I expected that my foot would have been injured by the end of the day, but it survived the ordeal unharmed.

That reminded me of a time when we first moved into the village of Yumielo. When I would walk to town with the locals, they were always behind me. They said the gravel road hurt their bare feet as they walked on it. I found that difficult to believe, since their bare feet had at least six millimeters (one quarter of an inch) of callus on the bottoms – they could walk barefoot on coral reefs! I was unable to understand why the gravel road would slow them down. On a trail, though, it was next to impossible to keep up with their pace. Could it have been that the jungle floor was so soft?

147

Once into the jungle and following behind, I sneaked a peek at my GPS to see what it was reading, and I again found it to be giving similar odd readings as it had done before. We would get close, then further away from the waypoint without seeing anything. At one time, the GPS read that we were within five feet of our target! I again played the hot and cold game for another hour as I moved in four different directions from the waypoint, so our trek recorded on the GPS seemed to have taken on a four-leaf-clover-like configuration with the unfound wreckage showing itself at the center of the clover leaf. Jared was getting tired of watching me move about in circles, and he made certain to tell me so. I too was irritated, but I calmly told him that I was actually useless in the jungle since I had no natural sense of direction and that I could only depend upon the GPS. I told him that if he had a better plan, I was all ears. Unbeknown to me at the time, my local "blood hounds" had stayed close to me, but just out of my sight. I thought that they had been searching the entire area, but to my surprise, that was not the case.

We had read that during WWII, US and enemy forces would sometimes be just 15 meters (50 feet) apart, yet they never saw each other. After having been in the thick jungle, I understood how that was highly possible. The difference between the jungle and forest was in the thick undergrowth. With that understanding, we could have feasibly been directly over the wreckage and yet not seen it.

To add to the tension, an old man who had come with us persisted in telling us about the time he had come to this area with a surveyor. He said that they had climbed up the hill to a clearing where a helicopter had previously landed. From that point, he said that he could overlook the ocean and look down to the villages on the coast. Unfortunately, we could not replicate that sight on this trip. While we trekked around, we reached a lower flat section where we could see outwardly, but our only visual was another mountain ridge. That made me think that we were still near another crash site, and I was convinced that there were two to be investigated. He, too, was confused as to why we could not see the coast line. On that note, the level of stress reached at a high point, so we decided to go back up to the road.

I concluded that we had used the wrong waypoint, so I frantically tried to contact Craig for verification. I used a satellite telephone to call our main center in Hoskins and asked them to contact

Craig by radio to verify coordinates and "downhill" direction. To our dismay, Craig was not available for that noon radio time, so we were left to use our imagination. We ate a biscuit and talked strategy while my son Jared returned to the wing site and then headed downhill perpendicular (which was parallel with the road) from the direction we had tried before. Although it still could have been considered downhill, it was not compatible with the direction which the GPS coordinates had indicated at all. As we rested, he returned with a large piece of aluminum that was like a rectangle air duct with about a 15 X 30 centimeter (6 X 12 inch) opening and a length of approximately 61 centimeters (two feet).

With that find, we were again encouraged and headed out once more, but this time, I kept the GPS in my pocket and returned to the wing area, stood on the road and said to my guides (who I seemed to be guiding), "Let's go downhill!" At that point, I let them take the lead. As local inhabitants, they grew up hiking in and around in the jungle. I had thoughts that they would follow the path of least resistance, but I did not want to give them any suggestions. I wanted them to sniff it out on their own. It was not long until I realized that I had brought the wrong blood hounds with me. In this case, they were not to be considered "AKC-registered" by any means. Although, under other circumstances, I would not want to be in the middle of the jungle without them as they knew how to survive in the wild. But now, they looked to me to see where the GPS was pointing, but I did not let it out of my pocket. So we stood there and looked at each other wondering, "What do we do now?"

By nature, these guides took the path of least resistance and, in this case, that meant that they would follow the road. As we walked down the dried mud road, we looked for paths through the bush that would have marked the trail that Craig had followed into the jungle. We were still on the timber company road, and we had almost reached its end at the bottom of the hill. My son, Jared, had gone back to the wing and again hiked in the bush parallel to the road. He found another piece of aluminum and we could hear him beating on it at some distance signaling his find. I then remembered that Craig had given Justin the coordinates so I went up the hill to call Justin. Surprisingly, my satellite telephone worked, and I was able to contact him. After I had reached him, he asked us to call him again in five minutes while he searched for the coordinates he had filed away somewhere. As I waited, my son came running up the hill, covered with perspiration, and he said, between gasps, that he had "found the nose." I had a difficult time connecting on the satellite telephone again, and Jared was getting impatient, but eventually I contacted Justin and he confirmed that the coordinates I had been given were the same ones that Craig had given him. Those coordinates, however, were 120 degrees different from where my son had just found something. It made me wonder what, exactly, had he actually found?

We headed into the jungle again. This time, I wore a slipper on my shoeless foot and a golf shoe on the other foot. We went down the hill and, not long afterward, Jared stopped and asked whether I had seen anything? At first, I could only see trees, but as I moved closer to where Jared was standing, I could see a large section of a fuselage; it was probably three-and-a-half to four-and-a-half meters (12 to 15 feet) long and had stubs of the wings attached to it. There was a small door on the side that was open. One old man had caught up with us, and he stood there and looked at the fuselage. He said he had not seen this section before when he had found an airplane with the surveyor. It was just what I wanted to hear, that it was, in fact, another airplane – a new discovery! (See page xi - NO. 23)

From where we stood looking down on it, I took a few photographs, then went down into the stream where the body section stood at a 45-degree angle and upside down. As I went around the side, I remembered having seen B-17 photos on the internet. I quickly recognized that the section was not the nose, but rather, the tail! The glass around the rear gunner was still intact although it was completely covered by moss. I then noticed yellow writing on the bent tail and quickly told my helper to clean it up so we could read the numbers. I was immensely excited because those numbers are what we needed to positively identify the aircraft!

As they cleaned it, I took more photographs and tried to get a GPS reading to mark the spot. Jared had climbed inside the fuselage. I could hear him saying, "Hey, there are bullets in here." Later he said, "Wow, there is a radio switch and lights in here." He climbed out through the tail end where the rear machine gun was, at one time, mounted – it was now gone. I took a photograph of his head sticking out from the assembly; I wanted to show a perspective of the size of the fuselage. He then commented that the open door was an emergency door and that he had found a sign next to the release handle. The handle had been pulled out of its clips, so we assumed the rear gunner had opened it and jumped from it. Of course, it could have been opened as a result of the impact with the ground.

By that time, Asap and Pasio had sufficiently cleaned the tail section numbers, and we were then able to discern that the numbers read "820" on the port side of the tail; on the starboard side there was a "1" at the beginning and then only the last digit "7" at the end of the tail. The middle section was too crumpled to distinguish the numbers. As we combined the two sides, they provided us with an almost complete number from the tail: 18207. I had not memorized the numbers of the airplanes we were hoping to find, so I sent Pasio back to our little camp next to the wing to get my folder out of my backpack.

While he was gone (and it seemed like hours), I shot more photographs and continued to try to get a GPS signal. The old man was inside the fuselage collecting 50-caliber machine gun cartridges. By then, I could not wait any longer. I dispensed with the GPS reading and climbed into the aircraft through the emergency door. Once inside, I could see that the interior was in nearly perfect condition. The aluminum was still shiny and looked like new. There were 50-caliber cartridges throughout the area. I picked up some cartridges and was surprised to find that the brass was still bright on some of them and the attached metal clips which still held them in line. They were strung with the bullet tips in a color-coded sequence. There were five black-tipped ones which were used for armor-piercing to penetrate the enemy airplanes' fuselages and engines. Three were red-tipped bullets which were used as tracers so the gunner could see where the bullets were firing, and finally, there were two with blue tips which were incendiary shells used for igniting the enemy fuel tanks.[53]

The two large boxes that once held the bullets were still attached to the sides and to the feed channel for the bullets which ran down to the machine gun. Unfortunately, the machine gun was missing. It may have broken off during the crash or, it might have been removed by someone who had found these remains earlier. Removing them would have been quite a feat, as they weighed approximately 68 kilograms (150 pounds) each. Overhead, we could identify the narrow walkway that was used by the rear gunner. The reason the walkway was overhead was because the tail section was now positioned upside down. I climbed up higher to try to see the intercom switch which was mounted on the fuselage wall; it had five positions. I also noticed the 13-millimeter (half-inch) iron plating that protected the rear gunner from enemy fire.

After I had looked around in the semi-dark, my helper finally returned with the folder. I climbed down to the open, broken-off end of the fuselage while Jared fumbled with the papers. I impatiently watched and waited for the announcement of what that number matched. Jared was rushing to find the page, flipping through the folder rapidly, but I could not control my excitement and grabbed the folder from him like a child taking his brother's lollipop. I hurriedly found the page that read, *Texas #6*, 41-9207. That did not match the numbers we had found, so I sent my helpers to look closer at the numbers and read them to me. They had been mistaken, it was not an "8" they had seen, rather, it was a "9." I had found myself inside the tail section of *Texas #6*, serial number, 41-9207 – it was just as Justin Taylan had told me on the phone. That was such a disappointment since we had sincerely hoped to find a previously undiscovered aircraft, perhaps even the *San Antonio Rose*.

Unenthusiastically, I reentered the aircraft with a flashlight; this time I searched for anything I may have missed previously. Since the airplane was upside down, everything looked strange, so I turned myself upside down and put my head in through the window area to get a feel of what it was like to sit in the rear gunner's seat and see what things looked like from that position. I wondered if the gunner might have written his name or some message on the fuselage around him, but I found no such writing. It was quite a sensation to sit there and contemplate the engines roaring along with the deafening booming of those 50-caliber shells fired so close to where I was sitting. I could only imagine how it would have sounded if all the guns were firing at one time.

Having seen enough and since I was bummed out, we glumly collected our things for departure. I was still unable to get a GPS reading even though there was now no tree canopy; I suspected that the reason must have been that we were located in a semi-deep ravine. We headed back toward the wing with hopes of finding additional pieces. Once out of the valley (about 500 feet up the hill), I was finally able to get a GPS reading. As we hiked, we found more aluminum at the base of a tree, it was partially buried but since we had to meet a truck to take us back to the camp, we did not take time to unearth it. After we had seen the number for *Texas #6* on the tail, our eagerness for identifying more pieces was, mostly, extinguished.

Earlier, I had found information from the *Pacific Wrecks* website regarding the *Texas #6*; it was shot down on June 1, 1943, while involved in armed reconnaissance. The crew of ten was attacked by 12 Japanese fighters after six hours of flight. The airplane was hit in the gas tank near the #2 engine and, within a minute and a half, it exploded. The explosion threw four of the crew members out of the airplane, of which only two had parachutes and landed safely. God only knows where the other two had landed. Other members of the crew went down with the airplane, four of whom miraculously survived the crash. Perhaps they survived, since the section of the airplane they occupied had slid down the mountainside, but even with that, it was almost close to a miracle. The villagers did take care of them at first, but eventually led them to the Japanese, and they were taken as prisoners (POW). Only one, SSgt Paul J. Cascio, who was the radio operator, survived the war. The crash site was investigated on March 12, 1946, and at least three crew members' remains were recovered.[54]

After we had returned to the camp and discussed our find, there were still some loose ends which remained to be tied up, particularly regarding the two older men who had traveled with us. It involved a couple of comments they had made, such as they were not able to see the villages from the site and had not seen this fuselage section before, that made me wonder whether there was still a second airplane in that immediate area? We had a discussion with them about taking us to the airplane they had seen, and we would use the route they had used when they had accompanied the surveyor. They said that they had followed ribbons that had been attached to trees in 1987 when Brian Bennett and a CILHI (Central Identification Laboratory in Hawaii) team traveled to the crash site in search of more remains. The problem with our plan was, because the timber company had now made roads here and there, the old trail would be obscured; therefore, my experienced guides did not believe they could find the route again. The only thing they remembered for certainty was a "galip" tree (Canarium nut) that they had seen on the way. That reluctance, and the fact that they probably would not be able to make the hike, made us abandon the proposal. However, as old as the one fellow seemed to appear, he was able to carry a bag full of 50-caliber cartridges up the hill and beat us all to the drop off point!

After that discussion, I was told by a younger man, Norbert, that he had asked his father if there was a second airplane crash in the area, to which he replied, he had known of one. Later that evening, I went to the village of Tokai and spoke with that elderly man, who was only about ten years old when the *Texas #6* crashed. So that would have made him approximately 75 years of age now. He had seen the airplane crash and went up to the site where he saw the four survivors, of whom two were seriously injured. One was burnt pretty badly, he said. They slept under the propped-up wing for a week and then carried the two injured men down the mountain while the other two were able to walk.

Still hoping to learn of another airplane, I then asked the elder if he recalled any other warplane wrecks at about that same time frame. He replied, "Yes, there was one afterwards." (SAR crashed before *Texas #6*.) The airplane, he said, was not shot down but rather had hit the mountain inside the valley. The locals went to the site and found that all the passengers had died. They then cut off the lower legs, forearms and heads of each of the passengers and took them to the coast for identification. He said that the airplane was high up in the mountains at the beginning of the Bergberg River, and, to his knowledge, no one has ever trekked into that area. Craig said that he had heard a similar story in his area. Research revealed that this was most likely a C-47 serial number A65-54 which crashed November 15, 1945, killing all 28 passengers on board. It was a tragedy, as the airplane had hit the crest of the mountain; it had almost cleared the top, needing only another 30 meters (100 feet) of altitude. Among those killed in that crash was a 29-year-old nurse named Sister Verdun Sheah.[55]

Craig Lowell with B-17 radio room machine gun. ENBP, PNG

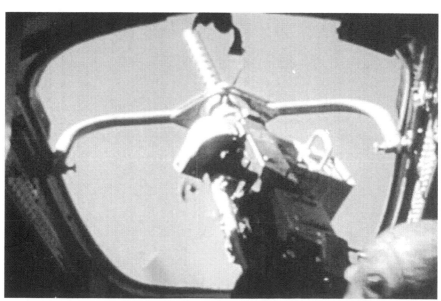

B-17 radio room machine gun.

Upside down B-17 *Texas #6* tail section. ENBP, PNG

50 cal. bullets from *Texas #6*. WNBP, PNG

Chapter 20

FOILED AGAIN

While at the timber camp, we had heard of another airplane wreckage up the coast; it was one that the timber company's head surveyor had seen. He told me that he had seen a large gun, a cannon, at least two meters (about six feet) long with a breech profile about 25 centimeters (ten inches) in diameter. When I questioned him further on the size, he retracted his story and said that perhaps his memory was a bit faulty. Later, Jared reminded me of an account he had read somewhere of a 75-millimeter (three-inch) cannon being tried out and mounted in the nose of a B-25. It had worked, but the concussion had slowed the airplane when fired and loosened the panels such that the ground crews had to re-tighten them after each mission. It took too much time to reload it, so although it was deadly in some instances, it was replaced as a viable weapon option by twin 50-caliber machine guns.

The camp manager agreed to allow the surveyor to take us up the coast. On the following morning, we made the two-and-a-half-hour scenic drive along the coast. We traveled into the cool mountains which presented majestic views. We then proceeded down along the muggy shoreline and stopped to get a drink from a flowing stream alongside the road by Korpun Village. There were other crash sites to see there, but Craig had already visited them so we did not bother. After we had passed the village of Wawas, we encountered a group of men who were milling timber with a portable sawmill. We asked them whether one of them would be willing to assist us in our visit to the crash site which was farther into the interior. Along with the men we had seen at the mill, there was a very elderly man who said that the "white men" had come there after the war and they "filled bags up with bones." After I heard that story, I lost some of my enthusiasm and excitement since I had hoped to find a new wreck site that possibly had human remains. Since we had come this far and were curious about the size of the gun, we continued our journey.

When we reached the turnoff and headed up the mountainside, we found that the side road had become completely overgrown. Timber operations had ceased in 2003, and in the four years of non-use of that road, the jungle had begun the process of reclaiming it. We hacked at the brush and small trees; after some effort for what seemed like a long distance, we found the road clear on the other side. The drive seemed fine for about one kilometer (.6 mile) until we were confronted with more brush. After we had cut it for a while, it was decided the road was severely overgrown and impassable by truck. We determined that we were nine kilometers (5.6 miles) away from our destination; that meant at least a two-hour hike, so we abandoned the search and reversed our direction. It was disappointing, but now believing that the remains had already been recovered, the journey became much less a priority.

Craig and I had heard small tidbits regarding an airplane crash farther to the east of Wawas; that was near a village called Milim. This was the closest I had ever been to Milim, so I asked around to see if there was anyone in the area who had ever been there. We learned of a small group of nationals in a nearby village and so went there to ask them if they had heard of any airplane crashes in their immediate area. Unfortunately, a man who was not a native of Milim said that he would ask about it upon his return home that night. He, typically, seemed to be a bit suspicious of my questioning. Later, he asked why I was looking for an airplane – to which I replied that it was possible that human remains may be in it and that their families would appreciate the return of them. He was, no doubt, probably thinking we were hunting for the airplane that had supposedly been "full of gold."

An interesting point to note was that the mountains interior from Milim Village rose to 2,286 meters (7,500 feet). That was the area an American miner had written about in a report, after he had reconstructed an estimated flight path and crash site of *San Antonio Rose*. After I had read his report and looked at the map, I surmised that it did seem feasible and convincing; still, as indicated earlier, I had my reasons to doubt the information.

After we had not found the SAR (*San Antonio Rose*) and having heard all the stories, Jared was eager to go to Milim and start hiking up that mountain. I cautioned him that, although he may have been lucky when he found the tail section of *Texas #6*, it seemed foolish to proceed without further investigation and without a guide to lead him to this crash site. His youthful enthusiasm was motivating and encouraging, but there were times when old fogey wisdom needed to be considered. I believe this airplane was the same one I had heard about, from the old man in Tokai village, that had almost cleared the mountain top.

Our return to the base camp was broken up by a relaxing lunch of boiled rice mixed with tin fish, so we leisured alongside a cool, clear river. Talking with Rudy, the surveyor, I learned that he was from the Philippines, as were many of the timber camp employees. What intrigued me was that Rudy had been working for the timber company for 15 years. Unlike my situation, where I had my family with me, his family was back in the Philippines. His contract allowed him to return home once a year. He was proud of the fact that he was able to provide for his family and even have the funds to send his children to college. Even though the timber company personnel had trucks to drive, beds to sleep in and fairly good meals, living at a camp was extremely rustic. They had no internet, telephones or even television. Some other workers I talked to did not even know what the internet was! Many had bought satellite telephones so they were able to communicate with their families. Most the time they were merely working or, during the rainy season, just sitting around with nothing to do. I saw one man who was making a large fishing net to keep him entertained. There were times I would get discouraged and wallow in self pity over the sacrifices we had made in coming to Papua New Guinea, but in reality, the sacrifices we had made did not compare to what others had given up.

I had read that when the US contractors were building airstrips and harbors on Guam and Midway, the main problem they had with the workers was boredom. Although the work was hard, they were paid well. They were provided with hot showers, good food, in some cases a daily ration of beer, and a way to communicate with their families. Even with all those amenities, the average worker had lasted for only four months! Rudy had already lasted 15 years. That is another example of how soft we Americans are in comparison.[56]

After lunch, we had to drive through that river and cross to the other side in order to proceed. It had a rock bed, and the water was flowing pretty fast. Even though the water was up to the middle of the doors of the truck, we crossed it successfully, without stalling. What a unique experience that was! With the river behind us, we bounced around on the bumpy road; it provided time for me to reflect back on our adventure. From a financial standpoint, including the $1200-plus it cost me just to hire the airplane to take us and pick us up again, and the multiple lacerations on my shins from unmerciful needle vines which had caused me to take a course of antibiotics – it seemed foolish. Yet from another perspective, where else could one spend so little and have such a magnificent adventure with one's son? Jared will not soon forget his jumping up and down on a hill in the middle of the jungle as his eyes first spotted the tail of *Texas #6*, nor will I forget the excitement of having found a lost airplane from the war.

Of course, none of this would have been possible without the cooperative assistance of the Malaysian-operated timber company. They had been most accommodating in every way, and they did not charge us a "toea" (PNG equivalent of 1/3 of a penny) for housing, meals or transport. I have predicted that, in the near future, they plan to remove more of the logs out from the area where *Texas #6* has lain for decades. I do not think they plan to go near the wreckage, since the large trees in that area easily fall over due to the softness of the ground. If they were to enter that area, I am certain that the machine guns lying there would eventually disappear. Within one year, the road will become totally unused, and just a few short years later, it too will be overgrown; the crash site will return to the tranquility that has surrounded it all these years. The remains of the aircraft represent a place of peace and serve as a hallowed ground wherein some of America's airmen can be honored in silence.

After I had traveled and physically searched for those wreckages, I have reluctantly conceded that there probably were not two wrecks up in those mountains as I had previously believed. There was, of course, that other known airplane crash, the C-47, with the gruesome story of remains being carried to the coast. Also, there was the report of the wreckage with the large gun near the *Texas #6* site. Then, too there was the airplane Craig had seen. I had concluded my trip with many unanswered questions and could not wait to get home so that I could talk with Craig and compare notes. I also wanted to get back to the surveyor who had told me about the fuselage he had stood in and ask him if, in fact, it had been the tail section I had seen, and whether he had followed ribbons that marked the path to the wreckage, as the two old men had related to us. Lastly, I wanted to ask him to again point out on a map where he said that he had searched. If he had not seen the tail section that we had found, I would continue to wonder whether there was a different mountain, and I was willing to return with him and have him show me what he had found.

Once back in Kandrian, I printed a few pictures of the tail section, and I went to speak with the surveyor. He related that he had *not* stood up in that tail section I had found. That coincided with the story the old man told me, as he, too, had never seen the tail section. I asked the surveyor if he had followed ribbons to the crash site. He said, "No." I found that to be intriguing, especially since the two old native men had told me that that had been the case. I then had him look at a map and showed him where we had gone, rehashing that the two old men said they had followed the ribbons to the crash site. He seemed perplexed as he studied the map. That meeting left me thinking he was turned around and that he really did not know the location of the mountain where he had spotted the airplane. Although, since he was a surveyor, I would like to think he did know. After that discussion, I renewed my curiosity about the location and identity of the airplane he had entered.

Also, after returning to Kandrian, we found the phone system inoperative, but I was able to receive e-mails by way of a radio modem. It was a slow connection; it oftentimes took two hours to download e-mail messages, but at least it worked – most of the time. I was happy to see that there were messages from both Brian Bennett and Justin Taylan. Mr. Bennett had been to that crash site in 1987 along with a US Army CILHI team from Hawaii that recovers remains. The team found the remains of the co-pilot, 1/Lt. Winslow G. Gardner, when they found the cockpit section. Most of the airplane parts were found over a period of two weeks of searching over a large area. Justin gave me the information he had received from both Mr. Bennett and his website. So, it appeared my friend Craig happened to have found the mid-section with the side guns and radio room, and I had found the tail section, but neither of us had found the cockpit section. It was quite possible that the cockpit was the section the surveyor had "stood up in." I sometimes wish I had taken him with me as this mystery has continued to haunt me – to this day!

Lunch of tin fish and rice alongside river. ENBP, PNG

Truck crossing river. ENBP, PNG

Chapter 21

REEF BOMBER OR A16-101

On December 29, 2007, just after Christmas, we had an opportunity to visit Gasmata again. Jared, some of the tall Diepenbrock family and I went to the airport where we found a group of young men hammering away at the starboard engine of the Japanese bomber that was by the airstrip. They had a long iron bar and were breaking off pieces of the aluminum casting. They had planned to heat up the fragments then quickly hit them with a hammer to make them explode. They were preparing their "fireworks" for the New Year celebration. I have even tried that myself using cast aluminum from a chainsaw cover, and it actually worked. I told them a bit of the history of that airplane and how it was one of only three left in the world. They listened politely then continued to break the engine apart. It seemed as if our attempt to prevent them from demolishing the rare antique was useless.

We returned to the airplane we were now calling the "reef bomber," which we had seen previously on the reef in May. (See page xiii - NO. 18) That involved sailing around islands and dodging hidden reefs. I wanted to have a closer look at it to see if it may be possible to identify what type of airplane it was. We parked the boat alongside the reef and snorkeled over to the wreckage. I closely examined the rear stabilizer and the one tail section there; I was convinced it was a twin-tailed airplane. The rear section of the fuselage was broken in two lengthwise sections along the seam. Because the entire section was upside down, we could see the rounded shape of the rear of the fuselage. It also had an oval hole on the bottom side toward the back, the purpose for which was unknown. I considered the possibility that it may have been a urinal port or perhaps an opening for ejecting bullet casings, but there did not seem to be a place for a rear machine gun as I had seen on a B-17.

As we swam around viewing the wreckage, I noticed a smaller-sized hydraulic strut, perhaps 75 to 100 millimeters (three to four inches) in diameter lying on the sand. That was when something caught my eye. I held my breath and went down a few feet to see something that was protruding from the reef. It was a large 15-centimeter (six-inch) diameter tube, and the item that caught my eye was a data plate that was spot welded to the tube. It was covered with a layer of algae, so it was not easy to notice. I used my fingernail to scrape at the plate and was pleased to see that the algae cleared off easily. As I scraped, I noted that the words "Lockheed Aircraft Corp" had become visible. I was excited with that bit of information to realize that the airplane had been made in America! I swam back to the boat to obtain the necessary tool from my tool box; Jared joined me and I handed him the tool without a word – he knew what to do with it. We had hoped to find a data plate with either English or Japanese writing on it. Such information was most important, since it represented the first piece of the puzzle needed to find an airplane's nation of origin. The next clue needed was information as to the type or model of airplane it was. And lastly, we needed to identify the most important recovery from an aircraft crash site – the serial number; it is a critical piece of information since, with it, records may then be traced back to ascertain passengers and/or crew.

I began to get my dive tank ready again as I wanted to have a more prolonged look at the large wing which was lying flat in approximately six meters (20 feet) of water. I took a hand brush with me and dived for the wing. It was covered with a 25 to 50 millimeter (one-to-two-inch) layer of sand and silt. I started at the wider end, brushing the layers off in both directions. I quickly had to abandon my effort since this brushing caused a cloud of sediment which blocked my vision, but soon I was able to return to the area to find that I had brushed it well enough to see the wing clearly. It was in fairly good condition, and interestingly, I observed a couple of places where the aluminum had been torn through, likely from anti-aircraft fire penetration. Upon examination, I was glad that I had used the brush; since had I been using my unprotected hand, some of the sharp edges would have likely sliced through my skin. I also noticed two longer, extended pieces which were the flap-guides used to guide the wing flaps along when they were extended.

My method was to brush clear a few feet, and, when the area became too clouded to see, I returned to the section where I had started. By then, the water had cleared sufficiently for viewing. I could see that the wing was black, but I could not discern any numbers. I continued this method working my way toward the tip of the wing. At about the halfway mark, there was such a cloud of silt around me that I was unable to see anything and became momentarily disorientated. After a brief delay, I began to examine the areas I had brushed, but there were no numbers. I did see some areas on the wing that were white in color. I continued brushing the sand from the leading edge all the way to the trailing edge. Occasionally, I hit a small, perhaps 20-centimeter (eight-inch) diameter, mound of brain coral that had attached itself to the wing, and as I moved forward, I was able to hang on to the coral as a point of reference. By then, I was again engulfed in a waterborne cloud and could not see anything. I kept my wits by assuring myself, after a quick glance at my pressure gauge, that I had plenty of air and even though everything had been temporarily obscured, I was all right. So, I proceeded to brush blindly. As I neared the tip of the wing, I could feel my sweep curving upward, and assumed that the tip must have been bent. I again returned to the area I had previously brushed, but it was still in a state of zero visibility. I decided that the best course of action was to swim back to the wreckage and allow the cloud to dissipate.

I brushed the side of the rear fuselage, and it, too, was white, but I did not find any markings or numbers. Later, I returned to the wing, but the cloud seemed to just hover over it. It was getting late and we had a long ride back home, so we reluctantly left the crash site and headed back to the boat with the data plate in hand.

Once back in Kandrian, I e-mailed my research partners Justin Taylan and Daniel Leahy. I also contacted a new e-mail acquaintance and WWII historian, Peter Dunn, to request assistance in researching that data plate, hoping to identify what type of airplane I had found. I had previously read a report of a B-25 in or near that area and thought that it might be that airplane, except for one glaring problem: the B-25 was made by Boeing, not by Lockheed. Later, when my phone began working again, I was able to go online and research things on my own. My effort began with a Google search of "Lockheed." From that research I learned that the twin-tail configuration was characteristic of Lockheed aircraft such as the P-38 Lightning. I recalled the one which we had already seen, in May, though that wrecked aircraft was tailless. My search led me next to a photograph of a twin-tailed airplane that had a rounded rear fuselage and a tail wheel. I then realized that the mysterious oval hole I had seen was likely one through which the rear strut protruded. I surmised, then, that the strut I saw laying close by was probably that extreme rear wheel strut.

Things began to make sense; pieces of the puzzle were taking shape. The model I had been examining was called a "Ventura." I was fairly convinced of the airplane's type because of the way the fuselage was rounded at the back end and the position of the hole for the rear strut.

I then reviewed some of my previous conversations with Justin and Daniel and read that a few Lockheed Hudsons had been lost in Gasmata as well. We had seen one of those Hudsons earlier on the island of Avurai. Another Hudson we had seen was by Zebu village where I encountered the bigman, Steven. The Hudson had twin nine-cylinder Cyclone engines. On the reef near this wreckage, we found a 14-cylinder engine; I began to wonder if another airplane had crash-landed on that reef as well. I had never seen a Hudson up close, nor had I seen a photograph of one, so I did not know how they looked. I performed a deeper search and found photographs of the Hudson aircraft. As it turned out, the rear fuselage of a Hudson had a rear wheel strut further in the back than did the Ventura, now convincing me the airplane we had discovered was a Hudson. In my research, I learned that some of the Hudsons were fitted with 9-cylinder Wright Cyclone engines, and others were fitted with Pratt and Whitney Wasp 14-cylinder engines. That further convinced me that the 14-cylinder engine on the reef was indeed from this type of airplane – maybe this one.

Additionally, I had discovered that the Hudson was equipped with 7.7-millimeter (.303-inch) Browning machine guns. In our dive, we found a box of 7.7-millimeter (.303-inch) bullets on the reef, but we thought that they may have come from a Japanese airplane such as the Val, which also had armament of that caliber. Those facts solidified my opinion that the airplane we had found was a Lockheed Hudson.

In a past conversation with Daniel Leahy, he had suggested the possibility of it being Hudson A16-101. Hudson A16-165 had been positively identified as the one we saw on Avurai Island that had been scrapped and lying in a boat waiting to be sold. Apparently, in 1946, a search team had found the wreckage of A16-165 and the remains of one crewman which had been in a lagoon. The natives showed them where another had been buried, and later, two more crewmen were found along the coast by the village of Akur. Paul "Eyeglass" was from Akur, and he had told me about those two graves. Both of those airplanes were lost on March 3, 1942, while carrying out a night raid on

Gasmata airstrip, having launched from 7-mile airstrip at Port Moresby; neither ever returned.[57] There is an update to the report that indicated A16-101 was, at first, assumed to have been lost in the mountains, but later the report was amended to read that it was now assumed to have been lost on this reef. Natives stated that the airplane on the reef and the one on Avurai Island had crashed on the same night. The four crew members from the one on the reef had never been recovered.

Later I had learned that the rear gunner from A16-101, Sgt. William "Bill" Coppin, was from Norseman, Western Australia. He had fallen in love with Beverley Dally when he was 18 years old and Beverley was 16. They were often seen by the townspeople riding bikes while holding hands. When war broke out, Bill enlisted in the Air Force, trained in Ballarat, Victoria, and became an Air Radio Operator/Air Gunner. He was then stationed at Pierce airdrome just outside of Perth, Australia. He and his love wrote letters and decided to get married in Kalgoorlie in November, 1941. Bill was then 21 years old and Beverley was 19. They had only been married one week before he got orders to fly out, and they were never to see each other again. One cannot comprehend how his new wife must have endured the years not knowing what had happened to her husband. Although she had received news that he was missing in action and presumed dead, she continued to write him with the hope that he was a prisoner of war and would one day return home.[58]

Further research revealed that a total of four Hudson aircraft had been lost in the Gasmata area. Two of them had been positively identified. That one on the reef was assumed to be A16-101 although it had never been positively identified. There was still another one missing, and that was A16-126 piloted by Flying Officer Graham (Ian) Gibson. My quest had now become to attempt to positively identify that wreckage on the reef, and if possible, locate the cockpit.

HUDSON A16-101   3/3/42   32 Sqd   Moresby - Gasmata
(See also A 16-165)   4/3/42

Departed from 7 mile Aerodrome, Port Moresby
Mission - Night bombing attack on Gasmata Aerodrome
Believed possible that aircraft attempted to fly through tropical storm
and crashed into one of the mountain ranges.
Request for D/F bearings between midnight and 0030 on 4/3/42 received
by Port Moresby W/T. May have come from this aircraft.
Bundle Report:
2/11/42 Wreckage located on reef 700 yards from MONTINGTONG Island north of
Gasmata Is. No bodies found. Not possible identify definitely but
was a Hudson - Natives say shot down same time as a/c on Urai Island-
Identified as Hudson A16-165 (Erwin's crew) Both aircraft A16-101
and A16-165 missing on 3/3/42 on attack Gasmata.
Deaths presumed   Confirmed further report 20/3/36.

RAAF Report of Hudson A16-101.

Ryan aeronautical exhaust date plate from A16-101.

Jared with bullet box from A16-101.

Chapter 22

ARE THESE REMAINS?

In the beginning of 2008, our telephones became useable again after being dead for six weeks. It was always quite frustrating when the phones were inoperative and I was forced to use a radio modem that could only send and receive e-mails. There was no surfing of the web and no ability to check E-Harmony to see how my son, Micah's love life was doing. Furthermore, the radio modem was slow and unreliable at best. Through e-mail communication, Justin had told me that the Japanese Embassy might be interested in hearing about my Val finds. In October 2007, there were reports of a PNG citizen who had found Japanese remains. He had created a little museum and was charging people to see the bones. I assumed that must have embarrassed the Japanese Government. I heard they set up a bureaucratic panel to respond to reports of remains found. I am not sure whatever became of the museum.

With that news as encouragement, I called the Japanese Embassy in Port Moresby, but the office was still closed due to the Christmas break. I also called a few other numbers and finally spoke to a Japanese lady who was not highly literate in English. To my surprise, not more than 30 minutes after that call, I received another call from a Japanese gentleman who was also less than fluent with the English language. I tried to explain to him what I had found, but he did not seem enthusiastically interested and did not ask many questions, so when the call ended, I was even more confused. Shortly afterward, I received *another* call from a PNG man who worked at the Japanese Embassy, and he informed me that the other man, with whom I had spoken, was unable to understand me, so he, instead, was calling to obtain the information. After I had apprised him of my aircraft finds, he told me that a Mr. Kimosawa would be getting in touch with me soon. Those phone calls made me believe that the Japanese may have become interested in hearing of the crash sites we had seen after all.

Well, as usual, the telephone failed again; this time it was inoperable for seven weeks! When service returned again, I immediately called the Embassy and was able to talk with a Mr. Susumu Kimosawa. He listened intently to my report, and we exchanged e-mail addresses to maintain contact. Without delay, I sent him the GPS coordinates and a brief description of the seven Val crash sites we had discovered. He replied to my e-mail that Rod Pearce had reported the one airplane in the water, and that the report had been sent to Tokyo a long time ago. He offered to make another report including these other six crash sites and send it to Tokyo for further response.

Soon afterward, I began to receive e-mails from Mr. Kimosawa, Rod Pearce and Justin Taylan. We had e-mails going back and forth and crossways as we kept each other up-to-date. Tokyo had replied, and they wanted to go to the Val in the water to retrieve the remains! But, they did not want to take the time to go to the other crash sites unless remains had been discovered. That was quite disappointing, as I was certain that at least four of the other crash sites would certainly have held remains and, to my thinking, it would have been a terrible shame for a team from Tokyo to travel all that way and not take the time to investigate all of the possibilities. I personally thought that the families of the missing crews might be interested to have any remains of their loved ones returned to their homes. My wife disagreed. She felt that the Japanese families would have said their goodbyes and would have buried their grief a long time ago. That opinion did have some merit as well; not all cultures react alike when dealing with such matters.

As the weekend was approaching, I remembered that Jared and I had been talking about his taking a motorcycle ride into the bush for a couple hours to a village. I was not able to recall for how long, but at least for a couple years, I had been hearing about an airplane wreck deep into the jungle. The men from Mang Village who occasionally hiked to the other side of the island had claimed to have seen it. Some rumors seem so bizarre as to be unbelievable. For example, there was the rumor about an airplane that had been brought down by a man who threw a spear at it. It was a good story, but it reminded me of my dad's story that he had sunk the Japanese Navy while riding on a whale and pulling the plugs from the bottoms of their ships. We believed him at the time since we were young, and it may be that the locals with their childlike minds and a limited world view would likewise believe that a man brought down an airplane with a spear.

In the previous November, I had given Edwin from Mang Village a disposable camera and asked him to take pictures of the airplane the next time he was in the area. A couple months afterward, he brought me the camera. I had to send it out for developing which would take a few weeks to complete. I also had Edwin draw me a sketch of the airplane he had seen. From the sketch, it became obvious that he had truly seen an airplane; thus my anxiety for the return of the pictures was intensified. As expected, it took a few weeks for the film to be developed, but finally word came that none of the pictures were viewable. That outcome left me greatly disappointed. I had assumed that there would be a few pictures of the airplane and a lot of pictures of his friends and family and I had prepared my mind for that, but I never envisioned the film would be blank! I concluded that I had not instructed him well enough on the use of the camera. I expected that it was going to be a long hike which I would not enjoy, and I also feared that I might be unable to complete the journey. My plan was for Jared to go alone and then hook up with some local villagers and hike with them to the crash site. Jared was all for going on the adventure, as he had been looking for an opportunity to hike a long distance. He had no apprehension of going alone. As parents, we too were not concerned, as we knew the Mang villagers. There was a church there and we felt we could trust them with our son.

Jared and I discussed his trip; I did not want to go because of the long hike, and the thought came to me of these other crash sites we had seen. I wondered about the possibility of locating human remains and whether an investigation team from Tokyo would then visit the sites. I asked Jared and later Mariko a question, "Of all the crash sites we have seen, which site do you think is most likely to have human remains?" It did not take much deliberation from either and they both said, "the Wako wreck." That was the one I would have selected as well. Although we had already traveled to it twice – once in 2003 and then again in 2005 – on neither occasion were we "seasoned" investigators, and we had not found any numbers to positively identify the airplane. The site was relatively easy to reach, and it held a special place in our hearts since it had been our first on-land crash site. I remembered that, when we found it, we were disappointed since it was scattered over a wide area and we had hoped to find an intact airplane. Now, having seen so many crash sites, I thought about how naive we were initially to expect to find an intact crashed airplane. I thought we now had better expectations and expertise to investigate crash sites.

That night as I lay in bed, I pondered the thought of a return visit to the Wako site. I considered that if we did not go to the Wako wreckage now, when would we get another chance? What if there were human remains at that site? I tossed and turned all night, and on the next morning, March 8, 2008, I awoke at 6:30 A.M. and lay there for a short time thinking about my choice of activities for the day. I considered other options that might be of more interest to me but was only able to think of one thing. Since my wife was still sleeping, I decided to leave the bed. I immediately began to ready our equipment for the trip. I boxed the food, filled the cooler with water jugs, packed my backpack with shoes and camera and gathered machetes, rakes and shovels. I also made a sifter from mosquito mesh to examine the ground more closely. Finally, I readied the portable TV with the video, *Attack! The Battle for New Britain.* An hour passed before I awakened my son Jared and said, "Let's go to Wako." Without a word, he rolled out of bed. Within the next hour, the boat was in the water, loaded, and we began the trip. Mariko had lost interest and ceased coming with us on our adventures, so it was just Jared and I.

One may have wondered whether Jared ever objected to these types of plans which I seemingly had made for him and, in this case, at last minute. His willingness to join me whenever and wherever I went was truly amazing. It also revealed something about his heart. I think that he wanted to accompany me to protect me and make certain I was not alone – even though his interest had begun to wane as well. It certainly was not a good idea to travel alone on such excursions; these trips included scuba diving or hiking, but loneliness itself was not a key factor and especially not on these types of excursions. Actually, the idea that one would be alone was seldom the problem, since most of the population were subsistence farmers and there were always plenty of people milling around looking for something to do, especially if they had the opportunity to be fed.

Before we left Kandrian, I did find a younger balding man, Ato Gelmus, from Wako, and we asked him if he wanted to join us – to which agreed. It was always good to have someone from the village to help alleviate any suspicions. We stopped at Yumielo Village and picked up Jacob Malis, a young man whom I had known since he was a toddler; his job would be to watch the boat while we headed into the bush. When we arrived at Wako, I sat and discussed my plans with the village chiefs (elders) and the people who had gathered on the beach. It is always a good idea to sit and talk for a while as it shows respect for the people and their ground. They had become used to me traveling through their village so I was welcomed and trusted. I showed them the video of the battle that had taken place in their area 65 years ago. While the video played, I went with another man to the top of the hill where he revealed that, under his house, he had collected a few bags full of aluminum and metal pieces. He allowed me to examine the material; I had hoped to find a data plate or stencil, but unfortunately, the pieces did not appear to have been related to the wing nor fuselage sections. Some pieces were thicker and had no paint on them – possibly made of stainless steel. The people said they were parts from a fuel tank. The teenagers who had found the pieces were there, too, and I questioned them as to where they had found them. From their description, it sounded to me as if they had found an airplane *other* than the one we had come to see, so I asked them to come with me and show me the airplane that they had found.

As we headed out of the village, I counted 11 persons who were escorting us on our trip. We drove the boat to a small shallow inlet as we had done previously. On this trip the guides encouraged me to go up a small stream that ran through the mangroves instead of anchoring and wading through the muck. To my surprise, the water was deeper than it had been in the inlet, though there were trees overgrown on both sides that threatened to rip and tear the boat canvas. We soon stopped the boat safely and deployed our rubber raft and loaded it with "guides" and supplies. I thought they were just going to the nearby bank, but they headed farther upstream.

We followed them and drove the boat even farther upstream. The overhanging trees became too thick to proceed, so we stopped as they paddled out of our sight. It seemed as if an hour had passed before the rubber dinghy returned to get a second load. We had not taken any paddles, so we used the rakes as paddles and a shovel as a rudder. The boat-load of teenagers really enjoyed our mode of propulsion; we took some photographs and had a few good laughs at ourselves.

After we had paddled for about 20 minutes, we stopped and began to trudge through the mud and mangroves to get to the shore. Of course, I almost fell as my feet were so tender and I had to remove my slippers because of the mud. We pressed on and, within five minutes, we arrived at the crash site. This was where the airplane pieces had been collected by the teenagers, so I did not believe there was another airplane in the area. Nobody from the first part of our group had done anything at the site, since we had the rakes and the shovel. It was 2:30 P.M., so I figured that we had to complete our search by 5:00 P.M. in order to get back home by sunset, which was typically about 6:30 P.M. The helpful workers started to clear the area while a few designated cooks began to boil the rice. I had always provided food as a motivator and friend-maker. In addition, I had learned they like coffee so I included instant coffee with lots of sugar, which was very high in demand. The entire packet was poured into a big 10-liter (two-and –a- half-gallon) pot; then, once brewed, the pot was then passed around so that everyone could have a mouthful.

Workers cleared the area around the engine as I went to look at what was left of the wings. The aluminum sheeting had long ago been peeled off for scrap. I had hoped to find a data plate or a stencil, because we had never even looked for them on our previous visits to this site. I was unable to locate any, but I did see a piece of Plexiglas. I asked the helpers where they had found it, and they pointed to a small mound to the left side of the engine. I told them that it was part of the canopy, where the pilot would have been sitting, and that we should begin to search more carefully in that area. Some workers started at that point, while others went to the opposite side of the engine and began scraping and digging the ground. They found many types of little pieces of aluminum, piping and wire harnesses. They were throwing the pieces behind them to where I stood. I scrambled to examine each piece and looked for writing in an attempt to identify them. After a cursory examination, I would place the pieces on the engine that I was standing next to. My helpers quickly found many pieces, and they began to lay them on the engine even before I could examine them. We were all aware of the short time we had to search, so the pace was frantic. From the corner of my eye, I saw that a helper had laid a square piece on the engine – I hurriedly picked it up. There it was! A data plate! I could tell by the Japanese writing that it was a type 99 model 22 made by Aichi (code name Val), with one noticeable difference. This plate had been made of brass whereas all the others I had seen were made of aluminum.

The excavators continued to dig and soon uncovered a dual-lever handle which I deducted had been the throttle control lever. I encouraged the workers and let them know that they were focusing on the right spot because that was where the cockpit would have been. They dug a little farther and found a piece of rubber which looked like the sole of a shoe. That greatly energized the search. The next object they found was a four-sided seatbelt buckle which had been used by one of the crewmen. When we found that, we were certain that we were searching in the right spot!

A little more digging revealed another seatbelt buckle, so we had both the pilot's and a crewman's seatbelt harness buckles. Things began to happen pretty fast, and within just a few minutes, a belt buckle was unearthed, then we found something suspicious. We examined it closely, and it appeared to be a bone. The inside had a white powdery substance. It was round – a finger bone or a clavicle? I placed it carefully into a plastic bag. Soon after that, another similar piece that looked like a bone fragment was also found. Quite honestly, I would probably not have recognized these types of fragments as bones, but the PNG nationals customarily dug up their dead, so that made them fairly keen as to recognition of bones. We found six fragments in total and wrapped them in plastic for protection. The weather was changing for the worse, and we began to hear thunder. It was already 4:15 P.M. so I said, "Let's go." My goal was not to find all of the bones that may have been there, but rather, proof that there were remains at the site and that we had found some. I finally had my proof to show to the people at the Japanese Embassy.

By the time we returned to the boat and headed for home, it was dark – pitch black is actually a more accurate description. The seas were calm, so I tried to move the boat rapidly, but I nervously watched the radar, the depth sounder and GPS instruments as we tracked and hugged the coastline. Once home and the boat was pulled out of the water, I went to my office to send an e-mail to report the finding.

What happened over the next few days was a bit disheartening. I assumed that the Japanese Embassy would be happy and eager to hear my report. The man with whom I communicated did seem appreciative, but was not eager to look at the artifacts, nor did he appear to want to send a representative to check it out. I had written to others who had replied with encouraging comments of "fantastic work," but I was reminded by some that the Japanese did not really want to remember the war. Toshi, the Japanese fisherman, had told me that there is only one paragraph written about the war in their history books. For public relations purposes and because of pressure from relatives, they did make an effort to retrieve remains when they were discovered. I explained to the Japanese Embassy that I had retrieved human remains from the crash site and hoped that they would come to recover them when their team came to collect remains from the airplane in the water. I also hinted that I believed that there were, possibly, additional remains to be recovered at three other crash sites that we had located, as well as from the Arawe battlefield where 150 Japanese soldiers had lost their lives.

I heard from an old man from Meselia Village, Madang, who said that, after the war, Japanese remains were found leaning up against trees and under rock cliffs. "They died where they fell," he said. It was possible that they had been wounded and then abandoned, so as not to slow down their comrades. He said that the remains were probably now covered with soil and foliage and branches after so long a time. Without a guide to find a specific location, it would have been next to impossible to find those remains.

There is a published work entitled *The Bone Man of Kokoda* which tells the story of a Japanese soldier, Kokichi Nishimura, who was with the 2nd Battalion, 144th Regiment of the Japanese Imperial Army. He had fought against the Australians on the Kokoda trail and was the sole survivor of his platoon. Wounded and starving, he left thousands of his fellow soldiers in shallow graves; he promised them that he would one day return and retrieve their remains. That was precisely what he did for over 25 years, and he has found over 300 Japanese wartime remains. Nishimura's story has been told in the book by Charles Happell, published by Pan-Macmillan in 2008.

The question remains, is the Japanese Government really disinterested in the findings of our searches? I have always been certain that their relatives cared, but it is probably true that Japanese soldiers knew that if they were killed on the battlefields, that is where they would stay. They may have never expected to be returned to their homeland. They did not have the motto of the U.S. Marines and U.S. Army Special forces, "Leave no one behind." Justin brought to my attention and Toshi directed me to the website of a well known Japanese patriotic song called, *Umi Yukaba*. This song was constructed to engender loyalty and warm feelings toward the Japanese nation; the song has been compared to *The Battle Hymn of the Republic* for Americans. It was sung by many Kamikaze pilots prior to their departures for their suicide missions. The song says, "If I go away to the sea, I shall be a corpse washed up. If I go away to the mountain, I shall be a corpse in the grass. But if I die for the Emperor, it will not be a regret."[60]

In addition, the Japanese kamikaze pilots would say, "See you at Yasukuni" as they departed on their one-way missions.[61] They must have believed that if they died in battle for the Emperor, their name would be put into the Yasukuni Shrine. In our western culture, such a mindset is difficult to fathom. Some have suggested that according to Shinto religious belief, once a person is enshrined, all his negative or evil acts are absolved, and their "kami" (spirits/souls) would have a permanent residence as a deity.[62] My Japanese friend Toshi elaborated on this matter, that "death cleanses the soul and enshrinement gives deity." Once a soldier or airman was enshrined, their families could find comfort and a place to go to mourn or pray, even though remains were never recovered.

So, a new question has arisen for me – should I pursue the search for human remains (especially Japanese remains) at other sites? And even if I found human remains in the wreckage of a Japanese aircraft, would the family members agree to DNA testing to identify those remains as a lost son or brother or father? The possibility of a refusal to test is strange to western thinking but seemingly acceptable to the Japanese. How different from the persistence of Douglas Walker who has been fervently investigating his father's fate, hoping one day to find his remains. Perhaps I should concentrate my efforts looking for the San Antonio Rose, I thought.

Once back in Kandrian, I took the suspected remains we had collected from the Japanese Val near Wako Village to the Kandrian hospital, in order to determine whether what we had found were truly bones and if they were human. After a number of different hospital workers had examined the pieces, most of them assured me that they were, indeed, bones. About two months later, there was an Australian pathologist who had been on a fishing trip and happened to stop at Kandrian to refuel his boat. I asked him if he would render his expert opinion on the specimens I had found. He had never before seen 65-year-old bones, so he deferred to say for certain what he thought they represented. The Papua New Guinea people customarily dig up their dead ancestors' bones, so I reasoned that they were actually more experienced at identifying old bones, and I accepted their opinion over that of the pathologist. I suppose there was no way of knowing for sure if they were animal, American or Japanese bones, but the location of the discovery made it rather clear in my mind.

Meanwhile, I had been corresponding with the Japanese Embassy and Mr. Susumu Kimosawa who said that, although I had "no obligation to find more Japanese human remains, it was *their* duty." Did that mean he preferred I not look for remains? He also sent me various forms to document the crash sites. That encouraged me, somewhat, to think that they might send a team to find the remains at the other crash sites we had located. I completed the forms as requested and returned them per instructions; I never received a reply or even a "read receipt" for my e-mail message. That left me perplexed at the seemingly lack of concern of the Japanese Embassy personnel, and I began to think that I had wasted my time in processing this notification.

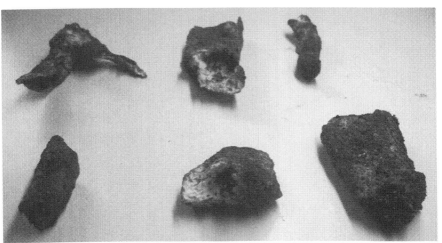

Deteriorated aluminum tubing disguised as remains.

Guides from Wako Village. WNBP, PNG

Chapter 23

JARED'S QUEST – VAL #8

The day arrived for Jared to make his planned trek to the interior in search of the airplane we had heard about for a couple of years. We had attempted to have Edwin, one of our national friends, take photographs of the airplane, but the film, for some unknown reason, was returned undeveloped and ruined. Jared had wanted to take a long hike, so he was definitely up for the challenge. He rode his motorcycle as far as Mang Village on March 16, 2008. That required a couple hours of off-road travel even though he was actually on the road. The government mud roads in the area where we lived were not maintained very well. After he had attended church with the believers in their village, a couple of teenage boys reluctantly agreed to take him to the crash site. The three of them set out just before noon and had hiked for three hours when they reached a bush shelter. It was still fairly early, but the two guides had noticed dark clouds and wanted to avoid the rain. So they spent what Jared described as a sleepless night trying to doze off while lying on a bed made of sticks. That was his first experience in trying to get comfortable on a traditional PNG bed, which he found to be an impossible task.

Morning arrived, not a minute too soon for him, and they set out on the trail again. After a couple more hours of hiking, they arrived at another jungle shelter. That one had some happy fellows already in it; they had been out hunting for wild pig. Their hunting trip was successful, so the three hikers were invited to sit down to enjoy some pig meat with them. Had they pressed on farther the first day, they could have had some company to share the shelter overnight. Once they had dined on pork and had a brief rest, they went on a little farther and arrived at the village of Walo. From there to the crash site, it was only a ten-minute hike. (See page x - NO. 1)

When they reached the site, Jared was beside himself because the airplane was *virtually intact*. It was broken-up, but no one had torn the aluminum from the wings and fuselage to sell for scrap metal. They found pieces of wreckage that we had never seen before, left there undisturbed. The cockpit, with both the pilot's and crew's seats, was intact. Even the canopy frame which could be slid back and forth was still attached. All the gauges and switches were still in place. The engine had been torn from the front and lay a short distance from the main fuselage. At first assessment, it appeared possible that the crew might have survived the crash landing, as it had apparently skidded down the hillside and did not impact nose-first. The tail section had broken off and was standing next to and separate from the fuselage. All the leading edges on the wings had big gashes made by the trees which the skidding airplane would have hit on its way down the hill. On one side of the tail, there was a number "2."

The locals' story of the airplane was that it was piloted by a white woman. She had a baby and a man with her. They had been seen drinking water by the river after the crash. The baby eventually died and was buried under the airplane. We had heard this story of a white lady pilot in many of the places we had visited in our travels. It seemed, somehow, like a convoluted version of Amelia Earhart's legend that had reached even into the deepest jungle.

Jared had calculated that he would be able to hike out and ride home before dark only if they spent no more than one hour at the crash site. I do not think he wanted to spend another night on a stick bed! With that thought in mind, he took as many photographs as he could, but did not have enough time to execute a more thorough search. The job of photographer was usually mine, so he did not relish the task. When he saw the number 2 on the tail, he did not give it much thought. Had he found more numbers on the tail, those would have made it possible to identify the airplane, its squadron and flight. He did find the identifying stencil which enabled us to know the model and production number. It was made by Aichi, type 99, model 22, manufacturer's number 3179. He returned home rather tired but excited to have made the trip and the discovery.

WING IN THE WATER

The next day, March 18, 2008, found us in the Gasmata area again. Although we had been there on official charter business for a rosewood timber cutting operation, our other agenda was to check out the Hudson wing which rested in six meters (20 feet) of water. We planned to search for identifying marks or numbers. If none were visible on the top side where I had brushed off a cloud of sand, we would attempt to flip the wing over for a look on the other side. We knew from the Hudson wing we had seen at Zebu that the numbers would be found on the bottom side.

We left early that morning and arrived at the site around 9:00 A.M.; Jared was still quite exhausted from the long trek the day before and slept most of the way. The water was thankfully calm, so we made good time getting to the wreckage area. When we arrived, I was somewhat stunned by how crystal clear the water was revealing perfectly the condition of the wreckage! The water was flat with the sun hitting it just right. The tide was in and the water was deep at the top of the reef, so after awakening Jared, I had him idle in slowly to get a closer look while I stood on the bow. We were able to approach somewhat near to the long twin-rudder tail section that lay upside down in approximately six feet of water. I could not stop taking photographs; I wanted to get just the right shot. I was rather excited to say the least! This was an unbelievable opportunity, not only for good photos, but also to make an in-depth and high-quality search that could lead to positive identification.

When a sufficient number of photographs had been taken, we anchored the boat and I hurriedly suited up for a closer look at the wing that was six meters (20 feet) below us. The wing, even as far down as it lay, was clear enough for us to see while standing on the boat, but not clear enough to warrant an effort to obtain a good photo. I dived in and examined the wing's surface that I had previously brushed clear of sand. Some silt had resettled on it, but not enough to cover any numbers or impair visibility. After swimming back and forth over the wing, I could clearly discern now that it was the top surface of the wing. As I examined it, I realized the curved section I had felt previously was not the tip of the wing, but it was the section that attached to the fuselage, and a portion of the side window was still intact. After I had seen the window, I realized that this was the inner section of the port (left) wing. The cutout section that once held the engine also enabled me to identify it as being the portside wing. It was in excellent condition compared to the wreckage that was lying in shallower water. At first, I presumed that the aircraft had crashed nose first, but it was also possible that it could have slid across the top of the reef, separating the wing from the fuselage, and it indicated that the engine must have been torn from it. One engine was wedged into the reef next to the tail section and surrounded by coral which made it difficult for us to see clearly.

I surfaced to retrieve a rope, then dived again and hooked it on the guide for the flaps. Jared tried to pull it up using the anchor capstan, but it did not apply sufficient torque. He then repositioned the boat in an attempt to flip the wing over with the use of power of the boat's propulsion; unfortunately, the wing seemed to be glued to the bottom. It was obvious we could not make it budge, and, because of the excessive time we would have needed to continue our efforts to flip it, we decided to quit and headed for Kandrian. Although we did not succeed in all our intended goals, I was content with the effort and satisfied that we had obtained so many photographs.

Val engine by Walo Village. WNBP, PNG

Val fuselage by Walo Villag. WNBP, PNG

Val cockpit by Walo Village. WNBP, PNG

Wasp engine on reef in Gasmata. WNBP, PNG

Hudson tail section on reef in Gasmata. WNBP, PNG

184

Chapter 24

JUNGLE BOMBS

March/April is a good time of year as the seas are generally calm and the weather is starting to cool down to low 80s during the day. I proposed to Jared the need for making a big push to investigate the many rumors we had been gathering. He agreed, so on March 30, 2008, we headed for the Pulie River again after hearing of an airplane in the jungle. We met up with our guides at Murien Village. Our primary guide was a young boy of only 13 years of age who had seen the "airplane" with his father. We moored the boat at the first big bend in the river, and then we proceeded on foot to locate the "plane." We had not hiked too far when we came to a timber company road and continued on it for 45 minutes before heading into the bush. After about ten minutes, I noticed that our guides were not certain where to go. As luck would have it, our search eventually led us to a bulk of rusty steel lying in the middle of the jungle. It had loops mounted to it as if it were to be attached to a wing or undercarriage. It appeared to have been round at one time and had the appearance of an external fuel drop tank, but I was reluctant to conclude that certain airplanes had used steel drop tanks. We searched around the area and soon found another one. They both had burst open and rusted, which made it difficult to determine what they represented – bombs? fuel tanks? Three years later while I was in Rabaul visiting a war museum, I saw a bomb that looked similar to these, as it had also burst open from the explosion. I now believe that what we had found were remnants of exploded bombs in the middle of the jungle.

In any case, it seemed that we had wasted a colossal amount of time, so we took the young boy and others back to their village and preceded with Plan B. Plan B concerned our examination of some filled bags of aluminum from an airplane. Some local people had ripped or torn the material from the aircraft sheeting and had packed the pieces into burlap bags. They had hoped to sell the aluminum, and so they had the bags loaded onto a dugout canoe. They departed the village, and as they passed the reef's outer edge, a large wave hit them broadside and overturned the canoe. All the bags of aluminum pieces fell from the canoe and sank to a depth that was beyond the people's ability to retrieve them with a free dive. We shared their disappointment. Our interest in the bags was greatly heightened once we found that the scrap had been taken from the Val in which we had excavated human remains near Wako Village. If we could have found the bags, we might have found the stencil with the manufacturer's number. We already had our scuba gear, so we made a dive and searched for approximately one hour back and forth along the reef's edge at various depths. Unfortunately, we were unable to locate the mysterious bags of aluminum. Had the sun been shining, it might have made the coral colors brighter. The reef had various crevices into which we could swim, and it would have been a most dramatic dive experience. So, needless to say, the day was rather disappointing regarding our efforts to locate something useful to our interest.

BROKEN RIBS AND DISLOCATED SHOULDER

The seas were rough on our return, and we arrived home almost at dark. After we had unloaded the boat and headed towards the house, I remembered something I had forgotten and returned to the boat. As I stepped from the dock onto the boat, a swell moved the boat, and consequently my foot slipped. I fell into the water (which could have been a comical scene) but on the way down, the edge of the boat caught me under my rib cage on my right side. I managed to catch myself before I could fall all the way into the water and somehow pulled myself back into the boat. I was enduring an immense amount of pain! I found myself lying curled-up, fetal position, on the deck, as I groaned and tried to catch my breath. I eventually climbed out of the boat very slowly and walked to the house. It felt as though I had broken a few ribs. I had never before broken a rib, but I had heard that it hurt severely and the usual downtime was six weeks or more; that did not make me happy. That night I hardly slept and, for the next two weeks, it hurt to sneeze or even blow my nose. In an attempt to alleviate the pain, I wrapped an Ace bandage around my chest to restrict the expansion of my chest cavity. I am not certain whether it helped or not, but my family said that I looked funny. Consequently, I was in no mood to go hunt for WWII wreckages during the downtime required to heal!

In the small town of Kandrian, there were no emergency rooms to go to, nor was there a qualified doctor, so I treated myself. It reminded me of the time when I was building our house. The scaffolding I had rigged collapsed, and I fell approximately eight feet, landing in an awkward position. My local carpenter helper, Waselio, was standing next to where I landed. He just stood there waiting for me to move, as he did not know if I was dead or alive. Once the dust had settled and everything was quiet, I told him I was alright, but my shoulder was dislocated.

I gently made my way to the truck and sat in the back seat. I had been teaching Waselio how to drive, but we were still on lesson number one so he did not know how to shift the gears yet. We slowly made our way to the "hospital." I was met by a "Doctor" who had me lay on the cement sidewalk outside the facility. He then pulled and twisted my arm until I could no longer withstand the torture. I thanked him for his efforts, then Waselio, slowly (in first gear), drove me to our house as I endured excruciating pain with each bump along the dirt road. Arriving at the house, I had Joan get me some of her headache medicine, and I swallowed three tablets. Along with a pain reliever, the medicine also had a muscle relaxant. I then tied a three-pound sledge hammer to my hand, hung my arm over the back of a chair and waited for Waselio. He had returned to the work site to put our tools away so they would not walk away on their own. While he was gone, I brushed up on how to deal with a dislocated shoulder as I read the book, *Where There is No Doctor*. After one hour, Waselio returned and I explained to him what we were going to do and showed him the picture in the book. I then laid on the floor while he stuck his beetle nut stained and calloused foot in my armpit. At the same time, he gently pulled and twisted my arm which caused it to pop back into its socket. It was amazing how soon the pain subsided once the joint was realigned. But I think I may have overdosed on Joan's medicine since I was nauseated and eventually vomited. That experience taught me that there was no advantage in going to the local clinic.

THE LOST CAVE

During this time of recuperating, I heard of another airplane crash site up the Pulie River. I also decided that another trip to the Arawe battlefield was in order. Perhaps, I would come across other old men who could guide me to the remains of soldiers who had been buried there years ago. Even though I had been there before and had asked around, I have found that often a second visit proves to be more fruitful. It has been my experience that the local village people are probably aware of the location of a lot of WWII relics, but they keep that type of information to themselves – unless they are asked directly. Furthermore, the real person "in the know" may not have been available on the first visit, so it has always been a good policy to consider a return trip.

We made our way to the village of Meselia. The seas were rough and there was no place to tie up the boat, so I stayed with the boat while Jared went ashore. His mission was to investigate a cave that was rumored to have jeep tires and other items in it. There was also reported to be a large snake in the cave, so the villagers were afraid to go into it. White skins were apparently dispensable so they summoned us to come explore the cave. We were interested in that area because it was the location where the Japanese had resided during the Arawe battle. From that battle, there were some American Marines who were missing in action (MIA), and we thought it possible their remains may have been hidden in the cave. Unfortunately, the young villager who had reported that cave to us was not at the village, so Jared never did find the cave or whether it even existed.

Reichman house construction, Kandrian. WNBP, PNG

Chapter 25

NARCOSIS

I had been monitoring the whereabouts by radio communication of the Au Timber Company chairman, Mr. Daniel Kovi. A year earlier, he had been extremely helpful by escorting us around to track leads on an airplane in the timber area near Gasmata. At that time, the crash site turned out to be a great distance away with no access road, so we abandoned the search. A surveyor had told me that he saw the airplane while he was marking the boundary of an area to be cut. He said that he had seen a propeller and a large tank, but he did not spend much time investigating it. To confirm that the surveyor was actually at the camp, I went to his father's house to find out if he had, in fact, physically travelled there, and I received assurance that he had. I had hopes that he would be able to guide us. We had heard rumors that the timber company road had now reached close to the crash site, and, since Daniel Kovi was to be present for a couple of weeks, my mind was made up. The weekend of May 4, 2008, arrived, and I realized that I had not personally hunted for any relics throughout all of April (I was still experiencing a bit of pain but I was finally able to sneeze), so we decided to head east toward Gasmata.

I spent the day before the trip getting the boat and supplies ready, since we planned to spend the night on the boat during the trip to give us plenty of time to search the next full day. It was like the preparing for a camp-out. Preparations included packing a little burner that operated with mentholated spirits, loading plenty of rations, and filling the back pack with a camera, the GPS, etc. Of course we could not forget to take the fishing rods and tackle box; those would certainly become useful in case we were to encounter rough seas and had to slow down to trolling speed. It seemed odd that we were heading out on what seemed to be only a camping trip with so much "stuff." The nationals must have shaken their heads at the extent of our preparations. When they planned a trip, they just concerned themselves with finding some petrol and jumping into their boat. They hoped that they could make it to their destination and, in the process, find food along the way. Little if any thought was put forth for the return trip.

Saturday morning I arose before daybreak, but I was disappointed to see dark clouds all around us. It apparently had rained during the night as the grass was wet. Large swells were hitting the beach. It did not bode well for our extensive plans. I walked all around and looked at the clouds over the ocean and at the mountains to contemplate my options. The last time we set out in bad weather, Jared became upset because he thought that these adventures were supposed to be "fun" trips. He would have said that rough seas and hiking in the rain were not fun! I was reluctant to wake him if it seemed as if the trip was going to be cancelled. In addition, I could not find our designated boat security guard we had identified for this trip. Our friend Alfi, who had led us to Zebu village, wanted to come along again on this trip so that he could visit his in-laws. I felt that his inclusion might help us to avoid any difficulty we might encounter with the locals. They had had endless suspicions of us, so our ability to have one of their own with us always helped to put them at ease. We never felt that anything was guaranteed though, since Alfi was not much help the last time when I met up with Stephen at Zebu Village. On that day, our friend, Alfi, was nowhere to be found.

I stood there and wrestled within myself as I pondered over the decision as to whether we should risk it and take the trip or play it safe and reschedule it for another day? The boat was loaded and ready to go, but the weather was not cooperating and Alfi had not yet appeared. Then, as I stood there, Alfi stealthily walked up behind me as if sneaking up on a fish or pig. His covertness was successful, and I was, indeed, surprised to see him. As I explained to him my hesitation about making the trip, some blue skies began to show slightly, but not in the direction we had planned to go. He tried to assure me that the rain during the night had ended and that the day would be nice. I was less than convinced of his meteorological skills, since many locals believe they have the power to make it rain or stop the rain if they choose to do so. I was not certain as to which "powers" Alfi had, or if he had claimed to have any.

We continued to watch the skies as more and more clouds rolled back giving way to blue skies; we made the decision to go. I awakened Jared and, shortly afterward, found someone to join us to watch the boat while we hiked into the jungle. One convenient thing about the high unemployment rate in PNG was that it was usually easy to find someone willing to work – even for an unbelievable low daily wage. I always paid more than the government's minimum wage and fed my workers well, which probably explained why finding people to accompany and help us seemed easy.

We had already fallen two hours behind schedule, but at least we were able to launch and were now under way. The seas were relatively calm, but as we made the bend around the point six miles east of Kandrian, we saw dark clouds in our path. That certainly was not encouraging, so I switched on our radar which showed the rain clouds. I was relieved to see that the clouds represented only a large local shower about a half-mile deep. We continued onward without a course change and experienced a few rain showers and a couple downpours. I was glad we were able to close the clears surrounding the helm and stay dry inside the enclosure. The main cloud was moving out to sea so we pressed onward.

Two hours later, we arrived at the timber company near Au Village. I was amazed to find Daniel Kovi, the fellow whom we had seen a year ago, sitting there, as if he were waiting for us. We shook hands and I explained our plan and what we hoped to accomplish. Unfortunately, the surveyor who had spotted the airplane had left the day before to return to Kandrian. It seemed as if we had been foiled again! What a disappointment! I inquired as to whether anyone had traveled with him when he saw the airplane wreckage and was informed that a younger, mid-twenties man named Boas Moses, who lived up in the bush, had accompanied him to the site. After a brief discussion, it was decided that we would wait until the next day to continue the search. The timber company road did not lead us to the actual crash site, so it was going to be a long journey, and since we had yet to find Boas, a delay was deemed prudent. In addition, our guides and helpers had some other activities happening in the village and they did not want to depart just yet.

I assumed all the excuses for not wanting to go had to do with their desire to hang out at the village with a visiting Local Level Government candidate in hopes of getting drunk. I realized my little excursion was not that important to them, so we opted to motor away and go see some of our fellow missionaries who were not that far away from Au in Gasmata.

Once we finally arrived in Gasmata, we considered once again our attempts to flip the wing of the Hudson in the water to find any numbers that might positively ID the airplane. I later learned that the RAAF stopped numbering the Hudsons after A16-100, so even had we flipped the wing, we would not have seen the number A16-101.

The records I examined showed that four Hudson aircraft had been lost. This was one of them, and I had personally seen two others. One with serial numbers A16-165 that had crashed on Avurai Island, and A16-91, which was near Zebu Village, piloted by W/Cdr. John Lerew. The fourth Hudson had never been found. I thought the airplane we were after might be the missing Hudson or a Boston, or even a Beaufort, but it is all speculation until the wreckage is examined closely and some sort of identifying numbers can be located.

We lingered at the "haus boi" (house where men and boys sleep). Those are convenient sleeping places when back-packing around PNG. As I talked to the locals, I began to get sleepy and considered taking a nap when I remembered that Jared had never seen the sunken Japanese ship in that area. Reinvigorated with the idea, we jumped back into the boat and secured approval from the locals who govern that sunken-boat area. They were agreeable and allowed us to dive, and some of the local villagers even wanted to go along for the ride. Five men boarded with us, and we proceeded to the location of the ship which was not all that far from their island of Avirin.

We motored slowly to the position and followed our GPS readings as we neared the site. Our eyes were fixed on the depth sounder for a sudden change in depth. We found ourselves over a flat bottom of 41 meters (135 feet), but then it became shallower and the depth reading changed to 35 meters (115 feet) quite suddenly. We knew that the sunken ship was directly beneath us, so we dropped anchor and floated back until we could feel the anchor had caught onto the side of that ship which rested on the harbor bottom.

We next suited up in our diving gear and dangled an extra air bottle off the bow to about nine meters (30 feet) as we had done on the previous dive. That was a wise practice for all of our deep dives, such as the time when we dived on the *Taka Saka Maru*. It actually served as a safety precaution to alert us in the event that our ascent might require decompression for a longer time than our diving air would allow. It signaled the level we should not exceed on our ascent and cued us to check our gauges in the event we had ascended too rapidly. Any diver would confirm the fact that it is never a good feeling to be underwater in the midst of a dive and have the airflow stop! With that extra tank suspended, we were assured that we would have back-up air should we need it. In the event a diver spends more time looking around than he should have, as he begins to surface, he needs to spend several minutes at different levels starting at nine meters (30 feet) in an attempt to decompress. That technique allows the body to release nitrogen from the blood stream, slowly so as to avoid the "bends" (nitrogen narcosis).

As we descended along the anchor line, it became quite dark very quickly, but we continued our descent. Jared was in the lead, and at 26 meters (85 feet), he turned around and looked at me wide-eyed and with a face that communicated, "Where is it?!" I motioned to move even deeper, and finally, the ship came into view. Our visibility was only about three meters (ten feet) and much of that was blurry. I took a quick photograph of Jared as he stood on the ship's edge. It turned out blurry, but it communicated easily the idea of how scary it was down there. Our anchor was lying on the starboard side of the ship, at the front edge of the forward cargo hold.

We swam along the starboard walkway and momentarily stood on the deck of the huge ship to look around. I wanted to go inside the cargo hold, but it was pitch black in there and rather spooky, so I abandoned that idea rather quickly. We swam toward the stern and came to a short ladder that led us up to the next deck level. We had vastly limited visibility, and schools of fish were within arm's reach. I am not certain who saw the other first, us or the fish, but we were all startled whenever a school of fish came into view. Our hearts skipped a beat and the fish scurried away! I think we were all scared.

We crossed over the raised deck area where we could identify the hole where the smoke stack once stood. There was also a small hip-roof-like structure that appeared to have openings for windows. As we continued toward the aft of the ship, we passed another spooky cargo hold and came to another ladder and a raised deck at the stern. The top deck was missing; it may have been hit with a bomb or merely deteriorated over time. We descended over the stern and stayed close to the wreckage to avoid losing orientation but we were a bit closer than what was comfortable. We were now looking at it in front of us instead of beneath us. Jared was, no doubt, sensing the same eeriness, as we swam so close together that we were rubbing shoulders. Normally, on a clear dive, divers swim nine to 12 meters (30 to 40 feet) apart from each other as they explore their surroundings. That was not the case this time; we might as well have been holding hands – we stayed pretty close to each other.

When we swam back up and over the stern and headed forward on the port side, I found myself at the ominous davit which was used for lowering a life boat. It, of course, was empty, so I wondered whether some of the crew had escaped before the ship sank completely. I went a little farther until I came to the other one. I was standing between them, confused as to why the davits were along the edge of the cargo hold! It did not make sense to me that they would have lowered the life boat into the cargo hold.

As I continued, I turned and motioned to Jared to follow me since I wanted to go explore the starboard side of the boat. We swam out a ways, but I was unable to see anything, so I motioned to Jared to turn around. I momentarily panicked since I was experiencing vertigo and did not know which way was up. I frantically looked around and turned toward what I had thought was the surface. I then saw that this direction was indeed a bit brighter as I looked up, and that confirmed the right way to go. I checked my tank pressure, but since it was so dark and I was without my glasses, I was unable to read the pressure gauge. I thought I was at 1000 psi which, according to the 10% rule and us being at 30 meters (100 feet), made it time to ascend.

I swam in a circular pattern keeping an eye on my dive computer to make sure that I was not ascending too rapidly. As we neared the surface, visibility began to increase and everything was brighter; I could see that I still had 1500 psi. When we had reached the nine-meter (30-foot) level, we could not yet make out the bottom of our boat, so we surfaced and found ourselves approximately 15 meters (50 feet) away from the boat. I dived back down to six meters (20 feet) and proceeded to swim toward the boat. After swimming for some time, I surfaced again and saw that we had passed the boat, so I collected Jared and we made our way to the boat together. We never did see the anchor line or decompression bottle until we were almost on top of them. Fortunately, because we had not stayed down that long and our dive computers had given us the green signal to surface safely, we did not need to decompress.

Once on board, Jared asked me laughingly, what I was doing down there? At first, I was a bit surprised at his question. Then he said I had been swimming off into nowhere away from the ship then came back and swam in circles. I explained to him that I knew that something was not right when I was down there, but could not figure it out at the time. Much later, as I reflected on the incident, I believe that I was suffering from narcosis at that time. Narcosis is a condition, similar to intoxication, that frequently occurs to divers at deeper depths. Something certainly affected me, and I finally realized that those davits were not along the cargo hold as I had confusedly thought, but on the edge of the boat, which makes more sense now to my "non-narcosis" (sober) thinking. Because of the narcosis, I was disorientated and confused, and it affected my ability to reason properly. Jared was the one who usually became tipsy at depth, but on that dive, he remained clear-headed. He did not recognize the seriousness of my curious behavior, so he did not attempt to come to my aid but innocently followed me. In retrospect, that phenomenon has led to many diving disasters, and but for God's grace, it could have ended badly right there. Since it all went well, we had a good laugh.

The entire memory of that experience was also mingled with a collateral event when a disgruntled old man, Ben, paddled over to us and yelled at me claiming that I had been diving in "his" water. As was indicated earlier, we had the permission of the Ward Counselor (Councilman) who was on board to conduct the dive. I had even paid the Counselor PNG K10 when the government approved fee for two divers was six Kina (US $2.35). Ben was, nevertheless, ranting and raving as the locals on board advised me, "Don't mind him." I still believed that, in order to get rid of him, I would have to give him some money, so I spoke respectfully to him and handed him five Kina (US $2). That seemed to satisfy him, and he quietly paddled away.

That had been my second dive on that boat, and on both of the dives, the water was not clear. On a previous effort, I had also taken some fellow divers there, but they said that the visibility was only three feet and they surfaced within minutes after beginning the dive. After my first dive on that ship with my older son Micah, I had to deal with another old man named Francis. He was the brother of Ben, and he also claimed to be the "Papa of the salt water!" Ben was "Papa of the ground," according to him. It was no wonder that there were not many tourists who visit PNG, since tourists were so often confronted by the locals in ways that left a bad taste in their mouths. That was really sad because most of the local people are so friendly and helpful. Unfortunately, there were other times when a fellow came along who just liked to yell at someone in the hopes that he would be paid to go away.

We returned to the wharf of our fellow missionaries' leased island in Gasmata and spent some time bracing the wharf. (See page xiii - NO. 22) Sea worms had been eating at the posts, and once they succeeded in riddling the post with holes, the wharf would lose its strength and eventually collapse. That night, we had dinner and fellowship with Ryan and Nicki Coleman and their two little children. It was an enjoyable evening, and I am reasonably certain that they enjoyed our company; after all, they lived on an island with only one other English-speaking couple, Adam and Julie Martin. We kept them up until the late hours as we talked about life in PNG and the depressing rainy season soon to be upon us, with its 76 to 127 centimeters (30 to 50 inches) of rain per month. After returning to the boat, I wondered all night long if our guides would still be willing or able to go search for the crash site in the morning.

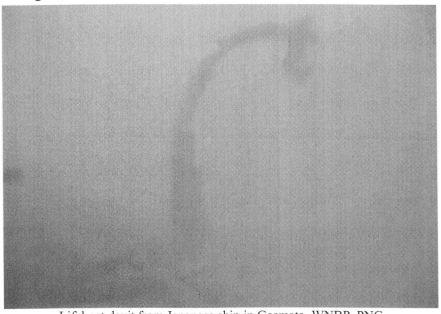

Lifeboat davit from Japanese ship in Gasmata. WNBP, PNG

Chapter 26

FOUND – HUDSON A16-126

After a good night's sleep on the boat, we awoke early and departed for Au village just after sunrise. The boat ride was uneventful and smooth as it often was in the early morning. The skies were looking bluer than they had the day before, so I was not expecting much rain, if any. As we approached the shoreline, to my surprise, we could see Daniel Kovi was waiting with a truck. That was certainly an encouraging site! After we anchored and paddled to shore in our rubber dinghy, we loaded Daniel's truck with our gear and rations. As usual, a few workers hopped onto the truck as well, and we started our journey.

Daniel drove conservatively on the karanas (lime stone) road, and after about a half hour, we met another truck which was traveling in the opposite direction headed for the coast. Daniel instructed the driver to join us, but first, he was to go and find Boas who supposedly knew the location of the wreckage site. We waited 15 minutes for the truck to return from a side road with a younger, early-20s fellow. He was a timid sort and did not say much. I asked him specific questions, such as how many propellers had he seen, and did he see a wing or tail? His answers made me suspicious that he had not seen the airplane at all. I mentioned my concern to Daniel, and he questioned the young man further with similar results and hesitation. Daniel also doubted that this fellow knew where to take us, and neither of us wanted to roam around in the jungle aimlessly.

I then asked him if there was anyone else who knew the location of the airplane. After he and another man had a discussion in their clan language, which I did not understand, it was decided that we should find one other person who may have seen the wreckage. We headed out, one truck following the other, and stopped at an intersection. Again we waited while the other truck traveled down a side road. When it returned, our companion brought along an older gentleman wearing tattered clothes who sat in the rear bed of the truck. After we had questioned him and he answered to our satisfaction, we continued the drive up the mountain.

As we drove, Daniel told me that the "bush guys" did not converse too much. I had already assumed as much from my own experiences. He added, "When talking to these guys you can't just start asking them questions. You have to go slowly, sit silently for a while, chew some beetle nut, talk about the weather, then eventually, get around to what you really wanted to know." I already knew this, but it was a good reminder of cultural norms. My investigative side wanted more immediate answers!

As we continued up the winding, rocky timber company road, we began to come to sections that were not so rocky. They were merely mud bogs waiting to capture us. The other truck raced through the mud and bounced violently, but it did get through it. Our driver was taking a more gentle approach and slowly "walked" the truck through the mud. That worked too, but on one hill we came to a standstill. The driver pushed the pedal to the floor, and the engine was revving at wide-open throttle so loudly that I thought it would blow up. The tires were spinning fast, but we were not moving. The guys on the back, including Jared, were jumping up and down, and I was wondering whether we could just back up and get a good running start. Miraculously, we started to move – slowly. We eventually made it up the hill, and we were relieved – but only temporarily, since we found ourselves at the foot of another muddy hill.

We finally reached the top and found a lineup of bulldozers which were used by the timber company. We parked the trucks, and everyone jumped into a few 'dozers and started them. It reminded me of the old days when we ran to choose a go-cart at a race track. Jared and I looked at each other with eye language that said, "Is this cool or what?" Eventually, all ten of us joined together on one 'dozer, and we "sped off" at about 2 mph. In order to keep myself occupied and to avoid falling asleep from the lulling rhythm of the engine, I quizzed the operator on how to turn the 'dozer and shift the gears. He seemed happy enough to teach me, and the conversation helped us to pass the time. We went down a hill for a half hour, then through mud that no truck would have ever been able to negotiate. It was an interesting experience, to say the least; Jared rode atop the wire roof of the 'dozer with a couple of other young men his age. That was fine until we ran over a large rock that shook the 'dozer back and forth and threatened to throw them off. Since the 'dozer had no suspension, the riders felt every rock and gum wrapper we ran over, but fortunately most of the passage was in the mud and the ride was relatively smooth.

We reached the end of the road and we all dismounted. The helper crew was in no hurry to proceed further, so thinking that we were almost there, I suggested that we boil a pot of rice. They said they would wait and eat at the river's edge. With that, Jared and I and a few workers started to go down the hill on a path a 'dozer had previously cut where trees had been uprooted. It was not a clear path, but it was certainly easier than walking through the virgin rain forest. We walked quite a distance when we reached the end of the 'dozer track and proceeded through dense jungle. After approximately a half hour of hiking while cutting branches and vines, we began a descent down the side of a mountain, and as we continued, I had difficulty with my footing, slipping and sliding as I went. I had a mental picture that someone was going to have to carry me back up this mountain – poor guy!

After another half hour of hiking down the mountain side, we reached the bottom and came to a stream approximately seven-and-a-half meters (25 feet) wide. That meant that I had to remove my shoes. As I stepped into the cool water, it was so-o-o-o refreshing, but my tender feet had a difficult time navigating over the stones and I nearly fell several times. I finally reached the opposite shore where I noticed that the ground was fairly soft, so that even a tenderfoot like myself was able to walk on it barefoot. In just a short distance, we found another river which was approximately 15 meters (50 feet) wide. By then, the other half of our party had already arrived and had crossed to the other side, even though they started walking after we had. They must have taken a shorter or better route. I again stumbled to the other side and was relieved when I finally made it, still dry.

We all sat around and waited for Daniel to arrive. Like me, he was not a fast hiker. The old man we had picked up on the way was sitting alone and I could not contain myself. I slowly walked over, squatted beside him and asked, "So how far is it to the airplane?" He had rather a surprised look on his face and a half smile. I then remembered that I was supposed to take things a little slower. Too late! He stumbled for words but I think he said it was by a village. I was not sure if he was saying a village name or the name of a man. The only thing I do remember thinking was that this guy did not have a clue either, just like Boas, as to where we were going.

I was mystified and sat next to Daniel who had just arrived and was sitting for a rest. I told him that I did not think that this old man knew where the airplane was located. His face had the same bewildered expression that I must have had on my face. We had begun to think that after all this driving and hiking, here we sat along the side of a river in the middle of the jungle and nobody knew which way to go! We were justifiably dumbfounded. Finally, Daniel, gently asked the old man, Malis, which way to go to find the airplane. He said something like, it was along a trail to a village far away, but that trail was not used anymore. To make matters worse, since the timber company had made roads all over the place, he was no longer sure how to locate that old trail! That bit of information really brought to light the seriousness of our present situation!

Daniel and I looked at each other in disbelief. Neither of us was in any mood to wander around in the jungle aimlessly looking for a needle in a haystack, which, for all we knew, could be on the other side of the jungle! We were, at that moment, tempted to give up the search and head home. I could not believe that we had come this far only to call it quits and head back home. In addition, I dreaded the climb back up that mountain. Finally, Daniel yelled to a few of the young men and told them to go find the airplane. He told them that we would stay here while they went ahead to find it and come back to show us how to get there. With that, four young men, obediently, and with no hesitation, started to head back across the river. As I watched them depart, my first thought was, "Why did we come to this side of the river if we had to cross it again? Had we crossed the river unnecessarily?" I called one of them back and tried to instruct him on how to use the GPS to mark the location should they find the airplane. He obviously had a difficult time comprehending how to use the thing, although he nodded his head like he was indeed understanding my instructions. I was so glad when my son, Jared, being young and adventurous, volunteered to hike with them; he knew how to use the GPS. That was a relief, because I do not think that there were enough hours in the week for me to give instructions to that young man on how to operate the device. Even I had not totally figured out all the ins and outs of how to use it, so how was I to teach someone else?

With the GPS in hand, they crossed the river, headed up the ridge on the other side, and were soon out of sight. The rest of us passed the time by sleeping on the rock bed along the riverside and strolling along the riverbank looking for gold. One never knew what one might find! I wondered if they dreamed about the pot of gold they hoped to find if we discovered an airplane. I tried to drum up some conversation and even suggested that we talk about girls, but that went nowhere. Nobody was in a talkative mood. I started wondering about Jared and if he were to break a leg – what would the guides do? I had forgotten our satellite telephone on the boat, so we had no way to contact our mission to send a helicopter. I caught myself before my mind ran too far amok with fear. I whispered a prayer and tried to reason, "What are the chances of anything bad happening or that we could survive this setback?"

Finally John, who had long dreadlocks, said, "It's going to rain, so I'll cook the rice." With that, he cut three thin sticks about four feet long and tied them together at one end. He then spread the other ends apart and stood the sticks upright like a tripod. He collected firewood and piled it neatly, then started a fire using a match. He seemed like the kind of person who could have started the fire by rubbing sticks together if necessary. I watched him fill a pot with rice, then go over and wash it in the river while checking for bugs. He then hung the pot over the fire on the stick tripod. He obviously had done this before, as he was quite adept.

After it had boiled for a while, the rice was ready to eat, but no one ate anything. They apparently wanted to wait for the other lads to return; I thought that that was most commendable. Actually, our little picnic along the side of the river could have been quite nice, but I think that I would not have hiked *here* just to have a picnic. It was not long before the rain began to fall, slowly at first. I decided to retrieve my emergency plastic parka from my backpack and covered myself and the cameras. The guides just stood in the rain, and I thought to myself, these guys have been raised with rough conditions, so they have learned to endure most situations, especially rain! Some of them have probably never had a hot shower in their lives. One of them did make an umbrella from a palm leaf, and Daniel found a little shelter under which he could hide. As the rain drops got bigger, the sun shone through, and it was quite a surreal experience to watch the heavy drops floating down in this valley. It reminded me of my childhood when I

201

saw big snowflakes slowly falling down. I asked John how he knew it was going to rain, and he replied in English that he was "connected to the environment."

The rain slowed, and we heard a noise from the other side of the river. It was Boas, and he slowly waded back across the river to us. He did not yell or anything. When he approached us, he calmly said, "We saw the plane, your son said to come." I was excited, and, in that excitement, I had a thousand questions for him, to which he only replied by repeating the same thing over again. I must admit that, in my frustration in trying to get Boas to talk, I visualized some comedies where the actor would grab someone by the neck and shake him back and forth to get an answer. I would not have done that, of course, even if that thought may have crossed my mind. Finally, I asked if Jared had said whether it was a Japanese or Australian airplane. He slowly said, "Australian," but, as I walked away, I heard him say, "American."

Well, my watch had broken somehow on the dive the day before, so I had no idea of the time of day. Someone said that I did not have enough time to go that far. We must have waited for at least three hours while they had scouted the countryside. I looked at the sun and estimated it to be in about the 1:00 P.M. position. (Camera recorded pictures taken at about 1:30 P.M.) Talk about being connected to the environment, that was me. Wow! I was telling time by looking at the position of the sun. I then thought that Jared would not have sent Boas if: one, he did not think that I could make the hike or two, it was too far away. With that, I stumbled over the rocks and made my way to the other side of the river. I sat down to put my shoes on; I could see that no one was following me. The nationals were all eating the rice! Perhaps they did not eat it before because of my presence. Could it have been that it was a cultural taboo to eat in front of the host?

I waited for what seemed like ages until finally John came across the river carrying the pot of rice that was still half full. I was impressed. He had thought about the other guides who were waiting at the crash site. He yelled back to Boas and asked him for directions to the beginning of the trail, and we eventually found it and headed up the ridge. For some reason, Boas did not go with us. He was obviously tired, but I was curious as to how John would know the route? As we continued, I observed small trees that either had a knife mark in the trunk or had been cut completely. Finally, I realized that apparently all we had to do was follow the cut trees. It reminded me of the Hansel and Gretel story where they followed a trail of white bread crumbs along a path.

Even though I could see the cut trees and was thinking pretty highly of my tracking skills, I was glad that John had taken the lead. After a half hour, we stopped and he yelled out and listened for a reply. There was none. I figured that we had not hiked long enough yet, so we continued, stopping periodically to yell and listen. My left shoe was cutting into the back of my heel, so I used my machete to cut a slit in the back of my shoe, hoping to release the pressure on my heel. In my rush, not wanting to lose my guide, my hand slid off the handle and I managed to cut my finger. What other oddities could have been added to this already bizarre adventure? To top it off, I lost John anyway as he had kept moving fast, so I became wide-eyed as I searched for those sticks they called "kutins." I called out and John answered, but since I had become deaf in one ear (nerve damage from a skull tumor when I was three years old), I could not tell what direction the sounds of his voice were coming from. I kept moving and, thankfully, I finally found John. He was yelling out and listening. He said to me, "I heard someone." I told him that that had been me because I had fallen behind. The trip had become quite a comedy of errors. It was a good thing he was "connected to the environment."

As we hiked, I asked if Boas had given him any instructions as to where to go. He said, Boas just said to "Go straight and it was a *long* way." That was not surprising to hear as Boas was a man of very few words. At a few points, we lost the cut-tree path and wandered around looking for a cut tree so as to resume our journey. Although the path was still visible some of the time, I think that even John had become a bit nervous. We searched for a long time to find the path, and when we could not find it, I became equally nervous. We hiked onward, and I kept mulling in my mind about the type of airplane they had seen. I also wondered why Jared had not sent me a note to tell me what he had found. I was curious as to why he had not given Boas a more complete message to relay to me. Boas may not have told me anyway. What if it was Amelia Earhart's airplane and that was the reason he said that I needed to come see it? I let my mind go wild with all sorts of strange thoughts to keep me from focusing on the stress of the hike (which I have always disliked).

We crossed a small stream and John yelled out again. This time, there was a reply! We moved toward the voices, and suddenly there were eight eyes staring us in the face. Jared was with them. He said it was a Beaufort, A16-126, but I immediately knew that it was not a Beaufort, but rather *the missing Hudson* I had wanted to locate. He said that it was ten minutes away and he asked if I wanted to see it. My reply was, "Of course, I did not travel all this way just to turn around!" I asked him if he knew the time of day it had become? It was ten minutes before 3:00 P.M. Jared had calculated that if I did not arrive there by three, he would assume I was not coming and would begin the return trip. Because it started to rain, they had decided to leave early. As I wanted to see the wreckage, they turned around and we all hiked back to the crash site. It seemed a bit surreal to hike so far with anticipation, then suddenly, the destination is reached! As I hiked up to the wreckage, the first thing I saw was the Hudson's tail section lying upside down, intact, with the rear tail wheel sticking up. (See page x - NO. 20)

Jared knew that I would want to see everything, and since our time was limited, he said, "Don't bother with pictures, I've taken a bunch. Let me show you the main parts." (Camera recorded his first picture was taken at 12:21 P.M.) While our guides meted out the rice onto leaves and filled their empty stomachs while eating with their hands, Jared showed me the rear section of the airplane with the numbers A16-126 clearly visible on the side of the fuselage. Forward of the serial number was the large, 124-centimeter (49-inch) RAF type A.1 roundel with a red circle in the middle, then white, blue and yellow rings around it. That provided us with a *positive* identification of the aircraft. It was not often that one could find such definitive identification. I was actually in awe and shook my head in disbelief. We had found the one that had been missing from the previously located Hudsons. I had already learned something about the history of this airplane from my research, and I knew that it had never been found. It was truly amazing! This aircraft was one of 247 Hudsons the RAAF had received. I could only envision how relieved the families of the four crewmen would be, if, after all these years (66 to be exact), the mystery of this airplane's disappearance was solved.

Jared continued his tour, and he showed me the large starboard tail that was also lying upside down. It clearly had the red, white and blue fin flash (tail striping) of the Royal Air Force (RAF). We had seen a portion of that type of airplane earlier in the scrap heap of aluminum inside the boat in Gasmata. The majority of those pieces were from A16-165, but it was unclear at the time how the wing piece fit onto the tail. Since we had now physically examined an intact tail section, we were better able to see how the pieces of the puzzle all fit. Further, the airplane on the reef also had a piece of tail section visible. That one was a near duplicate of what had been found at this site, so that helped confirm, to my mind, the probability that it was a Hudson as well.

I walked around the tail sections and then back to the rear fuselage section; I looked inside and noticed that it had broken off just ahead of the rear turret. The 7.7-millimeter (.303-inch) bullet boxes remained attached for the dorsal turret machine gun which was manufactured by Boulton Paul. A great many spent casings were lying on the ground, so it was obvious that the gunner had been shooting prior to the crash. It appeared that there had been a fire, as the green primer paint had burnt off inside. The fire might have been caused by flares stowed in the rear section. The side door was missing, and Jared pointed out the emergency release handle. We suspected that the gunner had bailed out; so the door was probably somewhere to be found in the rubble. I stepped inside to take a better look, but I was warned about a huge nest of wasps, so I backed off.

I continued moving toward the front of the fuselage where I spotted a machine gun lying on the ground. Jared had already taken a photograph of one of the guides, Martin, who had posed with it. There were bullets in the stainless steel feed mechanism. Farther forward around the fuselage, the distinctive side windows of the Hudson model were clearly visible. We also located a Very flare gun near the fuselage.

By the time I had scanned this wreckage thoroughly, I felt overwhelmed. Having seen so much, so quickly, I had not yet been able to examine any parts closely. As the tour continued, I saw the exhaust of the port engine jutting upward, but the three-meter (ten-foot) diameter propeller was out of sight, possibly having been buried into the ground upon impact. A short distance away was the starboard engine with a short 46-centimeter (18-inch) section of propeller protruding from the ground. The landing gear was still attached to a small section of the wing at a perpendicular angle to the buried engine. The evidence seemed to indicate that the airplane must have impacted the ground at a nearly vertical angle.

The huge wings, which at one time spanned just slightly over 20 meters (65 feet), were nowhere to be seen, nor was the cockpit, but as we walked around, we realized that we were constantly stepping on aluminum which we concluded to have been pieces of the wings. I noticed four gauges in a row that were facedown; I attempted to lift them, but the aluminum was brittle and began to fall apart, so I chose not to disturb them further. I wanted to leave the scene as pristine as possible. I was able to see the faces of the gauges, although the cloudy glass prevented me from determining the type and function of the gauges.

It was particularly important to establish a GPS reading; Jared and I spent what seemed like hours trying to get a signal on two different units. The tree canopy, though it had been cut back by our guides, was still very thick. We were unable to gain a fix from the necessary three satellites. I set my unit down and let it search while I proceeded to take some photos. I retraced my steps to examine and photograph all of the pieces. Because of the dim light from the late hour and the increasing humidity, the camera lens continued to fog up. Those factors made it nearly impossible to get a clear photograph. I also tried to take some video footage, but most of it was turning out dark due to the onset of twilight. I returned to the GPS and was relieved to see that, despite our impatience, they were now functioning and the units were able to establish a precise location. The altitude of the crash-site was defined as 305 meters (1000) feet above sea level.

We began our hike out of the area, lest we be caught in the jungle for the night. We hurriedly packed our gear and headed down the trail. As we hiked, Jared and I talked about the wreckage incessantly. One thing I learned was that when he had first come up the mountain, he had hiked for over one hour, then his team split away from Boas. That was probably why John and I had temporarily lost the trail. Boas went down one side of the ridge, and the other three guides went along the opposite side. Even though Boas had said that he had originally seen that airplane many years ago when he was small, it had taken him only 30 minutes to locate the site of the airplane crash. My previous thoughts regarding his intellect were apparently premature. It truly amazed me that he was able to find it at all, even though it was in his "back yard." His innate ability surely contributed to the success of my day.

The return hike, for some reason, seemed a much greater distance. It was not long before my right shoe began to cut into my heel so that every step I took was painful. It seemed to have become an endless hike. Eventually, we started on a downward sloping of the trail until we finally arrived at the river. Of course we had to cross it again, and I removed my shoes since the hard soles made them nearly useless when walking on slippery rocks. I decided to continue to wear my socks as a cushion for my feet against the rocks; I was then able to step into the cool water. The refreshing coolness was quickly masked by the hundreds of stinging sensations I had on my legs. Although I did not have as many cuts as when we hiked in our search for *Texas #6*, there were still a great many tiny gashes that reacted to the cold water. The coolness was welcomed anyway, since it more than offset the pain.

I did not take time to enjoy the stream like the locals who had decided to take a bath, so I kept moving. Since I had continued to wear my socks, it really did work well in cushioning my feet. When I reached the opposite shore, I replaced my shoes and then began to climb that mountain. I had dreaded that part of the hike back up and, as it turned out, for good reason. It was not long before everyone was out of sight, having scaled the terrain with apparent ease. I had stopped regularly to give my heart a rest, as I could hear the familiar pounding in my (one good) ear. At one point, I had asked Alfi, my guardian angel who was following me, if his heart was pumping hard. He replied that all was "normal." I thought to myself, "Normal? How could it be normal? Maybe I needed to someday do a stress test to see if I had any arteries blocked in my heart."

Surprisingly I made it to the top in half an hour, but it seemed as though it had been hours, days, or even weeks, physically speaking. By the time I had arrived at the muddy road, my shirt was drenched and both my heels were on fire with large blisters which had broken and exposed raw flesh. To my utter surprise, the rest of the party was already sitting on a bulldozer. I was overjoyed to know that the operator had returned and had waited for us. The road back to the truck would have been unbelievably miserable to hike because of the sticky, thick mud. The 'dozer then crept up the hill which was half masked in fog as we made our way back to the truck.

Since I had forgotten my satellite telephone, I was unable to contact Joan. I had hoped to get to the coast rapidly so I could board the boat and utilize the radio during our mission-scheduled radio time ("sked"). I knew that after not hearing from us all day, she would be anxious about what we had been doing and if we were OK. Once in the truck, we went back down the mountain as the sun slowly set. It seemed that the darker it got, the more our "conservative" driver increased his speed. It reminded me of horses returning to the barn. They tend to go faster and faster and become harder to rein in, until they hit the brakes at the corral gate. I assumed that the driver must have been pretty familiar with the road, but what bothered me most was that the truck's right headlight was shining up into the trees to the left, making it almost useless as we sped through fog on the winding road. Needless to say, I was just a tiny bit nervous. If Joan only knew the harrowing, death-defying experience we were now enduring!

I have always considered myself to be somewhat physically fit since I have not gained any weight for the past 25 years, but my children did not agree that I looked that fit, since my weight did appear to have "shifted" a bit. So as we cruised down the mountain, I took the opportunity to ask Daniel how he had liked the hike back to the bulldozer. Alfi had already told me that his heart rate was "normal," when my legs were rubbery and completely opposed to carrying my weight much further no matter what I weighed. I was pleasantly surprised to hear Daniel say that he must have stopped ten (if not twenty) times to catch his breath. After I heard that, I felt that I had done pretty well, since I had only stopped a few times.

The ride down to the coast, for some reason, seemed longer too even though it felt like we were traveling at lightning speed. My knuckles were white and numb from clenching the dashboard as I speculated the possibility of us having a wreck after having just found a "wreck!" I was so relieved when we started to see the lights of the timber company camp in the distance. It was like a small town coming into view. We finally passed through the camp and made our way along the coastal road and stopped at our original point of departure. I slowly off-loaded myself from the truck and was relieved to find Jared was still onboard. I had supposed that he would have bugs stuck in his teeth from our harrowing race down the mountain – but he didn't.

The sun had set, and without a moon it was pitch black. I could not even see our white boat at anchor which had been moored not more than 30 meters (100 feet) away. At first, I had an adrenaline rush when

I thought it had left without us. The headlights on the truck did not help because I had not parked the boat up in the tree branches where the light was shining. I approached each of the guides who had accompanied us on the hike and paid them for their day's work. I had also provided them with lunch and snacks during the day. I was grateful for their assistance, and they left happily. When I approached the "talkative" Boas who was hiding behind a post, I thanked him fervently and gave him PNG K50 (US $20) for finding the airplane. He did not say anything (was I surprised?), but he did smile, so I knew he was happy.

We said our good-byes and made our way to the boat in our rubber dinghy, taking care not to puncture the bottom with our machetes. We raised anchor and sped away at 7.5 knots (8.5 mph). I checked the GPS computer and it indicated that at that speed, we would be home in six hours! I wanted to go faster, but it was so dark that we were unable to see a thing in front of us, and I did not want to meet up with a log or reef while cruising at 21 - 25 knots (24 - 29 mph). Thankfully, the seas were calm and the stars were majestic in the clear night sky. They seemed so close and beautiful; it provided another moment for us to be in awe over God's creation.

Once we were on our way, I attempted to call Joan on the satellite telephone, but since the telephone did not ring at her end, she would not have known if I was calling. I questioned myself as to why I had even tried. I probably did it so that I could say that "I did try" while she *interrogated* me. I then tried to call her on the radio, even though it was past our normal radio time. There were times, for contingency reasons, that we called every hour on the hour until we made radio contact. We had not discussed that plan when we left this time, so I doubted that she would be standing by anxiously waiting to hear from us. After a couple of hours, I gave up and concluded that she was probably watching a movie or she might have had her mind on other things. Surprisingly, I was able to reach my son, Micah, in Hawaii, and tell him of our find. Later, I asked Joan if she was ever worried about us and she said, "No," but only because we had always returned.

After those attempts at communication, I went down below and supplemented my boat security guard's pay and boiled them some rice on my little mentholated-spirits burner. They were pretty impressed with how fast the rice cooked compared to their open wood fires, but they were not impressed with the watery rice I had made. After having been married for 28 years, I seemed to have lost some of the cooking skills I may have once had. By my fourth or fifth attempt, I was able to cook the rice correctly, but by that time, everyone had eaten their fill and was ready to bed down. The droning engine and slow rocking back and forth of the sea had made everyone sleepy. I dimmed the cabin lights and went to check on our Captain, Jared, to make certain that he was not too sleepy to continue guiding the boat. There were times while trolling that he had been known to drift off. We would realize it when I noticed that we were heading straight for the shore; that was usually a signal that he was checking his eyelids for cracks. On the current trip, though, he was wide awake and carefully monitoring the radar, depth sounder and GPS to assure that he avoided the reefs and stayed in deep water – and off the land!

It was, actually, rather enjoyable to run strictly with the use of instruments only, debating over what setting to use on each electronic device, what route to take and how close to the shore we should allow. We continued to be blinded by the darkness, unable to see anything in front or to the sides of the boat. Jared finally suggested that I go check on the crew. I was getting the idea that he did not desire my input. He had come a long way since his big brother Micah had returned to the United States, and he had become quite efficient in everything he attempted to do. Navigation in the dark was just one example of his expertise at the age of 18. I was awfully glad that we had bought the radar for the "just in case" scenario, such as the one in which we had now found ourselves. I was also grateful that the seas were calm or it would have made a long trip seem even longer.

To our mutual surprise, the GPS performed accurately. It took us, in fact, six hours to get home. It was 1:30 A.M. as we closed in on our home port, and we radioed Joan on the VHF radio. She answered and we asked her to turn on some lights. As we pulled up to the dock, my passengers remained asleep. We let them sleep and left the boat in the water while Jared opted to sleep the rest of the night on board. I personally made my way to the shower and found my way to my pillow without the help of any GPS! As I was lying there, I mulled over the events of the last two days. I reviewed all that we had seen and done, and how much it had cost. I thanked God for the success and safety on the trip and the time I had spent with my son. As with our trip to see the

Texas #6, it was worth it all. And to think, I almost decided not to go because of the inclement weather.

Daniel Kovi and bulldozer operator.

Wreckage of rear fuselage of Hudson A16-126. WNBP, PNG

211

Wreckage of tail section of Hudson A16-126. WNBP, PNG

Jared with guides to Hudson A16-126. WNBP, PNG

Chapter 27

BABY ON BOARD

That time of reflection with Joan now asleep not knowing of our adventure reminded me of when we lived in the village of Yumielo. One night, at approximately 3:00 A.M., I was awakened by people calling out to me. A pregnant lady, Apangme, was about to give birth, and they wanted me to take her to the hospital. I quickly dressed and started the truck, she slid into the rear seat, and we headed for the clinic operated by the Catholic Church. Another girl was seated next to her, and I listened to their conversation. I was still in the process of learning their clan language, so I was not yet fluent in it, but I did hear her say, "paul guut" which meant, "it already fell down." I looked back to see what was happening and noticed that the other lady was trying to hold the baby's head back to keep it from coming all the way out. I rolled my eyes and stopped the truck. Then, I hurriedly got out and opened the rear door. I instructed the lady to lie down as I tried to remember which way our children had turned when they were born. Had they turned clockwise or counter-clockwise when they exited the birth canal? There was no time to discuss the matter or to consider the various technicalities! I held the baby's head and instructed the mother to push. The baby came right out – clockwise. I did not have the means to suction his mouth or anything, but he started to cry – and that made me enormously grateful. I handed him to his mother who was still lying on the rear seat, and I headed towards the clinic. The dirt road was rather bumpy, and it took almost a half hour before we arrived. The mother sat up and exited the truck and carried her newborn baby with the umbilical cord still attached and placenta still in place.

Once they were under proper medical care, I drove back home. The rear seat and floor were, of course, full of blood and water, so I spent a great deal of time cleaning it. I then cleaned myself and slipped back between the sheets again to finish my night's sleep. Joan remained asleep beside me and had no idea as to what had just taken place. I was lying there reviewing the events of the night and thinking how glad I was to have risen from bed to help the situation. If I had not awakened and left my bed, the baby would have been born along the side of the road or with the mother lying perpendicular on a log on the beach where the baby would fall onto the sand (which I have witnessed previously). It was another graphic example of the rough life people in PNG live. We later learned that the lady named the baby Mark, after the "Midnight Obstetriciann" who had delivered him.

After returning home from finding the wreckage, the next morning I sent e-mails to all my WWII enthusiast friends and research partners, knowing that they would be interested in hearing the news of our discovery. I worked the rest of the morning communicating back and forth with Justin Taylan who originated and maintained the website, *Pacific Wrecks*. It had been his influence and enthusiasm over the years that had kept me going. Without his encouragement, I no doubt would have discontinued my searches. So he was the first one I contacted. I sent him photographs of the wreckage, and he gathered information about the airplane for posting to his website. Next, I contacted the Australian Embassy; unfortunately, I only reached an answering machine. It *was* lunchtime, so I left a message and my e-mail address. An hour later, while checking e-mails, I found a message from the Embassy! They were highly interested and wanted to hear more; they wanted to see the photographs and obtain the GPS coordinates; I gladly obliged them. E-mails passed back and forth, and within one month, they asked me to return to the site in order to prepare a helicopter landing area. They wanted to send an advance investigation team in to see the wreckage and develop a plan of action. If the team felt there was a possibility of human remains at the site, they would send in a full forensic team and do a thorough excavation of the site for human remains and personal artifacts.

To this day, I must admit, I was quite impressed with the swift response of the Royal Australian Air Force. After all, the Japanese still had not even responded to a report sent five years earlier, but the Australians replied within an hour and began developing an investigation into our report.

BELIEVE IT OR NOT

The following was a coincidence worthy of the "believe it or not" category. May 2nd, 2008, when we were making plans for a search up the coast, down in Australia, David Forrester had been talking with his friend whose father had been a fighter pilot in New Guinea. That conversation motivated him to learn more about his own Uncle Bill who had been lost during the war. That same day, his brother James Forrester, had decided to search the internet for any information regarding his long lost uncle, Sgt. Barton Irving Coutie, better known as Bill. Bill, as it turned out, was the rear gunner on the airplane we had recently discovered. The next day, May 3rd (the day we had set out to find the airplane), out of the blue, David received an e-mail from his brother James with only some links that related to their Uncle Bill! James had mysteriously been searching at the same time David had. Also coincidentally, on May 3rd, their mother, Barbara Forrester, and her twin sister, Elizabeth Cutler, daughter Helen, and granddaughter Alice had gathered and reviewed photos of their relative, Uncle Bill, who had been lost during the war! To the twins, Bill was like a big brother. Barbara had no idea that her sons were seeking information at the same time until she returned home and checked her e-mail. She found some "interesting links" that James had sent related to the mission flight associated with her uncle's lost aircraft. One of those links he cited was from the *Pacific Wrecks* site of Justin Taylan. That was before we found the wreckage and the pictures were posted on the website. The website did have basic information about the crew, the mission and the fact that it had been declared missing in action. David had also sent her some information he had found at *www.adf-serials.com* confirming that their Uncle Bill's airplane had crashed on 11/2/42 (February 11, 1942) near Gasmata Island, PNG. E-mails went back and forth during that day as they collectively researched and put together the many pieces of the puzzle. They sought to learn the purpose of the mission, the number, type of aircraft involved and the number of aircraft that had been lost on that fateful day.

On the next day, May 4, the day we had discovered and taken photographs of the wreckage, Barbara looked over photos of Bill, newspaper clippings, and letters that Bill Coutie had written. She had never read them previously but something was moving her to read them now. As she read, she felt as if she were prying into his life, learning that he was sending most of his money home to be invested as he did not gamble or drink. He did admit to spending some of his pay on milkshakes.

When I learned of all these "coincidences," including others not mentioned here, it made me feel as if there had to be some kind of unexplainable "spiritual connection" in play. At the same time we were getting ready and setting out to find the wreckage on the ground, the Forresters were searching cyberspace. The day we discovered the wreckage and were taking pictures of it, Barbara Forrester was looking at photos of her Uncle Bill. Some have referred to such events as pure "coincidence." Others do not believe in such occurrences; rather, they believe that God is the cause of all things that worked together for good. In either case, these events seemed to have come together in a very "coincidental" fashion, for the good!

In the week that followed, when the Forresters did not know that the wreckage had been found, they continued their research and David wrote his "Mum:"

> Despite the slight discrepancies and vagueness of the records, it is clear that these men displayed enormous courage and commitment to duty in the face of overwhelming odds. I am sad that their deeds are not more widely known but am very proud that I am related to one of them and bear his name. Lest we forget.

To which Barbara replied:

> Many thanks for these [internet links] David. I have looked at them on Dad's computer and have printed both out. I was proud to be able to call you after Bill, for in fact that is what I did. He was my hero from the time I can remember, he was a very nice person, just as you are. Lots of Love from Mum.

Barton David Forrester never knew, until that moment, that he had been named after his lost Uncle Bill, Barton Coutie. He had always thought that he had been named only after his great-grandfather, Barton M. Coutie. As it turned out, Barbara named him after both of them. Barton David Forrester was known by his second name, with his first name, Barton, more of a family name. After he had learned of his uncle's history in the war and that he was named after him, the name Barton now had a special sense of significance. He was proud to be called "Barton" after his uncle (with whom he was just beginning to become acquainted).

Unbeknown to the Forresters, as they searched other sites for more information, I had just contacted Justin Taylan, the webmaster of *Pacific Wrecks,* upon my return, and I sent him photographs of the

Hudson wreckage we had discovered. He quickly updated the web page with the discovery, including the photos I had sent him, and posted it on his website on May 5th for all to see. (http://www.pacificwrecks.com/aircraft/hudson/A16-126.html).

Then, on May 16th, while David continued his search on the internet, he again looked at the *Pacific Wrecks* site and was indeed shocked to see that Hudson A16-126 had been found! He immediately wrote his Mum. She, too, was surprised to hear the news, and they both wondered whether James (who had started his "just fooling around" search almost two weeks earlier) should be tested to determine whether he had some ESP skills!

David then did a Google search and found my e-mail address and wrote me. I was extremely excited to hear from him, and I was encouraged by his message. After he introduced himself, he went on to say:

> Thank you for all you have done already - just the fact that the aircraft has finally been found is a great relief for my family and has caused quite a bit of excitement. Regards, David Forrester.

It was especially encouraging for me to see that people still cared about these losses and were grateful for our efforts! They only needed some information to lead them forward. It was quite a contrast after our experience with the Japanese when we had submitted information to report the airplane we had found in the water. Their lack of response caused an ongoing discussion in our home about why do we bother to search for these crash sites. My wife contended that the lack of response from the Japanese indicated that nobody cared anymore. I refused to believe that and thought, surely, the Japanese, American and Australian families have continued to care about MIAs. My wife felt that the families had probably already said their goodbyes and did not want to be reminded of their loss. I remained unconvinced by her argument, and so the debate continued every time I returned from a search for an airplane crash site. Thus, when I received the message from Mr. Forrester, I could not wait to tell my wife – and gloat, at least a little bit.

A couple of years later, we saw a movie about the remains of an MIA who was returned home. When we saw the American flag draped over the casket as it was taken from the airplane, carried by men in uniform, and the tears of the on-looking family, it was then that my wife truly realized the significance of finding the airplane and what it meant to the families, as she, too, mourned with them.

The sister of the lost gunner Bill, Mrs. Dora Dance, was still alive (92 years old), and it was reported that she "went into shock for a couple of days" after she had heard the news, saying "They told us he went down in the water." She had never spoken about her brother and, taking her cue, her entire family had never mentioned him. The hurt was too much to bear. The niece of the gunner, Mrs. Barbara Forrester, mother of Dr. Barton David Forrester who had first written me, was also distressed. Apparently, she was awfully fond of her Uncle Bill and was very distraught when he was declared missing in action. She had never spoken of him either, but as we came to learn, she had named her son, Barton, after her uncle. They then sent me a photograph of Sgt. Barton Coutie who was remembered by his niece Maree as "tall and handsome." He had joined the RAAF on April 1, 1941, and was single and only 23 years of age when he was lost in World War II.

BLANK CHECK

The Australian RAAF had contacted me about clearing an area for a helicopter to land. Since I wanted to return to the crash site as soon as possible, before our rainy season hit hard and would prevent it, I communicated that desire to the Australian Embassy. To my surprise, they quickly gave me the green light to go and asked me to send them a bill of my expenses! That meant (to me) that I had a "blank check" signed by the RAAF! Well, since I was frugal, they really had "No Worries," but I did think it exceptionally trusting of them.

We made plans for the weekend of May 17, 2008, to travel back to the site, and began to make all necessary preparations. Then, that Saturday morning when we awoke, it was raining. To top it off, because of the rain, none of my boat security or guides had appeared, and even the seas looked rough; so we cancelled the trip. Later in the day, the weather cleared, so we opted to make the journey on the following day, Sunday, and were indeed able to depart. The seas were somewhat rough, but we went slower and made it to the timber camp in fairly good time. Fortunately for us, Daniel Kovi was there, and we told him about the RAAF planning to come and investigate the crash site. He, too, was interested to hear the news and was agreeable to assist in the effort. It was too late in the day to head out for the wreck, so the plan was to start our trek early Monday morning.

THE MYSTERY AIRPLANE

We had the rest of the day to kill, so we decided to go to Gasmata and attempt to locate that mystery airplane in the water everybody seemed to know about, but no one had ever seen. David Forrester was now becoming my main researcher in Australia, and he had been feeding me with reports regarding downed aircraft. He was exceptionally enthusiastic about the task and demonstrated outstanding skills in digging up information from the past. He sent an Australian military report from RAAF Squadron Leader Keith M. Rundle who had conducted his own investigations in January of 1946, regarding crashed aircraft in the Gasmata region. Rundle had been guided by a native from Avirin Island, named Orio. They went to a spot in the Gasmata Harbor where Orio said a B-25 had crashed. He said that the airplane had crashed on the same day that another B-25 had crashed on Avirin Island. I had previously found the engine from that second airplane when I investigated the area, and my research revealed that the B-25 was serial number 42-64846. Now the question became – which airplane was in the harbor and *where* was it? This new information may have been related to the mystery airplane we had been trying to find, for which the locals could never provide a pin-point location.

Rundle's extant report provided a description of what "appeared to be a plane" in about six meters (20 feet) of water. He had written a three-point description of the wreckage location. "1 & 3/4 miles NE from Gasmata, 50 yards NE of Umbo Island and close to the shore approximately 25 yards south of the New Britain coast." With that report in hand, I was enthusiastic that this time we were going to find that elusive airplane which rested in the water.

After we had conferred with the locals in an attempt to ascertain the location of Umbo Island, we proceeded to the location that we assumed Rundle had described. As we arrived at the desired location, we lined up as best as we were able with the three points of the description. We were dismayed to find that the water was only four feet deep and murky. Our guide, David, said that he had dived along the perimeter of that area frequently, and he had never seen an airplane. Our next move was to find Ben, the son of the guide, Orio, who back in 1946 had shown the airplane to Sqn. Ldr. Rundle. *This* Ben, as mentioned earlier, was the same Ben who had complained to me when we had previously dived onto the Japanese ship and to whom I had paid PNG K5 (US $2). Our hope was that his father, Orio, would have shown him the airplane, but unfortunately, he told us he had never seen it. He could only share his father's explanation regarding its location. From his description and his pointing in the general direction, it appeared to be the same location where we had twice previously dived and, on both occasions, came up empty. In addition, it was also far away from Rundle's description, so it seemed we had returned to square one again.

Sgt. Barton "Bill" Coutie

Chapter 28

THE MAKING OF A HELO PAD

That night, we had dinner with the other missionary couple, Adam and Julie Martin, on old Gasmata Island, and then we slept on the boat. On the following morning, I awoke at daybreak to rain and a heavy cloud cover, so I decided to go back to sleep. I reawakened at 6:30 A.M. to the same inclement weather, so I again returned to bed until 7:00 A.M. The weather had not changed much, if any, but it was getting pretty late, so saying our good-byes to the missionary families, we shoved off and returned to the timber company to find some guides. By the time we arrived, the rain had stopped and the people were beginning to peek their heads from their houses. We ferried our supplies to the shore with a rubber raft and met with Daniel again; we then waited for a truck to come for us.

We headed out with ten carriers and proceeded up the bumpy timber company road, driving for about an hour. At the end of the timber company gravel road, the dirt road became muddy much sooner; this meant our 'dozer ride would be considerably longer. We loaded the bulldozer and, flanked by two other 'dozers, we moved onward through a sloshy mud which was at times two feet deep and came over the top of the tracks. It was really quite amazing what a bulldozer can penetrate. The three dozers moving along this muddy, sloppy road made it seem like a surreal go-cart race, with 'dozers neck to neck, but in slow motion. I think that the other 'dozers had accompanied us in the event we became stuck, since the road was that unbelievably muddy.

After a one-hour 'dozer ride, we arrived at our drop-off point which was just short of the upcoming steep mountain climb. I asked the 'dozer operator if he could penetrate further into the jungle. At that request, he jumped onto another 'dozer without any passengers and he led the way, steering back and forth, knocking down 15 to 20-centimeter (six to eight-inch) diameter trees as if they were match sticks as he plowed a path through the jungle. It was quite a spectacle to see, and I could only wonder what the conservation officers would have to say if they had seen this. He did shorten our hike considerably and, "tree-huggers" notwithstanding, that made me happy.

The hike down the hill was not so bad this time, and within a half hour, we reached the stream at the bottom and crossed over to the other side. We then proceeded up the ridge and through the jungle, following the cut trees that we had seen on our previous trip which marked the "road." I usually started the trek at the front of the line, then ended up somewhere near the back as, one by one, I got passed by the guides carrying chain saws or other heavy items. My actual strategy was based upon my view of the guy in front of me; when he had almost vanished from sight (no more than 15 meters or 50 feet away), I let another lad go ahead of me until he was almost out of sight; then I let another person pass and so on and so on. I did that because I could have easily gotten lost had I lost sight of the guide in front of me. It was no wonder that the Japanese and American forces could sometimes be in close proximity to each other and yet not see each other.

Even though I lagged behind and delayed the work party, we arrived at the crash site in fairly good time. As most of these carriers were part of a new crew, they were anxious to hear the story of the wreckage and were eager to see it, since they had not been involved in the first trip. One of these carriers, Dixon, pulled out a belt of bullets from the ammunition box and draped them around his neck. I photographed him adorned in bullets as he held the machine gun, and we nicknamed him "Rambo."

Jared and our guide, Martin, immediately began to search for a location that could serve as a possible helicopter landing zone. Martin returned and asked to show me where he thought he had found a good spot. We also met Jared who wanted to show me a potential site he had found. We decided to survey Jared's spot first, which, after viewing it, Martin agreed was a better location than what he had seen. As we walked around, Jared suddenly disappeared; he had fallen off a cliff! Fortunately, the drop-off was only about two and a half meters (eight feet) deep initially, but continued down even more deeply into a valley. He was fine, thankfully, but once again, we were made to realize just how our limited vision in the dense jungle could become tremendously dangerous. On a positive note, this valley made it possible for a helicopter to make an approach without having to make a vertical landing, and that would enable it to carry more weight. Immediately, the men began to clear the area while I returned to the wreckage site only 183 meters (200 yards) away. At that point, I sent the other group up the hill to assist in clearing and cutting trees.

I was then left alone to earnestly concentrate on the wreckage, which was something I had not had a chance to do since the initial discovery. I had promised David Forrester that I would gather some spent bullet casings for him from the machine gun turret where his great-uncle had served. At first, as I searched, there were some large flying ants that appeared to be vicious. This made me nervous, but they later huddled around their nest and left me alone so I was able to relax. In my search, I found a Philips screwdriver and what I believed to be a bone fragment, but at the time I could not be certain. It was rather fragile and broke in my hands, so I put it back where I had found it, laying it gently on a leaf to be shown to the forensic team later. After an hour of surveying the wreckage, I snapped a few more photographs then I went to check on the landing-zone crew. They had cut many trees down and had cleared them away, for which I praised them but they had left stumps sticking up one to two feet above the ground. I explained to them that the stumps needed to be cut down flat with the ground surface so that a "chopper" could land safely. This meant that it made double-the-work, but it had to be done.

We continued to work until approximately 5:45 P.M. Jared shared with me that the workers had asked if we would be sleeping overnight. Unfortunately, darkness was expected in about thirty minutes, and a return trip required at least a one-and-a-half-hour hike, so I told him that I felt it was better to stay and that we should start setting up camp. The guides cut small trees and made a simple frame, fastening it with vines. We hung the tarps over a center ridge pole and tied them down using jungle "rope" (vines) just as darkness fell upon us. Fires were built at both open ends of the "tent." I was certainly glad that these helpers were along with us, since this was everyday living for them, and they built the tent and fires with ease. To my mind, we were going to sleep in the middle of the jungle on the ground; no toilets, no water, no TV or radio!

Actually, it was not all that bad. Some of the locals had made traditional beds by laying sticks close together so they were much like home. I rested on the ground and discovered that it was not much harder than the mattress Joan and I slept on at my home. When we first arrived in PNG, we had brought a water mattress along, and I made a frame out of bamboo. The bugs ate the bamboo and the mattress, which caused it to leak in many places, so we eventually purchased a proper mattress. I made a frame out of rosewood and trimmed it with black ebony. The first night we slept on it, it seemed so hard I thought the store had sold us the box spring!

My eyes were burning, though, from the billowing smoke of our camp fires. I slipped on my coveralls and a fresh pair of dry socks and then lay my head down. I had expected that we were going to get a downpour of rain, but the moon and stars came out and it turned out to be an especially nice night. It did get rather cold, (must have been below 70 degrees F), a common occurrence on cloudless nights. Our bodies were accustomed to 90 degree days with at least 85% humidity. Nights were rarely in the low 70s. Jared was asleep and stretched out straight using his nylon hammock as a blanket. He looked cozy, warm and sleeping well. I, on the other hand, was curled up in the fetal position breathing down into my coveralls in hopes of producing a bit of warmth. I was freezing and just could not get warm. Needless to say, I did not sleep well and was glad to see first light so I could get up. Jared felt badly when I told him that I had frozen all night, because he had slept comfortably. One thing I had found pleasantly surprising was that in the jungle at 309 meters (1015 feet), there were no mosquitoes or flies.

On another note, when one hikes, eats and camps with the locals in their teens and early 20s, one gets the illusion of being one of the guys. That illusion faded when Jared told me later that when the workers had asked about either sleeping in the bush or heading back to the coast, they had said that they thought *they* could make it out before dark, but they knew the "lapun" (old man) could not. Old man! Was that me? I guess that meant that I was not one of the guys.

I may not have been one of the guys, but by no means did I feel threatened by them. Some people might think that in a country such as Papua New Guinea, which had a fairly high crime rate, that it would have been nearly insane to go hiking in the jungle with locals with whom one was not acquainted. Some of these lads' grandfathers could have been head-hunting cannibals. If they wanted to steal everything we had and abandon us in the middle of the jungle, they surely could have done so. We were totally at their mercy. There have been certain times when dealing with some of the people that I have felt threatened, as with Stephen from Zebu Village. In the jungle, though, the locals were always seemingly considerate. They even slowed down on the trail to wait for the slower hiker, namely me. They helped to carry my load and that of others if they sensed the onset of our fatigue. I have developed the confidence that if, somehow, I was to break a leg or become immobile for some reason, they would have carried me out on a stretcher fashioned from jungle material. It was no wonder that during the war, these jungle dwellers, many with bulging muscles even though they had never set foot in a fitness center, were affectionately referred to as "the fuzzy, wuzzy angels."[63]

As the next morning arrived, we spent another three hours clearing the area for the helicopter pad; we leveled the ground and enlarged the area. It had an excellent approach up the valley to the southeast. Once we had broken camp, at 10:00 A.M., it began to rain as we started back down the ridge. As we hiked, everyone stopped in their tracks because there was a python snake curled up at the side of the trail. We kept our distance and one of the guides went close to the snake and talked to it. Apparently, he was telling it we would not hurt it and that we were merely walking on the trail. That conversation, I was told, was to calm the reptile so he would not attack us now or in the future.

Even with our delay, we made good time, and I was not even the last one to the river for a change. At the river, many of the boys took the opportunity to bathe, which did not make sense to me. A hike up the steep mountain faced us, and any gain from cleanliness would have been quickly lost in the blood, sweat and tears expended in reaching the top, making a bath seem useless. I suppose that this bath actually served as a refreshing stop before the real work of climbing the mountain began.

Since I did not feel the urge to get any wetter than I already was from rain and sweat, a couple of carriers and I started the trek up the mountainside and left the bathers behind. Just as in the previous trip, my heart was soon pounding, and I needed to take a few rest stops along the way. I was truly relieved when I finally saw the 'dozer we had left sitting at the top, knowing my misery was soon to be over, but to my shock, I ended up being the last one to get there! All the bathers were there, sitting on the 'dozer and waiting. I think they must have known of a short cut, because not one of them passed me on the mountainside, nor did I see or hear them pass me on my flanks. Perhaps they *could* have made it out before dark the day before, maybe even if they had had to carry the "lapun!"

The bulldozer ride took over an hour to arrive at the truck. The workers were sitting or standing all over the giant machine as we drove. One fellow was even sitting on the engine cover. Jared and another worker were up on top of the cab. Four of the crew were standing in back on the drum of cable that was used for winching logs. I sat next to the driver, and behind me were some levers. As we bumped along, my head was nodding and I slid back and bumped the lever that controlled the cable drum where the four guys were standing barefoot. It started to turn, and they all scampered to keep from getting their feet caught in the drum. I did not understand how they managed it, but all of them evaded disaster, for which I was so immensely grateful and apologetic. I made certain that I did not ever bump into that lever again, and they certainly kept a closer eye on me.

Guides/workers on bulldozer "taxi." WNBP, PNG

Snake on trail. WNBP. PNG

"Rambo" w/machine gun and bullets from Hudson A16-126.

Worker w/machete clearing helo pad. WNBP,PNG

227

Bush Camping. WNBP, PNG

Worker with chainsaw cutting helo pad. WNBP, PNG

Chapter 29

THE STUMBLER

After I had returned home, I sent word to the Australian Embassy that the helo pad was cleared and ready for use. All up for fuel, food and local labor, the bill was PNG K3,732 (US $1,530). I did not charge for Jared and my labor. Three weeks later, a four-member team of the Royal Australian Air Force (RAAF) was scheduled to meet me at the Gasmata Airstrip. I was instructed to take them to the timber camp as we were to be air-lifted into the site on the next day.

Before the RAAF team arrived, I received e-mail messages from the family members of two of the other three Hudson crewmen. They thanked Jared and me for our discovery of the wreckage and our report of it to the authorities, which left me with a nice feeling of satisfaction and accomplishment. Of course, I had to taunt my wife a bit with each new message of appreciation that arrived. Although the RAAF had not officially contacted them, the Forrester family had tracked down the families and made them aware of the news. At that time, the RAAF thought they were the only ones who knew of the wreckage and its whereabouts. Unbeknown to them, it had already been posted on the *Pacific Wrecks* site for the entire world to see! (http://www.pacificwrecks.com/aircraft/hudson/A16-126.html)

Another "believe it or not" situation was in relation to Fiona Thorn, a relative of Frank Thorn. We had started to correspond and she wrote:

Hello Mark,

Thanks for your email. It has been an incredible experience to learn of your discovery. I never knew Frank Thorn as I was born post-war. His younger brother Les was my step-father, who was devastated with his death but never really talked about him to me. In fact I always thought he was killed in Europe. It was sheer "coincidence" that I had found an article by John Carew that my mother had torn out of a magazine 20 years ago and tucked in with some photos about two hours before James Forrester tracked me down in the phone book. Frank had four brothers, all now gone. They would have been so relieved that his plane has been found. I felt quite emotional looking at the photos and have thought constantly about what it must have been like on that last mission. Also what it must have been like for his new bride of only a few months and his parents and siblings, all now dead. His niece Betty is alive at 79 and remembers him. Thank you for your efforts. I really feel they were ready to be found especially by someone who shows such care. Best regards, Fiona"[64]

Later, Tony Gibson, the son of the pilot, Ian Gibson, wrote:

Dear Mark,

So good to hear from you. You have accomplished a wonderful thing for us all especially me as my father was the pilot. I was only one and a half months old when he went down. We have always believed that the plane was shot down in the sea so it was a double thrill to not only have it found but so recognizable. You have done a wonderful job of documenting the site. David Forrester sent me the C.D. My father was called Ian and was 26 years old and had been married a year. His only brother was captured at Singapore and died three years later at Sandakan P.O.W. camp. I have four children and five grandchildren. I will keep in touch with the RAAF to find out their intentions. Kindest Regards, Tony[65]

Tony later sent me pictures of his father, and I learned that he was featured in the Western Australian newspaper of June 28, 2008, with the story of the find. I had a good laugh when I read the account as the reporter, Gabrielle Knowles, described the finding of the wreckage as I "had *stumbled*" upon it. I pondered that perhaps the title of this book should have been *The Stumbler,* but that would certainly not have reflected the time, effort and work involved in such an endeavor.

I never did hear from the fourth crewman's relatives, although the RAAF had located a kin of Arthur Quail who was living in Cairns, Australia. Mr. O'Brien was a successful business man who was made a Member of the Order of Australia (post nominal: AM) in 2006 for service to Cairns through youth development, cultural and sporting organizations, events and philanthropy. He was very grateful and interested in the history of the aircraft.[66]

The families also started communicating among each other. Tony Gibson wrote to the Forresters:

> What incredible news we have recently received - I was only two months old when my Dad was shot down and as his brother was also killed as a P.O.W. at Sandakan, I am the only remaining Gibson. His sister Roy is still alive at 91 and I do see her regularly. I have four children and five grandchildren who are very proud of their grandfather as you must be of your great uncle. Please feel free to pass on my email to Fiona Thorn and I would welcome any contact from either of you. Kind Regards, Tony Gibson

I sent a CD with pictures of the wreckage to David Forrester who made copies and circulated them to the other families. Included with the CD, I sent the account of our finding the wreckage. I also sent an open note to the families as follows:

NOTE TO THE FAMILIES

First off, I want to express my sympathy to you all for the loss of your family member and loved one. I wish we could have met around other circumstances.

In my searches for WWII crash sites I have grown from the excitement of finding a bullet, to being able to identify a plane, to finding a lost plane and help bring closure to some who may still be wondering what ever really happened to their Son, Sibling, or Uncle.

In one sense, I'm glad to have found Hudson A16-126 but in another sense, I understand its discovery although for some it may be a blessing, it will be a shock to others.

My family and I have gone over the ramifications of finding a lost plane over and over. We are not agreed either about the issues involved. Some say "bring em home" and others say "let them rest in peace."

Resting in peace may have been possible for the past 66 years, although the villagers knew of their whereabouts, they did not go close to it for fear of spirits. Today, there is a timber company within a few kilometers harvesting trees and soon a road will be pushed into the area and possibly right to or over the wreckage. Reckless bulldozer operators will have little solemnity as they push the wreckage away to clear passage for a road, trees will be felled and probably even on top of the wreckage then later, scavengers will come and tear or hack every piece of aluminum they can off the fuselage hoping to get rich. All the while the plane and any remains of the deceased will be trampled underfoot. It should be a crime, but it isn't.

With this in mind, I am thankful to the Lord that He allowed me to find this plane before its resting place was desecrated. I'd like to think the crew made it out alive but that is unlikely and even if they did, we know they never came home.

Someday, we too will come to the end of our days. Our bodies will turn to dust but does our soul and spirit just disappear as well? I don't believe so. I believe in a heaven and hell and that we will meet our loved ones again, hopefully in heaven.

I've included a book, "By this NAME" written by John R. Cross, a missionary to Papua New Guinea. In it he tells the story of the Bible in a chronological order like I have told the story of finding Hudson A16-126. I trust you will read it and consider its story … the Greatest Story ever told. Sincerely, Mark Reichman.

P/O Frank Thorn and F/O Graham Gibson

Chapter 30

SEA MONSTERS AND MERMAIDS

When the RAAF finally arrived, I had to go meet them alone, as my family, including my "chief engineer," Jared, had gone to the north side of the island to do some work there. That left me to fend for myself. I did not enjoy that situation, so it was an opportune time to lose some weight, seven pounds to be exact. I thought I would shock my family upon their return and did not shave, so I was beginning to look like a wild man.

I left one day early to go to Gasmata so I could have a look around for the mystery airplane that I was beginning to obsess about finding. That afternoon, I told several nationals that I would pay them with PNG K100 (US $41.00) worth of food if they could show me that airplane. That is how obsessed I had become about that aircraft. Later that evening while talking with the locals, I again rehashed Rundle's report and "three-point coordinates" with them in order to try to locate the area where he said he had seen something that "appeared" to be an airplane. With that, two older men began behaving rather excitedly, then told me that they had seen it! They claimed that they knew where it was located.

Early the next morning, we had some time before the RAAF team was to have arrived, so I took these older men to the locale where they said that they had seen something that appeared to be an airplane. We were headed in the same direction as we had before, but then they motioned for me to slow down. They marked a spot in the water, so I circled back to get a better view, and sure enough, we were able to see a whitish shape in the six meters (20 feet) of clear water. Could this be it?! We dropped anchor and the two men eased themselves into the water. I moved to the bow of the boat to observe them, as one of the two men had dived under the water then immediately came back up like a breaching whale! His eyes were wide open and it was evident, from the look on his face, that something had scared him. I thought that he must have been thinking about that PNG K100 (US $41) reward I had promised him when he suddenly changed and seemed to have forgotten the fear that he had just expressed. He called to his friend in the water, and they agreed to go down together almost holding hands. Down they went as we anxiously waited for what seemed like hours. The water was so clear we could see them swimming below. Finally, they surfaced and said, "It's just a reef." That was disappointing. What they had seen was a white, flat, table-top staghorn reef that, from above, "appeared" to be an airplane. We all had a good laugh as they got back into the boat, and I awarded them for their heroic actions with a couple packages of *Hi-Way* beef crackers which are large, hard, beef-flavored crackers. They were quite tasty and filling, almost making a meal in themselves. They were also a good deterrent for sea sickness.

I had to wonder, how many years they had seen that white thing down there and were afraid to dive down to have a closer look? That incident brought to mind another characteristic about many of the locals; they live in fear. They had fear of the unknown, fear of myths that have been handed down from generation to generation, fear of dying and many other fears. From the outside, they appeared to be a happy-go-lucky people, but on the inside they are very fearful.

While my brave divers finished up their "Hi Way" rewards, we motored back to the location Rundle had noted, but this time, after much thought, I decided not to use the three-point location from Rundle's report, but a "straight line" location method with the same benchmarks. We positioned the boat one and three-quarter miles from Gasmata, (See page xiii - NO. 22) 75 yards off Umbo Island (See page xiii - NO. 21) and 25 yards off the mainland (shoreline). Two things had to be kept in mind: the first was that when Rundle used Gasmata as his point of reference, he was not referring to the Airstrip, but rather to the old Government post located on Old Gasmata Island; and, his reference of "25 yards from the mainland," may not have been the actual mainland, but another island entirely. One would have not been aware of it unless they were close to the passage between the mainland and that other island. It became feasible that Rundle may have mistaken it for the mainland. When we lined ourselves up in a straight line, to my amazement, the water *was* 20 feet deep!

I was certain that I had found the place and instructed my two courageous divers to jump back into the water. "No way" was the unspoken response that I could see on their faces. The water was murky and, what was worse, they believed that there was a sea monster that lived in that area and had never dived there. With that unexpected response and time growing short before the RAAF team was scheduled to arrive, I grabbed my mask, fins and pony bottle (small scuba tank) and jumped into the water. I dived to the bottom, but because the water was so murky in that area, I was unable to see anything, except the silt-covered bottom that was one foot below me. I swam for just a short distance and, I must admit, it was a spooky short distance, so I thought to myself, "I need Jared along on this dive; this is too scary." When scuba diving alone with severely restricted vision, it was of upmost importance to maintain focus or the imagination can lead to visions of being eaten by sharks or crocodiles. Since the water was so eerie at depth, it was no wonder why those other two "cowards" did not want to enter this water – I really could not blame them!

I surfaced and swam casually back to the boat, not wanting the locals to see any fear in my face and the fact that I had just about 'pooped' my pants. As I rested at the back of the boat still in the water hanging onto the ladder, I casually told them, "I saw the sea monster." They were all ears as I described what it looked like how it had a large, long tail and a body of a woman with long flowing yellow hair. They were eating up the story until I said that the monster had motioned to me that it wanted to kiss me. At that point, the cat was out of the bag and we all had a good laugh. I still had to assure them that I did NOT see a mermaid! They probably thought I actually had but tried to cover it up. I wondered if they would go diving there now just to look for the monster that I had seen.

XXX RATED MOVIES AND TALKING DOGS

Before I continue on with our meeting of the RAAF team, here is a story about an incident that happened at home with the local people. When we first built our "bush" house in the village of Yumielo in 1986, we did not have many amenities. We did have running water from a water catchment system for showers and cleaning dishes. Joan also had insisted on having a "flush toilet" IN THE HOUSE to alleviate having to use the public facilities, so I dug a large septic hole and installed a toilet. The villagers had never seen a toilet before and when they came in the bathroom, they asked if the sink was the toilet. The villagers had designated separate toilet areas for men and women in the mangroves along the beach. This is what Joan objected to using. We also had a refrigerator, which operated on kerosene but did not get too cold. We even used kerosene lamps at night. In 1988, my parents in the United States sent us a 23-centimeter (nine-inch) RCA TV and VCR through the mail, and to our surprise, it still worked after we received it! What a delight it was to be able to watch a movie every Friday night, even if we had seen it a few times already! My Mom and sister also recorded movies regularly and sent them to us; our video library slowly grew.

Most of the locals in the village had never seen a movie in their lives, so we thought we would show them some. We had to decide which one to show, and that took some thought. It required a great deal of discussion and, since we did not want to offend the culture, we finally decided to show them *Karate Kid*. It was rated PG for family viewing, and even though the people were unable to understand the English language and probably would not be able to follow the story line either, we felt that the karate fighting would at least be entertaining. So, over 100 people (men, women and children) all sat excitedly in front of that tiny RCA TV!

Something we did not anticipate was their reaction to a scene in the movie where the actor, Daniel-San, kisses a girl. It was just a simple kiss in a public place (at a Carnival) but you should have heard the people roar! One thing we had forgotten to consider was that the villagers believed that one should never show public affection. They also decried the holding of hands in public, and in their culture, they never kissed. In my opinion, that was possibly because their mouths were always filled with beetle nut (a nut chewed along with lime and mustard seed that gives a mild buzz, but left their mouths salivating a bright red mixture which is then spit out). Seemingly, everyone in PNG chewed beetle nut called, "buai." To them, it was as natural as walking. To westerners, it appeared to be like chewing tobacco, and to some, it was a disgusting thing to see! But of course, they had *heard* of kissing, and the younger generation, no doubt, may have even experimented with it, but that too, would have been done only in extreme privacy. So, when they saw the act of kissing on the TV screen, they could not hold back their whoops and hollers. Joan and I were devastated. Because of the outburst from the people, we felt that the kissing scene, to them, was like a XXX movie, and we were supposed to be missionaries! The people thought that it was hilarious that something usually done in private was being done in public right before their own eyes!

Well, they were hooked on watching movies, and they wanted to see more and more. I learned to use "movie night" as a motivator to get them to help me with some work during the day. But from then on, we really *scrutinized* our library and decided that we would show them cartoons only. Those should be safe. So, we showed them a Disney movie, *Lady and the Tramp*. They enjoyed it, although there was sort of a "kissing scene" when the two dogs were eating a string of spaghetti. But, besides that, we felt fairly comfortable with showing that movie. Not long afterwards, I had a curious man ask me, "How do you get your dogs to talk in America?" I realized that what they had seen on the TV was thought to be real. After the talking-dogs incident, I had to suppose that they would have thought our vegetables talked and walked if I had I shown them a *"Veggie Tales"* movie.

I had acquired a huge video camera that rested on one's shoulder with an external box for the VHS cassette that hung by the cameraman's side with a strap over the other shoulder. It was a "State of the Art" clumsy contraption, but it worked. So, I decided to show the people how a "movie" was made with actors and what was visible on a screen was not always real. I filmed my "actor" climbing a coconut tree, and once on top, he yelled and threw down a branch that whizzed by the camera lens, simulating a falling body. While the camera was on pause, the actor then climbed down from the tree and lay on the ground. Camera began to roll again and focused on the limp body as another teenager acting as a witch doctor ran up to him and used "white magic" that involved rubbing his chest. A close-up on the blinking eyes indicated that he was beginning to awaken and, lo and behold, he stood up and walked away! From that simple "movie," (which the people enjoyed watching over and over again) even if they no doubt had thought that the "white magic" worked, they hopefully understood that movies were not real, and "acting" took on a whole new meaning.

Afterwards, when they saw movies, they were overheard saying, "It's only acting." So, in the end, I think they understood the idea of movie-making. It was interesting to learn that the most popular movie was *Swiss Family Robinson*. That was probably because of all the interaction with the animals and the jungle setting. That was just one example that served to illustrate why I have had a lot of fun living with these people, and they, no doubt, got a kick out of me.

The people are continuing to be introduced to modern inventions both by missionaries and businessmen or technology coming into the area. Another missionary, Tina Girard, relayed stories that revealed how the people have begun to acclimate to the affects of civilization. Her husband, Bryan, was visiting some friends in a village and was, in their hospitable way, given a plate of food. He politely requested a fork and was told that they had thrown them away because the cook kept using them to comb her hair. Another story involves how an older lady named Rose, who was well into her 60s, reacted when she first heard the word "mobile," as in, "mobile telephone." She was, of course, confused as to its meaning, since she had never even seen a telephone in her life. Once it was explained to her (which I assume she did not comprehend), she said that she loved the sound of that word; so they now call her "Mobile." The best story though, was about the day someone came and told Mobile (Rose) about one of the big men from the area now living in the capital city. He had gone to the hospital and had a "battery" placed in his chest; it was a pacemaker. Apparently, the pacemaker had a ten-year battery. When Rose heard that, she asked her husband, Saio, if he could go to town to buy another battery. She was thinking that he had had a D-cell battery installed, like the size used in a big flashlight. She wanted a doctor to come and install it in her, as she would like to live for another ten years!

One must keep in mind that much of the population in PNG continued to live as their ancestors. The approximate 820 languages in the country had hindered progress as ideas could not be exchanged and tribal warfare was the norm. The people cook in a house with a grass roof using an open fire burning on a dirt floor. They did not wear shoes, and clothes were difficult to afford, since they did not earn money but survived primarily from the harvest of their gardens. In some remote locations they dug up their dead ancestor's remains for spirit appeasement, and some older women in remote locations had continued to wear grass skirts. Many people slept on beds made of sticks. When I first moved into a village in 1986, I was asked if someone had actually gone to the moon. Later, as I studied their language and culture I realized that many of them thought that the earth was flat. No wonder it was so difficult for them to comprehend mobile phones and pacemakers. But they seemed to learn quickly – especially those of the younger generation, although some speak into a cell phone as if they were speaking into a radio microphone, quickly putting it to their ear to hear the response.

Boy with ancestor's remains, Myu Village. WNBP, PNG. Photo by L. Tillitson

Man climbing coconut tree. WNBP, PNG

Woman wearing grass skirt, Myu Village. WNBP, PNG

Bed made of sticks, Mang Village. WNBP, PNG (1986)

Chapter 31

WE ARE THE GOVERNMENT

After boarding our boat, we sped off for the airstrip to meet the RAAF team. As we moored the boat at the shoreline, the Cessna Grand Caravan circled us, so we ran down the road toward the airstrip, which was a considerable distance away – a half hour away to be exact; I had thought it was closer! By the time we arrived, the airplane had already departed and there was no one around in the area. There were a few locals standing around who said that the RAAF team had hitched a ride on a timber company truck and had gone to the camp. I was so ashamed of myself for the lateness of my arrival to meet them. Even though I had the thought that, "Oh well, this is PNG" (where timeliness was not exactly a common trait), it did not help to assuage my guilt. I consoled myself with the realization that it would have been quite a hike back to the boat with all of their gear, so it turned out for the best.

Since they had all left, we headed back toward the boat, but I was stopped by an older gentleman who asked me what we were doing there. I explained to him about the bomber that was in the bush and that the RAAF team was here to investigate it. With that, he became belligerent and ranted about how the PNG Government did not do anything for the people. I told him that four men had lost their lives defending PNG and that their families are still mourning their loss and that their remains could still be found and returned to them. Even with that explanation, he was still in an upset mood and said he had wished the Japanese would have won the war as they would have taken better care of them. I could not reply to that statement as I was still digesting the thought. I stood there for a while and listened to his rampage; I tried to remain polite, but I then pardoned myself, walked away and left him standing there. I concluded that what he wanted was money. I have read that, during the war, there were pockets of Japanese sympathizers and, obviously, from that experience, some have remained to this day.

As I walked to the boat, I wondered about PNG and whether it could have become a better place to live had the Japanese won the war or had the Allies not pushed them back to their homeland – it was something to ponder. If one were to take a cursory view of the Gasmata area in its postwar condition and compared it to war-time pictures of the area, it appeared that there has been little new development over the last 65 years and, in fact, the road network and houses that existed during the war have disappeared. The town has remained without electricity, water, or telephone and has little or no services in shipping or infrastructure. The people have had virtually no way to sell their copra (dried coconuts used for making soaps and health products) or cocoa (the seed of the *Theobroma cacao* tree – the source of chocolate). As a result, the plantations have become overgrown and idle. Once, when asked about the government, their reply was, "What government? We are the government." In many ways that was true. They have had to take care of themselves.

From that standpoint, it made it easier to understand the man's frustration. He may have lost a relative because there was no medicine at the hospital, or perhaps, there were many other circumstances that could have embittered him. I am certain that, over his life, he has had to beg, borrow and even steal to get a pair of shorts to wear because of lack of jobs or the development of an economy that could have provided him a decent existence. It may have been the reason some of the local people have such a dismal attitude toward their Government. The inability to make money no doubt, was the reason they have exploited tourists by charging them to take photographs of the Japanese airplane relics which were displayed alongside the airstrip. I was certain that was the reason Ben had made such a fuss when we dived in "his" waters; he complained until I paid him. One had to wonder what other means they had to find money to pay for clothing or school fees or a bag of rice. Maybe that grumpy old man just remembered a time when life seemed better, and he associated that time with the period of Japanese occupation or Australian administration.

Those conditions were not confined to Gasmata; Kandrian, too, had very little development over the past 22 years that I lived there, and the Arawe Isles have had none (that I can remember). In reality, services and housing conditions appear to have actually deteriorated. These were not only my observations. During a visit by Provincial Governor Peter Humphrey, the Education Inspector, speaking on behalf of all the public servants, read all those issues, and more, publicly to the Governor so that he would be reminded of their conditions. It is no secret that the government has a lot of work to do under difficult conditions.

If it were not for the Malaysian timber companies in the area, the people would have had little money nor few means to get money. Furthermore, there would not have even been much maintenance on the road system. But all the lack of development cannot be blamed completely on the Government, as the people here have been free to be productive and enterprising should they so choose; but they have not. In a way, the time warp had a beneficial effect, since the area has retained its natural beauty. The lack of development has provided them with a lovely place to live in, but it also left them with somewhat difficult and frustrating living conditions. Even though timber companies have been accused of many inappropriate actions, my personal experience with all the companies, Rimbunan Hijau, Cakara Alam and Feflo, has been positive, and I have found them to be helpful to me and many of my co-workers.

So, the big question remained, would the people have been better off if the Japanese had won the war and had taken control? After deep consideration, I have come to the opinion that, had the Japanese been allowed to keep PNG for themselves, there might be better infrastructure and services but at the cost of freedom. The Japanese people would not be the ones we know today. Possibly, they would have been the same as the callous wartime soldiers who shot and beheaded local people for simple insubordination. The people of this land might have become slaves and third class citizens. There would not have been an independence declared, such as the current one, which allows claims for water or land ownership. The Japanese may have governed all of the land, and in all probability, become tightly or dictatorially controlling. The people, more than likely, would not have remained free and would have had to talk secretly about the good ol' days that their tabunas (ancestors) had once enjoyed. In some ways, the people might have benefited positively and, in other ways, possibly many ways, it could have become much worse.

IN SEARCH OF A BOMB

By the time we had piloted the boat back to the timber camp, the RAAF team, dressed in their official uniforms, had eaten a lunch. Daniel Kovi and I introduced ourselves to the team, and we all had a friendly chat while a large group of curious onlookers stood by watching us. Since it was still early in the day, I suggested taking the boat back to Gasmata to view some of the wrecks we had found there. That suggestion seemed amenable to all. When we arrived at old Gasmata Island, I wanted to show the RAAF patrol some Japanese anti-aircraft guns and projectiles, since Flight Sergeant Sean Cranfield was an Armament Technician. But we could no longer find the ordnance, and none of the locals claimed any knowledge as to what had happened to them. It amazed me that projectiles that had been lying around for 66 years could suddenly disappear. I had personally seen them less than one year ago. The locals might have hidden them with the fear that we would take them. Instead, the locals did show us an anti-aircraft gun that was overturned on the side of a hill and told us of a bomb that was lying on the beach.

We set out to see the bomb on the beach, which I thought would have been fairly close. We walked for what seemed like miles; it was approximately two-thirds of the way around the island. We walked on coral and, at times, sand. The military men wore heavy boots and spiffy uniforms, and I can presume, while sweltering in the high humidity and temperature, that they must have been wondering about the character who was wearing flip-flops and sported a scraggly beard? The long hike was somewhat enjoyable in that it allowed us to become better acquainted with each other. Squadron Leader John Cotterell commented at the surreal nature of this experience, since only a few days earlier he had been at a funeral in Tasmania and now suddenly he was hiking on an almost deserted island trying to locate WWII ordnance – it was mind-boggling to him. There is a great contrast between being in civilization one day, then in remote areas of Papua New Guinea the next; it is like being quickly transported back in time. The sudden loss of fast food stores, shopping malls and cell phones has surprised many a visitor. But, by contrast, as another RAAF officer told me that he had "Never seen a place as beautiful as this."

Finally, we arrived at the spot where the bomb was supposed to have been, but we did not see a bomb; rather, it was a *mine* lying on the reef. It was rusty, had a hole corroded through the top, and still contained explosive material inside, which appeared similar in composition to brown sand. The local guide said that they would take the "sand" out of it, lay it in the sun to dry, then pour it into a tin can, light a fuse and throw it in the water. After it exploded, all the dead fish in a 15 to 30 meter (50 to 100 foot) radius came floating to the top. I wondered, "How in the world do these guys learn these things?"

After a quick but disappointing look at the explosive, we began our return hike. Thankfully, we did not go around the perimeter, but we cut through the middle of the island on a coral rock trail made years ago by prison convicts – or so we were told. I could not help but think that it had to be true; who else would have lined coral rocks five feet wide from one end of an island to another unless it was people who were forced to do so? The locals were not likely to have had a reason to be that industrious. We eventually made it back to the boat, and I was glad I had some cold water to offer to the team. Despite this arduous hike as the RAAF's first initiation to Papua New Guinea, they thought it was great!

I next took them to see the Hudson in the water on the reef. We then proceeded to the site of the other Hudson, A16-165, on Avurai Island. At this crash site, there are still burst bullet cartridges (probably split open in a fire when the airplane crashed) lying in the area where the cockpit would have been after the crash. This too was quite an experience for the airmen, as it was always greatly moving to see a crash site and realize that men, in some cases still just boys, had lost their lives there. It is difficult to realize today, when things are so peaceful, that during the war the area was swarming with men in uniform carrying guns. Large ships would have been anchored in the harbor and full of ammunition. Bombs fell almost weekly, as more than 125 bombing raids were conducted against the Japanese at Gasmata, with some sorties including over one-hundred bombers.[67]

Dugout sail canoe by Kauptemete Island. WNBP, PNG

Truck on government road, Kandrian. WNBP, PNG

Timber company jigger. WNBP. PNG

Chapter 32

RAAF RECON MISSION

We returned to the timber camp, and early the next morning there was extremely poor weather. It had rained from 4 A.M. until about 8 A.M. We were considering whether to hike in or not when the weather suddenly cleared and the helicopter arrived. I rode on the first shuttle flight. The pilot, Colin Greenwood, had already seen the landing area we had prepared and had landed on it to test its safety and to blow away loose debris. It was a short eight-minute shuttle from the timber camp as we flew just above the tree tops and landed in the morning fog. It was a pretty neat experience and certainly not as tiring as it had been when we hiked our way into this area. As I pondered that eight-minute flight in a slow-flying helicopter, I concluded that the Hudson could have made the trip from Gasmata to this point in less than five minutes! For some reason, I previously had presumed that after the bombs had been dropped, the subsequent chase by the Japanese fighters would have taken a long time. I noted the short distance of our flight, and I dreamt how it must have seemed like an eternity to the crew of the Hudson.

Once we had landed and the helicopter had departed, the remoteness of our location in the middle of the jungle became obvious; and the RAAF military men were the first to make mention of it. We wondered about those who may have survived a crash and which way they would have trekked? Each step of the way would have been made with caution, moving a few feet at a time then stopping to listen for enemy patrols which may have been out looking for survivors of the crash. As the hours passed and the sunset came, they would have found themselves in a black jungle so dark that even an attempt to see the stars was not possible through the dense tree canopies. It would have been a lonely feeling, and one that certainly would have brought many a downed airman face to face with God.

After all the team had arrived at the crash site, Colin Greenwood, the chopper pilot, asked whether he could stay for the duration of our time on the ground. This was naturally agreed to for safety reasons and in the event the weather might start to close in. Sqn.

MIA

Ldr. John Cotterell, Flt. Lt. Mark French, Flt. Sgt. Sean Cranfield, Flt. Sgt. Gavin Willmett, Daniel Kovi, Colin Greenwood and I gathered together, and the seven of us hiked down the path approximately 183 meters (200 yards) to the Hudson crash site. I was glad that Daniel Kovi was able to join us on the helicopter since he had been so instrumental in assisting us in the discovery. Without his assistance, it was impossible to envisage a scenario where we would ever have found this wreckage. This was his first time to see it.

As we continued to walk, with me in the lead, we found ourselves only 30 meters (100 feet) away from the site. I decided to make the hike interesting, so as we approached it, I asked them all to locate the actual wreckage like Jared had done to me with *Texas #6*. That was not an easy task in the thick underbrush, and, unfortunately, the Squadron Leader, who was nervously opposed to playing such a game, "encouraged" me to move ahead. Suddenly, one of the team witnessed the wreckage to our left. We made our way over to it and stood in solemn silence for a couple of minutes. The first sighting of a crash site was always a sobering experience, as I have previously mentioned. It was similar to standing in silence at a grave site.

The first order of business was to form a line and walk through the area to search for any unexploded bombs. Some round cylinders were found in the ground and unearthed, only to be identified as oxygen tanks. We found at least eight of them, and there were two more in the tail section. During the search, a wing tip was discovered approximately 12 meters (40 feet) away from the rest of the wreckage. We had not found that on our previous trips. Once we felt assured that there was no live ordnance in the area, we began an examination of the crash site itself. The number A16-126 was clearly visible on each side of the rear fuselage, which was the airplane's identity. That satisfied one of the goals of the Air Force reconnaissance team. There were a few bullet holes in the side as well. It was easy to estimate where the cockpit area would have been, because both engines were stuck into the ground. Thus, the cockpit, which was nowhere to be seen, would have been in between and forward of those engines. The secondary purpose of the Air Force team was to actually look for the crew's remains or personal items. So we then started digging in that designated area.

As we excavated, we immediately began to find all sorts of artifacts buried just 15 centimeters (six inches) down. A curved sheet of

248

13-millimeter (half-inch) thick iron, likely the bullet-proof back of the pilot's seat, was found. We also found an RPM gauge face which was partially burnt. In addition, we discovered a flap-control lever, a cockpit window handle which still had some Plexiglas on it, seat belt buckles and pieces of strapping. We were definitely in the right area to explore the cockpit. Next, a pair of binoculars was found and also a green military-style flashlight. Those were most likely personal items. While we were digging, a group of ten local young men arrived, having trucked and hiked in to help work alongside us.

The area became crowded, so I spent some time looking closely in the rear fuselage where the ball turret was located; once again, I did not want to disturb too much. Whenever I picked up something to examine, I replaced it in the same spot so that the forensic team to come later would find things in-situ, i.e., as they were.

After I completed my search of the fuselage, I returned to where the team was digging. I was a bit surprised at the manner in which they had dug in the cockpit area, as they were disturbing the ground so much and moving things around. I thought that the RAAF forensic team would be upset once they saw how things had been moved around. I suggested that we diagram the area with a grid and draw a map to show the location of the items being found. The Officer in Charge did draw a diagram of the crash site to ensure that all the major parts had been located, like the wings, fuselage, main cockpit and engines. I then began to dig in a different area than where the others were digging. Surprisingly, I found a Lewis machine gun buried just under the surface of the ground, which I found both fascinating and rewarding.

We dug for about five hours and found a number of cockpit items, some personal items and a verification of the serial number of the aircraft. As it was getting late, we headed back to the helicopter with a bucketful of parts from the wreckage, and we were then shuttled back to the timber camp. As we ate dinner at the timber company mess hall, we chatted about our experiences of the day. A truck eventually rolled up with our helpers who were just now getting back after their long hike. They were all well paid, given food and baseball caps, for which they were all very grateful. I, too, was presented with a ball cap, but also a lapel pin, pen, and a clock, on behalf of the Chief of Air Force of the Royal Australian Air Force. They actually conducted an informal ceremony which I considered to be a gesture of international gratitude for my part in all of this.

In the early morning of the next day, it was raining rather hard and there appeared to be a mix-up in communication; for some reason, a truck did not bring the RAAF team down to the boat. I was supposed to have taken them back to Gasmata to meet their exit airplane, and time was running out. We waited nervously for almost an hour; I was prepared to hike up to the camp to find out where they were located, but before I could do that, a timber truck arrived and the driver asked me about the status of things. It was obvious that things must have been messed up, so I asked the driver if he would go back to tell the squad that I would meet them on the coast near the wharf. When we did meet later, I felt that it was important to contact Daniel Kovi. I thought that he had acted strangely when he did not send the team down in a truck earlier.

The Squadron Leader and I went to search for Daniel. We did find him, and appreciation for Daniel's assistance was expressed with the award of a ballpoint pen and lapel pin. Those items, along with a ball cap, appeared to have pleased him somewhat. It was getting rather late, so instead of my taking the team with all their cargo by boat followed by a hike to the airstrip, the timber company truck transported them by road. Daniel Kovi then took me back to the boat, and I thanked him for all the help he had given. Since I was confused and concerned that he had not sent the truck for the team earlier that morning, I spent a considerable amount of time encouraging him over the important part that he had played in this 'recon' mission. I have remained uncertain as to the reason for his neglect in sending the transport for the team earlier. In retrospect, I have pondered his behavior and wondered if he was disappointed at not finding the airplane that, supposedly, contained gold.

A couple of days following the RAAF team's departure, our rainy season began and, WOW, did it pour! It rained continuously for four days, so it was a good thing that we had made the Hudson 'recon' trip when we did. The rainy season was unusual that year, with a couple weeks of sunny and cloudy days with rain only at night, then several straight days of rain. Even with the odd rain cycle, we received a total of almost one meter (over three feet) of precipitation in just one month on the coast. There would have been more rain in the interior jungles.

Not long afterward, once the report had been received back in Australia, an official public announcement of the bomber find was made. I then received a phone call from the *PNG National Newspaper* asking to interview me for my side of the story. In my story, I included Daniel Kovi's name as well as the forgotten government post of Gasmata, which were then mentioned on the PNG radio and television news and in the newspapers. This gave Daniel the recognition he deserved, for which I was immensely grateful; without his help, finding the wreckage would have been, by any measure, much more difficult, if not utterly impossible. The Gasmata locals were excited to hear that their own town had been mentioned on the radio. They felt that they were so small that nobody ever heard of them. That was probably true. There were times when we would go to the main town of Lae, and local townspeople would ask where we lived. When we answered, "Kandrian," they would question, "Where's that?" Gasmata was even smaller and more insignificant, but as a result of all this notoriety, the little town finally was touted as an important place on the map.

The find was big news in Australia. It was on the nightly TV news, in the newspapers and on the radio stations across the country. Some thought that it was highly regarded news due to the fact that one of the missing crew members, P/O Thorn, had been a well known cricketer in his home state of Victoria and his grandson was a member of the Australian Olympic team that year. Unfortunately, no one picked up the story, and news of the discovery dissipated rather quickly. The *Fiji Times* ran an article on July 5, 2008. In America, as far as I know, the story only made the news in my home town months later, after many e-mails were dispatched to the *Joliet Herald Newspaper*.

Mark and Sqn. Ldr. John Cotterell

251

Flt. Lt. Mark French with binoculars from Hudson A16-126.

Flt. Sgts. Sean Cranfield and Gavin Willmett with Hudson radio antennae.

Chapter 33

OH MUCK

In the last days of August of 2008, the RAAF contacted me about checking on the jungle helicopter pad to make certain that it was still usable for a chopper to land on the following month. On September 5, 2008, while under way and just before reaching the Au Timber Camp, we came upon a pod of pilot whales. That experience was both amazing and educational! Pilot whales move much slower than dolphins, but they are about four times larger. At first, they were only nine meters (30 feet) away and fairly close to the boat. As we took photographs and made a video of them, more were sighted on the port side, followed by dolphins frolicking off our bow. All in all, there were probably over 200 dolphins and pilot whales. That was a breathtaking experience that we had never had before and one most people will never have. It was no wonder Papua New Guinea claimed to be "The Land of the Unexpected."

To our dismay, when we arrived at the camp, we found that the timber company had not resumed work due to the heavy rainfall. They said that even one of their 'dozers had become stuck because the road was so muddy. This meant that we could not reach the wreck site. That was pretty discouraging, but while we were in the area, we decided to go further to Gasmata to investigate reports of a couple of other airplanes.

We went to the village of Kalagen and talked with Leo, who had previously been a chain-saw operator back in 1994. He and another operator (now deceased) had seen an airplane that was teetering on a cliff northeast of Gasmata. He said that he had stood on the starboard wing, and as he walked toward the fuselage, the airplane shifted, so he did not go any further to get a closer look into the cockpit. As he stood on the wing, he noticed that the single tail was intact, but he did not see any engines or propellers. He also noted that there were windows along the side of the nose. That was about the extent of what he was able to remember.

I found that information hugely intriguing since I had on file the record of a Bristol Beaufort, serial number A9-186, that went down seven to eight miles northeast of Gasmata. The Beaufort did have windows along the side of the airplane's nose. I had never actually seen that type of airplane other than the pieces of A9-204 which we had seen in the mangroves of Gasmata (previously mentioned in chapter 14 of this book). That airplane reportedly had crashed with its bombs still on board which explained why there were only small pieces that had remained.

The disheartening blow to my plans came when Leo told me that he would not take me there that day. I tried a number of different ways to convince him to go, but he dodged each attempt. I was forced to postpone the trip for some other time. That episode was awfully disappointing since the RAAF (i.e., Australian Government) had paid for my fuel to get there and check out the helicopter pad and it turned into an impossible task. I had hoped at least to be able to report to them that I had found another airplane. To return later on my own meant I would have to buy the 60 gallons of gas myself, and at just under US $8 per gallon (inflation having pushed the price from US $6.50 to now US $8 per gallon), it would be a costly trip.

There was no convincing Leo to take us, so we decided to search again for the mysterious, elusive airplane in Gasmata Harbor. On our way there, an old man from Akur Island told me he had seen the airplane. So, I decided to take him along as well. We went back to the mouth of the Legom River and lined ourselves up 46 meters (50 yards) NE of Umbo Island (which the local people call Aumwo). We were 23 meters (25 yards) off the mainland, which was actually another island called Aglimbo, and the distance was one and three-quarters miles from the old Gasmata Government Post where the water was six meters (20 feet) deep. We made several passes in the area which ranged from six- to 11-meter (20 to 35 foot) depths, and we carefully marked every "high spot" as shown on the depth sounder. We located five such "high" points for further investigation.

The old man from Akur then took us to a point nearer to Umbo Island off the tip of the island just beyond the reef. He stood on the bow of the boat and led me to the precise location where he said that he had seen the airplane. When he said, "Here," I marked it on my GPS. I then circled around again and we followed the same procedure two more times. To my surprise, as I marked each pass, all three points were relatively close together. From that, I gathered that he knew where he was when he had seen it. My skepticism was raised, though, when I realized that the water had become 15 meters (50 feet) deep! There was no possible way that a guy sitting in a dugout canoe could have seen down into that water to a depth of 15 meters (50 feet).

It was getting late and everybody was tired from the search, so we took the man back to his island. I thanked him for coming along and showing me that location. By now I was rather cynical and thought that this was another something that "appeared" to be an airplane. But I looked forward to the next morning and a chance to check out those five dots on my GPS.

Neither Jared nor I were able to sleep well on the boat. Jared said that it was the mattresses because they had a vinyl cover which made them hot and sticky. I was constantly being awakened by the occasional banging of the boat against the wharf post which caused a slight jolt. I also knew that if it started to rain, there was a deck hatch opening right above my head from which I would inevitably have felt drops on my face. On the other hand, the slow rocking of the boat and sound of waves rhythmically hitting the bow were relaxing.

As morning dawned, we loaded our guides and returned to the site of the mystery airplane. It was the same area where I had dived previously by myself and had aborted the dive due to the fact that it felt too closed-in and had given me a creepy feeling. We placed the boat directly over the dots on the GPS which marked the "high spots" on the bottom, and we then threw out the anchor. We hurriedly suited-up in our dive gear and stepped off the swim platform into the water. At three meters (ten feet), our visibility was fairly clear and I thought we were going to have an un-obscured dive. When we reached six meters (20 feet), our visibility started to alternate between clear and cloudy. We used a compass and followed a heading that paralleled the island as we held a depth of six meters (20 feet). My compass was broken and I had forgotten my dive computer which calculates the depth, so I was totally dependent upon Jared. That was good training for him, and he did a great job.

As we swam along just above the silt bottom, our hands occasionally touched the bottom. What a strange feeling that produced!

255

The bottom was not sandy as one might have expected. It was more like a superfine powder, almost like flour, so the touch of it felt somewhere between creepy and disgusting. It was so weird that had I not been under water, it could have made the hair on the back of my neck stand up. Jared soon took his knife out and was sticking it in the muck to pull himself forward while he also tried to feel for anything that would make a clanging noise from metal hitting metal, such as a fuselage or wing. I had my knees bent to keep my fins away from the bottom so as to not stir up that powdery stuff and obliterate what little visibility we did have.

After several passes at different depths, we did see why the depth sounder had given us a reading that something was there. We found those things were only rocks, however. While I was impressed that the depth sounder had picked them up, I was really disappointed that they were not parts of an airplane. The more we swam back and forth over the area, the cloudier the water became and the lower we had to descend to see, until we were actually only 15 centimeters (six inches) from the bottom. We were barely able to see it as we slowly passed by. I had my elbow sticking out touching Jared to maintain contact so that I would not lose him. As it turned out, I did not have to worry, because he was, likewise, maintaining close proximity to me. We have always tended to stay close under such conditions. Then too, there *was* the story of that sea monster in that area ....

As we passed over the terrain, I thought about Rundle's report which read, "We saw what *appeared* to be an airplane and pulled out pieces that did not look like a RAAF aircraft, so we reported it to the Americans." Those words continued to cycle through my mind, and it made me begin to wonder about the pieces he had salvaged. Did they even look like they were from an airplane? Back and forth we swam until we had covered an area from three meters (10 feet) deep to 11 meters (35 feet) deep parallel with the island shore. We found nothing but the rocks that were sticking up occasionally. It turned out that the reason the water was getting more and more smoky was because Jared was sticking his fins into the muck as he pushed himself forward, stirring up the silt. I was disappointed to realize that, but had there been anything down there, even though we could not see, we would have certainly run in to it with our heads!

After we surfaced and returned to the boat, we still had quite a considerable amount of air in our tanks because we had not dived deep (nor long). We then decided to have a look at where the old man said he had seen an airplane. We positioned the boat about 46 meters (50 yards) from our previous spot, which placed us approximately 23 meters (25 yards) off Umbo Island and just short of the reef where the water was 15 meters (50 feet) deep. We threw the anchor out and suited-up. Because the water was cloudy, we decided to follow the anchor line down as our point of reference.

As we descended, the water became increasingly murky, and visibility deteriorated to only about six feet. We reached bottom and looked around, but of course we could see very little, so we decided to proceed in the direction of the reef and swim back and forth on it, starting at a depth of 11 meters (35 feet) then getting shallower with each pass. The visibility cleared up as we got shallower, but we did not see an airplane. It turned out to be a terrible looking reef with only a little color or coral. Hardly worth a dive compared to many other sites in PNG, so we were glad to return to the boat. With that disappointment, we opted to temporarily abandon our search for that airplane.

On that same afternoon, we cemented in new posts on the wharf at Old Gasmata Island, since the original mangrove posts had been badly eaten by sea worms, and we knew it would not be long before they would give way. As usual, while we were working, there were a lot of local guys just hanging around watching what was happening. At approximately 5:00 P.M., as we cleaned and swept the area, my boat security man, Steven, coyly told me there was a young man who had a story he wanted to tell me. I made my way through the crowd over to this young, cocky fellow who was slowly puffing on his cigarette and acting proud and cool with his back to me. We began talking, small talk at first, when he finally said, "That plane you're looking for, you're looking in the wrong spot. I know where it is." I questioned him a bit, and he seemed fairly competent and confident. With about an hour of daylight left, I said, "OK, show me." I told him that if he could show me an airplane that I have not seen before, I would pay for PNG K100 (US $41) worth of food.

With that, he quickly conversed with some other spectators on the wharf and headed for the boat. I briefly explained to Jared the new plan, but he was skeptical (having heard many similar dead-end stories previously) and not interested, so he opted to stay behind.

We launched our boat and made our way, eventually arriving at a reef not far from the airplane wreckage on the reef. The four fellows jumped from the boat and into the water while the rest of us waited onboard. They swam around and around and made their way to the other reef that had wreckage on it. I yelled, "I saw that one already!" They came back towards the wing which was in six meters (20 feet) of water and I yelled, "I already saw that one, too."

By that time, it was getting dark and the swimmers returned to the boat – shivering. My young "story-teller" wanted to save face, so he told me that part of the wing and the fuselage were out further, but it was getting too dark to find it. We would have to return at some other time. I motored back to the wharf at dusk, and Jared was not the least bit surprised to hear that we had returned empty handed.

WILD GOOSE CHASE

When morning arrived the next day, we headed back to Kandrian but stopped along the way at Melenglo. A man named Apaulo saw us coming through the passage and was waiting for us as we moored the boat. He told us that the timber company road now led to the site of another airplane wreckage. We gathered our things, packed some food, jumped into a truck and headed out. We drove up and around the winding timber company roads headed basically north and toward the interior of the island. We had traveled 26 kilometers (15.6 miles) when we turned off onto a small side road and proceeded a fair distance to the west. Finally, we arrived at the village of Akimbu and walked over to the haus boi. There was an old man lying on a customary bed made of sticks. I have tried to sleep on that type of bed before, but I have never had a good night's sleep on one. Inevitably, there always seemed to be a knot or stub sticking me in the back, and I spent a lot of time adjusting the sticks by turning each one so they would all lay even with no bumps. In addition to that, I was afraid to roll over for fear the sticks would fall off since they were not nailed down. Even the use of one of those 13-millimeter (half-inch) foam mattresses was useless. The final discouragement for sleep in such conditions was the smoke from a fire inside the house which always made my eyes burn.

The old man, Simon Ukli, sat up, and since I always tried to respect local cultural mores, I attempted to "ease" into the reason we were there. But Apaulo could not wait for the small talk and interrupted with, "We came to see the airplane." Well, that took the suspense out of our trek, and after further explanation, the old man said, "Yes, I saw that plane – a long time ago. The Village Chiefs were afraid to go near it. It had made a big hole." The only problem was that Simon was too old to show it to us himself, but he assured us that the younger men in the next hamlet could show us how to find the right location.

With that, we started our hike toward the other hamlet over a winding, muddy trail. After 15 minutes or so, we found the hamlet of Aumun, where there happened to be a Mission Church. The Bible teachers were Jack Sukiali and Maikal Likia, who had been evangelized in the early 1990s by Mark and Donna Archer while they lived in Palmalngen Village. I used to carry supplies for the Archers up the Andrew River, using a dinghy loaded with 500 kilograms (1,100 pounds) of cargo. I also took a pair of water skis and pulled Mark up and down the river for entertainment. That was something he enjoyed, but had had little opportunity to do while living in the jungle. Those days of my life were an entirely different story in themselves, but it was encouraging to see that the Church was still functioning after all these years.

We told Jack, one of the Bible teachers, what we had come for, and he, too, had seen the big hole at Kawahapei Village in the garden area called Pulalo and added that there was no airplane in it anymore. He said that it must have sunk down into the ground or it had been "choppered" out. He had never actually seen the airplane, but when he was a child, he had passed by the hole and the older men told him that the large cavity had been made by an airplane that had crashed at that spot. Jack also informed us that it was a good four-hour hike away.

When a story like that preceded a trek, and it happened often, it was necessary to apply sound judgment tempered by previous experience. It was easy to understand how one's reasoning could become clouded by one's zeal to find a wreckage site. So, after I had heard of a big hole I thought, "Big bomb." But when that was followed by, "The plane is gone," and "Someone must have used a helicopter to lift it out," it became necessary to use some of that gray matter between the ears and make the wisest decision. To Jared's relief, I opted to abandon the search because, even though if a big bomb had made a hole approximately 12 meters (40 feet) in diameter and four feet deep as it had been described to us, one would have expected that some airplane fragments would have remained lying around. The part of the story that really clinched my conclusion to depart was the suggestion that, "A helicopter had lifted it out." Even though we aborted the search, I still wondered what made that big hole ....

That wild goose chase and failure to locate a crash site was quite a disappointment. Unfortunately there were many such experiences which I have not recorded in this book. It was a long drive back to the boat and then on to Kandrian and home. Even though I was anxious to tell my wife about all of our exploits of the weekend, she had little interest other than the part that we made it back safely.

MORE INTEL

Rundle's statement in his report that he had seen what "appeared to be a plane and after salvaging for an hour only to bring up pieces that did not look like a RAAF airplane, so he reported it to the Americans," haunted me. I wrote my new friend and researcher, David Forrester, and told him of my dilemma and my recent unsuccessful attempt to find that airplane. He responded with a new twist to the hunt. He located Rundle's report to the Americans in which he had reported that the airplane had "crashed into the harbor approximately 20 yards from the southern tip of Umbo Island at the mouth of the Logom River and that the aircraft was in approximately 40 feet of water." When I read that report, I could have strangled David (so to speak), for not sending that tidbit of information to me sooner! It was the same twenty yards from the southern tip of Umbo Island where the old man had showed me and I had marked it three times on my GPS! The 15 meters (50 feet) of water was also close in depth to Rundle's report of "approximately 40 feet deep." It dawned on me that had Jared and I swum *away* from the reef instead of *toward* the reef when we followed the anchor line down, we would have possibly seen the crash site!

I was very anxious for an opportune time to travel to Gasmata again. David Forrester and Justin Taylan continued to check historical records for what airplanes were determined to have been missing at the end of 1943. They uncovered one report of a B-25 Mitchell, serial number 42-64846, that had been shot down on November 22, 1943. That airplane crashed on Avirin Island, and I had already seen one of its engines there. The natives in Rundle's report said that the airplane in the harbor had crashed on the same day as the Mitchell. David did not find any other B-25s that had crashed in Gasmata that day, but there was report of a B-24 Liberator, serial number 42-41043, that was determined to be missing on December 16, 1943. The natives also stated that one of the B-25s had dropped its bombs and the other one had not. It appeared that they were relatively certain that it was a B-25 and not a B-24 and that it had crashed on the same day. The mystery was that there were no other reports of military aircraft lost that day, and the area mentioned in Rundle's report did not seem big enough for a B-24 crash site. But Rundle also mentioned in his report a Catalina, serial number 264-846, that had never been recovered in the Gasmata area. Perhaps that could be the type of airplane that had fallen there? For the time being, I had no other reason to go up to Gasmata, so the solution of that mystery would have to wait.

Pilot whale. WNBP, PNG

Dolphins. WNBP,PNG

B-25 *Mitchell.*

Chapter 34

REMAINS RECOVERY

It was an exciting day when the RAAF team arrived on October 3, 2008. We had been anxiously awaiting their return throughout our rainy season so the operation could proceed, hopefully without torrential downpours. The team consisted of returning officers, Sqn. Ldr. John Cotterell as Officer in charge and Flt. Lt. Mark French as Second in charge. Two forensic specialists came this time, Sqn. Ldr. Alain Middleton and Sqn. Ldr. Alan Cala. A photographer was also on the team, Flt. Sgt. John Carroll. From the Australian High Commission in Port Moresby, came Flt. Sgt. Gavin Willmett, who had come previously and was instrumental in finding many personal effects. Lastly, the Papua New Guinea Government sent a representative from the Port Moresby museum, Mr. John Lelai.

They arrived in Kandrian on two Cessna Grand Caravans chartered from Port Moresby with all of their supplies for living in the bush. That not only included food and water, but also tents, cots, chairs, utensils – you name it, they had it! The week-long operation, called "Kovi Moses," was so named in respect for the Chairman of the local timber company, Daniel Kovi, and for the land owner of the site where the wreckage was located, Boas Moses. John Cotterell commented that, unconsciously, the name "Moses" could also refer to me, as I apparently reminded him of Moses the first time we met and I had my white, scraggly beard. This time I was clean shaven. On Friday afternoon, we weighed everything for loading the helicopter shuttles scheduled to begin early the next day.

On Saturday morning, October 4, 2008, the Heli Niugini helicopter, piloted by the owner, Bill Lusty, arrived at 6:45 A.M. and began the first of what would be four shuttle trips to the crash site. John Cotterell, John Lelai and I were flown out on the first shuttle trip. After the second group arrived, I knew I had at least an hour before the third group would arrive, so I decided to take the opportunity and show this group of men the crash site. After a cursory tour, which was always sobering as one attempted to visualize the events of the day of the crash, I examined a wing tip for possible data plates. To my surprise, lying underneath the wing next to the flaps was an aluminum pen on top of the ground! At first, I thought someone must have dropped it when we shot a few photographs of team members as they stood by the wing. I carried it up the hill and gently scraped the corrosion from it. Dr. Alain Middleton, who was a forensic odontologist, used his magnifying glasses to examine the pen more closely. To our surprise, it had a name, F.O. __IBSON, emblazoned on the side. It turned out to be the pen of Ian Gibson, who was the pilot of the Hudson! Imagine the excitement! How in the world could it have laid there for 66 years? Our answer to this question was to conclude that it had been overlooked, since only a few people had ever seen this remote crash site.

After the last group arrived, we set up camp in the helo pad area because it was already cleared and relatively flat. The local workers rode in by truck, then 'dozer and lastly they hiked, and so finally everyone had arrived. Four shelters were set up using tarps. On that same afternoon, we went to the site and cleared it of loose wreckage and leaves. I was a bit surprised how we cleared and moved everything, especially after I had previously taken such care to replace even the smallest items I had found back to its exact spot. I had assumed that the forensic team would have us go over the area by hand with a fine-toothed comb, but instead we used *rakes*. To maintain a degree of organization, we established grid lines using stretched ropes, partitioning off an area of about 334 sq. meters (3600 sq. feet).

That night, as I lay on my cot, unable to sleep, I wondered *how* that pen might have gotten under the wing, which was actually outside the search area. My imagination ran wild, and I envisioned the possibility that Gibson had somehow miraculously survived the crash. That had happened before: Wing Commander John Lerew had survived the crash of his Hudson A16-91 when he parachuted at 122 meters (400 feet). It also occurred on the Hudson A16-165 that had crashed on Avurai Island; in that case, Flight Lieutenant K. Erwin had survived with a broken leg. So it was not totally beyond the scope of reality. I could further see in my mind's eye that Gibson had survived and had slept on the wing. As time progressed and he became weaker from the elements, he realized that he was not going to make it; he wrote a note to his Mum and Dad, or maybe his wife and son Tony. He then buried it and placed the pen on top of it to mark the spot.

Sunday morning did not arrive a bit too soon, and I was the first to return to the site. I went directly to the wing. Anxiously, I dug under where the pen had been to find the note, but to my disappointment, it had only existed in my imagination. Later, the wing was flipped over and the entire area was scanned with a metal detector, which did not reveal anything significant. What a discovery it would have been had we found a note! Real life does not always have such endings.

The rest of the workers soon arrived at the site, and we began to practice the scraping/digging method we would be using to excavate the ground. Our training was hampered by a bit of rain which finally passed about one hour later. We proceeded, in the mud, using pointed cement trowels to scrape the ground down to an old layer of dirt that was harder and of a different color than was the top soil. To reach that layer, it required digging to a depth of between five to 30 centimeters (two to 12 inches), depending upon the location. That variant depth was due to the fact that the wreckage site was on a hillside, and that made it natural for the many years of rain to gradually wash the topsoil away. Accordingly, we were instructed to start digging in the lower grid and work our way up the slope.

While our band of amateur archaeologists dug and scraped, others looked around the wreckage. As a section of the fuselage was lifted, right there, just inside the folded aluminum, was a .38 caliber revolver. It was rusty and fragile, but it was a meaningful artifact! Research has led me to believe that the revolver was a Smith and Wesson Military and Police model with a 100-millimeter (four-inch) barrel developed from the Smith & Wesson .38 Hand Ejector Model of 1889. It had a swing-out cylinder for loading the cartridges and a lanyard loop at the bottom of the grip frame. An interesting note is that a debate surrounded this model as to how much stopping power a .38 caliber cartridge could effect.

The Thompson-LaGarde Commission of 1904 was assigned to test hand guns to settle the disagreement. After they had tested various rounds on live cattle, the commission concluded that the .45 was "the best bet for a combat handgun."[68] As a result of the commission's findings, this model chambered the .38 S&W Special cartridges that had an increased powder charge from 18 to 21 grams of black powder. Later on, the model became known as the Smith and Wesson Model 10, and there have been 6,000,000 of this type produced over the years making it the most popular revolver of the 20th century.[69]

While some or our team was digging in an inner grid area, a couple officers scoured in and around the outside perimeter with a metal detector. They found the port side propeller approximately nine meters (30 feet) in front of the engine and buried totally beneath 15 centimeters (six inches) of earth.

At approximately 8:30 A.M., the RAAF photographer, John Carroll, said he had found a denture. It was located in the area between the engines which we assumed to be near where we estimated the cockpit would have impacted. Everyone stopped to look at the upper denture with two false teeth still attached. The RAAF odontologist, Dr. Alain Middleton, had brought with him copies of the forensic records for each of the crew. Those records revealed that Sgt. Quail was the only crew member to have had dentures. This was the first indication that airmen had been killed at the site. John Cotterell requested that I provide a prayer of condolence for the crew, which I respectfully did.

That find encouraged us all to dig more solemnly, and a little over one hour later, two dog tags were recovered with the name of the pilot, G.I Gibson, stamped on them. That led me to conclude that Gibson had not survived the crash and could not have slept on the wing. It was still strange, that his pen had flown at least 12 meters (40 feet), and the wing had landed on top of it.

As the day wore on, a coin was found, a wristwatch, another coin and another revolver. Gavin discovered a pocket watch and small pocketknife in the rear fuselage. I dug up a handful of bullets stamped REM-UMC 38 S&W. The .38 caliber bullets were made by Remington Arms-Union Metallic Cartridge Company.[70] Other members of the team, including Mark "Frenchy" French found many harness buckles and other paraphernalia from the airplane. After lunch time, about 1:00 P.M., there was still more excitement as Gavin, who seemingly found something wherever he looked, unearthed the dog tags of B I Coutie, service number 405543, under the ball turret. The dog tags revealed he was of the Presbyterian faith.

Interestingly, about one-and-a-half meters (five feet) away were pieces of leather from soft-toed boots. Could this be where the body lay, or did it lie in the fuselage where the pocket watch and knife were found? When the fuselage was rolled away for continued excavation, another revolver was found. It was also corroded and fragile from having been buried in the ground. All of those things, along with many other artifacts, were found on just the first day of digging! It was exciting to find artifacts since they convinced us that we were on a successful run and made us more attentive as we dug, knowing that at any moment we might unearth our reason for being here, namely, human remains.

On Monday, after a cool night with no rain, we began the digging process promptly at 6:30 A.M. The day's efforts brought fewer artifacts to light, but we did recover, along with many pieces of strapping buckles, two four-point harness buckles, three deteriorated leather boot toe sections, one boot heel and various leather boot fragments. A watch was found with a date stamped on the back. The date read: 16-8-32. That date coincided with the 20th birthday date of P.O. Frank Thorn, and it was assumed to be his. Shortly afterwards, a RAAF ring was discovered.

Tuesday's recoveries were even less eventful, with only the recovering of more coins, another knife and a plastic comb which may not have been from the missing crew. In addition, I counted over 400 expended bullet casings from the ball turret dated 1937. I remembered that one of the bullet-feed boxes still had quite a few bullets in it until "Rambo" removed them on our second trip to the site. That made me wonder if one of the twin-mounted machine guns had jammed, and I speculated that the turret gunner, Bill Coutie, may have run out of bullets on one of his guns while the other one malfunctioned.

In total, we found six 7.7-millimeter (.303-inch) machine guns which included: two in the ball turret, one in an engine cowl (one engine cowl gun was buried with the engine), one gun that fit into the retractable belly pod and a Lewis machine gun with a round magazine that was mounted on the top. Two extra magazines for the Lewis machine gun were also found with the bullets still in them. The local helpers had their eyes on them. Those also made me wonder why there were so many bullets left in that Lewis machine gun. Had the other gunner been hit early in the air battle and was unable to shoot at the approaching enemy?

There were many times, as we were digging, that we found things that appeared to have been bone fragments or were at least of a questionable nature. Whatever they were, these items were quite different from tree sticks or rock or corroded aluminum. We passed those fragments to the pathologist, Dr. Allan Cala, who along with the odontologist, Dr. Alain Middleton, examined them closely. Apparently, none of those fragments were deemed to have been human remains, since after the two had a discussion over the pieces, they were tossed outside of the grid area. I personally felt that those items should have been collected in a bag or container for future cleaning and examination by scientific equipment which is more reliable than the naked eye. But I had not been trained to recognize old bone fragments as these two very experienced Doctors had. To a layman like me, many of the aircraft parts looked like potential bones.

Once we found Sgt. Coutie's dog tags under the fuselage and eventually rolled the fuselage out of the way, I used sifting pans along with the locals to sift as we dug. I felt that even if no bones had survived the wet, damp ground, surely teeth would have remained. We tediously sifted for about an hour, which is a rather slow process as the sifters we were using had fine mesh screens similar to mosquito netting. The locals soon tired of the effort and put their sifters down.

Although we did not perform a great deal of sifting, our method of scraping and the keen eyes of the PNG amateur archaeologists revealed many minute things, even as small as a safety pin. It was disappointing that we found no obvious human remains. That was my first excavation, so I had nothing to compare our efforts to, but it seems that had we sifted more, we might have found some teeth or other artifacts. The ground was fairly soft and wet, so even with my limited knowledge and experience, I would have to say that the bones had likely deteriorated over the 66 years from being exposed to the elements or possibly had been carried away by wild animals. Because of the overwhelming evidence of a near straight-down crash, revealed by, among other things, the engines buried halfway down into the ground, survival would have been next to impossible. Furthermore, personal items from each crew member were found in close proximity, mainly in two grid sections with a total area of 500 square meters (546 square yards).

It was interesting to note that the fellow from the museum, John, had found several rounded metal fragments, which appeared to have been a helmet-shaped item, outside the search area near the base of a tree. A quick metal detector search was conducted, but no signal was heard so there was no digging. I wondered if it was possible that a survivor sat there while wearing his helmet. Had airmen even worn helmets at that time? I recalled that we had only found three revolvers, and we mused that the fourth must have remained there somewhere. It at least made one ponder the possibility.

During the recovery effort, on a couple of occasions, it started pouring rain, and we were forced to take cover under a tarp. It usually became uncomfortably muddy, and as a result, we were reluctant to start digging again, but the Air Force team was keen to keep moving ahead as they wanted to get the job completed ASAP! Camping in the middle of the jungle, even with all our equipment, did lack some creature comforts. We were fortunate to have found a stream close to our camp site where we could bath after a day of digging in the mud.

By Tuesday afternoon, after not finding much in the way of artifacts and no human remains were uncovered, we were instructed to go back over a couple areas that had previously been excavated, where the pilot's dog tags had been found. Some locals started excavating while I commandeered a few workers and decided to dig up the propeller that was buried about 15 centimeters (six inches) down. It was reasonably heavy and required five of us to lift it up out of the ground. We stood it upright, and propped it up with a stick – we propped the "prop" (pun intended!).

We dug for three full days, during which we were able to find personal items connected to each crew member. For some reason, I felt, perhaps wrongly, that after finding the personal items, the RAAF did not actually want to find human remains. I developed that perception because during the recovery effort, it was mentioned to me that they estimated the entire operation had cost over PNG K125,000 (US $51,250). That amount was conceivable, as the helicopter hire alone was PNG K6,000 (US $2,460) per hour, and I did charge them for the petrol I had burned using my boat.

But the overall cost of the exercise was not an issue. The emotive issue for the Air Force team was that they wanted to find either all of the remains or none of them. They desired that the four airmen stay together, rather than be apart.[71] We did find many personal items, and it was clear that an honorable crew had died there on that day in service to their country, and maybe that was all that needed to be confirmed. I have remained grateful to have been included in the operation, and I felt privileged to have been part of the recovery team.

In addition to digging, we cut out an approximate 46-by-122 centimeter (18 by 48 inch) section of the fuselage that had the serial number A16-126 on it. A more accurate description was that we hacked it out because we had no tin snips or other such proper cutting tools; we used a machete and repeatedly hammered on it with an ax. We noted soberly that this section of aluminum also had a bullet hole in it. That fuselage piece was specifically sent to the RAAF Museum in Melbourne, Australia, so that paint samples could be taken. In the event that they rebuild a Hudson aircraft sometime in the future, the correct paint mixture/type could be used.[72]

That Tuesday afternoon, when the operation was officially completed, we took a group photograph with that piece of aluminum in front of us. I was honored when I was asked again to say a prayer, so we stood in a circle around the area where the cockpit would have impacted. It was also the spot where most of the artifacts had been discovered. I prayed in English, then again in Melanesian Pidgin (Tok Pisin) for the benefit of our local workers. I prayed that even though we had not found human remains, our Heavenly Father knew the location of the crew's spirits.

We had completed the operation to the best of our ability and to the satisfaction of the RAAF, so we broke camp on Wednesday morning, October 8, 2008. John, from the Port Moresby museum, was given the belly pod machine gun to take back to the museum for display. John had confided with me that oftentimes the museum employees were propositioned with offers of "thousands of kina" (hundreds of US dollars) for museum items to be used in private collections.

The PNG workers were paid exceptionally well for their labor and given the leftover packets of food rations (Meals Ready to Eat = MREs) and the metal containers the MREs had been transported in. I actually enjoyed eating those MREs and was glad to receive a few packets myself. They seemed greatly appreciative, and we were extremely thankful they had assisted us. As they began their hike, the helicopter landed at approximately 7:00 A.M. and began the first of four exit shuttles. I boarded the last flight, but before my departure, I returned to the crash site one last time, and fighting back tears, I said my final goodbyes to the crew of Hudson A16-126. I knew each one by name. We had, in some strange way, become mates. The flight back to Kandrian was somber as I reflected on all that I had experienced regarding the crew of the missing Australian bomber.

The whole experience was particularly memorable and emotional. It was an experience of a lifetime. I only regret that no human remains were found, but I know it would have been a circumstantial impossibility. That regret was at least partially based on the knowledge that if human remains had been found, they would have to be buried in Bita Paka War Cemetery in Rabaul. The Australian government would have flown me, as well as all the family members, there to attend the interment. I had strongly hoped to meet the families of the crew at just such a funeral.

RAAF EPILOGUE

The planning and the recommendations formulated from Operation KOVI MOSES shaped the foundation for the plan of the Australian Defense Force's July of 2009 search and recovery for the final two personnel listed as missing from the Vietnam conflict. The lessons learned from Operation KOVI MOSES ensured that the Royal Australian Air Force was prepared, ready and able to undertake and successfully close a significant chapter in Australia's military history in Vietnam.[73]

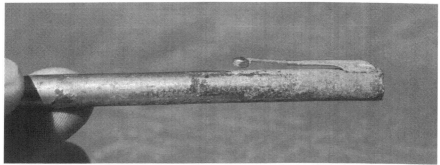

Inscribed pen of F/O Graham Gibson from wreckage of Hudson A16-126.

Watches from wreckage of Hudson A16-126.

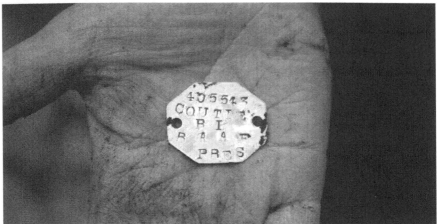

Dog tag of Sgt. Barton Irving Coutie from wreckage of Hudson A16-126.

RAAF ring from wreckage of Hudson A16-126.

Sqn. Ldr. John Cotterell at wreckage of Hudson A16-126.

John Lelai with S&W pistol from wreckage of Hudson A16-126.

Sqn. Ldrs. Alain Middleton and Alan Cala with propeller of Hudson A16-126.

Remains recovery team of Hudson A16-126.

CHAPTER 35

THE FINAL FLIGHT

I have often pondered scenarios that could explain the wreckage evidence we had found of Hudson A16-126. A thorough investigation of the rear fuselage revealed a half-dozen bullet holes at the end of the tail section. There were also bullet holes on the side of the fuselage. Although there were two engines half-buried into the ground, we never did locate the two wings. The one wing we did discover was from the port side, and it was in two pieces. The Hudsons could fly on one engine but *not with only one wing*! I also observed that in the bulkhead, directly under where the ball turret gunner would have sat, were about 20 holes in a small cluster. The oddity of that was that those holes were actually fired from a gun *inside* the airplane. The ventral gun would have been pointing right at that spot if the belly pod was up, but I could not find any exit holes.

Another mystery was that of the belly pod (ventral position called an "A Tunnel" in the manual) that had a Browning machine gun mounted in it. On the retractable belly pod, there was a track in the middle into which the machine gun fit, enabling it to slide from front to back and front again. Once the pod was manually lowered by winding the operating handle fitted on the starboard side of the cabin, the gun would be slid to the end with the barrel projecting out of the pod and toward the rear of the airplane giving them defense from the rear and downward. The confusing issue was that the belly pod track had no sign that the machine gun had been mounted in it. The track was not bent in any way which would have been necessary to allow the gun to come out of the track due to a sudden impact.

With the belly pod (ventral position) extended, that would have slowed the airplane down some, and possibly to approximately 148 kts (170 mph) which was the maximum speed for dropping flares or while the undercarriage was down. Since they had attempted to escape from fighter aircraft, they no doubt needed all the speed they could muster. I assumed that after the bomb run on the ships, the belly pod could have been cranked up to allow the aircraft to reach its maximum limitation speed of 291 kts (334 mph), although high speed rate at sea level was only approximately 213 kts (245 mph).[74] After a close examination of photographs of the wreckage, more specifically, the mechanism for lowering the belly pod, it was determined that the belly pod was indeed in the extended position before the crash. The Japanese fighters had a maximum speed of 237 kts (272 mph), so with the belly pod lowered, the Hudson would likely have been flying slower than the attacking aircraft.

In Book Two of *The RAAF Hudson Story,* by David Vincent, is the account by Sgt. Fred Thies, the gunner in A16-103. This was the third aircraft that got away; it was piloted by "Pedro" Pedrina in the attack on February 11, 1942, when A16-91 and A16-126 crashed. Thies was lying in the belly pod while it was extended. This was his account:

> The plan was to go in at mast height. Weather was fine – on the way over we tested our guns and one felt very vulnerable in my belly gun position. The visibility was very limited and the one hope was that we would surprise them and get in and out quickly.
>
> I could not see the other kites as we started the dive – saw some smaller craft – started firing – flew right above one transport and saw hits on deck and fire started – think they had drums (of) petrol on deck – all over very fast – Pedro (the pilot) kept right down to tree tops – heard Morrison firing from turret and engines flat out – back to Moresby – waited for news of other two kites but eventually realized that (they) had gone in.[75]

In David Vincent's book, on page 204, is an account of a Japanese Zero that attacked a Hudson. That account was written by Saburo Sakai, as recorded in his book, *Samurai*. The air battle was fought on July 22, 1942, in the Buna-Gona area on the mainland of PNG, and it occurred only about five months after A16-126 had been downed. It involved the Hudson A16-201 piloted by Pilot Officer Warren Cowan. The circumstances were similar, but there were six or more Zeros involved. In successive attempts, none of the Zeros scored hits on the Hudson as it was thrown around in the sky taking evasive action, with the turret gunner returning fire all the time. In individual passes against the Hudson (Sakai had made at least four), the combination of the speed, maneuverability and firepower of the fighters meant that the Hudson crew had little chance of escaping their attackers. The fighters pursued the Hudson for nearly ten minutes, but once the turret gun had been silenced, the aircraft was defenseless from the rear. Here is what Sakai wrote after the turret gun stopped firing:

> He closed in to 20 yards and held the gun trigger down, aiming for the right wing. Seconds later flames streamed out, then spread to the left wing. The pilot stayed with the ship; it was too low for him or the crew to bail out. The Hudson lost speed rapidly and glided in towards the jungle. Trees sheared off the two flaming wings and the fuselage, also trailing great sheets of flame, burst into the dense growth like a giant sliver of burning steel. There was a sudden explosion, and smoke boiled upward.

A combination of the evidence and Sakai's account brought me to this hypothesis. I assumed that the crew of A16-126, like A16-103, had tested their guns prior to the bombing run. But it was possible that the belly gun (ventral position) had malfunctioned and inadvertently fired before the pod was lowered leaving about 20 holes in the inner bulkhead. The gun was probably removed from the track that held it. As the airplane neared Gasmata, the aircraft decreased airspeed and the belly pod was lowered. While they aligned themselves with their target, and as they were diving, four Claude fighters attacked the Hudsons. The most vulnerable angle of attack would have been from the side and underneath. Sgt. Quail may have positioned himself to the side window and manned the Lewis machine gun. He may have been wounded, perhaps fatally, and ceased firing; that might have explained why there was plenty of ammunition left in the magazine as well as two other completely full magazines. The airplane continued its attack on the transport ship and made a direct hit. After he cleared the harbor, the pilot, Ian Gibson, navigated straight ahead for maximum speed, probably keeping close to the tree tops as they headed north-northwest. He may have been seeking cover in the clouds over the mountains. Unfortunately, the belly pod was still in the down position which hindered the aircraft from reaching its maximum airspeed as they were pursued by three enemy fighters. In that circumstance, they were unable to outrun the Claude fighters.

There were plenty of bullets remaining in one of the two bullet feed boxes for the twin ball turret guns, while the other box was empty. That fact made me assume that, in the last minutes of the battle, Sgt. Bill Coutie, sitting in the ball turret firing at the enemy airplanes, was only able to use one gun, as the other had probably jammed, leaving bullets in the box. In addition, he was only able to fire at an enemy airplane which approached from level or from above his aircraft. He would probably not have been able to fire at an enemy which approached from below. But he could swivel to each side. Nonetheless, he fired over 400 rounds and may have downed one enemy aircraft. When he had depleted his ammunition on the operating gun and/or suffered a wound himself, he would have stopped firing, and the Claude pilots realized they were able to close in on him unopposed.

I also believe that the pilot, Ian Gibson, was possibly fatally wounded. That reasoning arose as I concluded that the wreckage had nose-dived into the ground. That was also the way Hudson A16-91 had crashed *after* the pilot, John Lerew, had bailed out. I remembered Lerew's account when he had tried to squeeze out of the window. The aircraft went into a dive, so he had to push back on the wheel with his foot to level it out. The wreckage of A16-165 also had nose dived into the ground, and there are reports that the pilot, Ken Erwin, had *bailed out* and was later found near the wreckage with a broken leg. He was captured, interrogated, and then executed. His remains were later found in a lagoon by the Gasmata airstrip. The wreckage of A16-101 was scattered over a large area, so I assumed it had slid across the reef or it had exploded in the air. The Japanese pilot, Sakai, mentioned that the Hudson glided in, and that caused me to assume that the pilot, P/O Cowan, was still alive at the controls when the aircraft crashed into the trees. So, my theory is that once the pilot was wounded or had bailed out, and no one was manning the controls, the airplane crashed in a nose dive.

Other scenarios could have been that the outer starboard wing was blown off. With only one wing remaining, the aircraft would have entered into a fatal nose dive. Or, some action may have ignited a fire and the pilot attempted to escape the airplane as it nose dived uncontrollably.

Because Gibson's and Quail's personal effects were found in the same area, it implies they were together up front in the aircraft. When the airplane impacted, the rear section severed behind the wings and eventually fell to the ground, about 12 meters (40 feet) away. Thorn's wrist watch, with his 20th birthday date on the back, was found midway between the nose section and the tail section, so he may have been operating a machine gun or trying to send a message on the radio in the midsection of the bomber. Bill Coutie may have been strapped into his gunner seat so his body stayed with the tail section. His dog tags were found under the ball turret. This speculation has been based upon my perception after much consideration as to how the air battle might have occurred.

THE MEMORIAL BOXES

We returned to Kandrian, and Thursday we rested. Then, on Friday, we proceeded to Gasmata by boat to recheck the Hudson in the water. We incurred some engine troubles, so it was a slow trip, but we did spend about one-and-a-half hours at the site.

Jared and I did conduct a dive on the wing in 12 meters (20 feet) of water and found a data plate, but it was so fragile it disintegrated when we tried to remove it. We had also failed to take a photograph beforehand, which in hindsight left us feeling rather inept. I did give the data plate I had previously removed from the exhaust pipe to the Sqn. Ldr. so that he could try to trace it back and identify the airplane. Previously, Rundle had also removed a data plate in 1946, so with the two pieces of evidence, they might be able to determine if that was the missing A16-101. Someone even suggested that the Royal Australian Navy could go there and make an attempt at identifying the airplane – that remained to be seen.

After the RAAF returned to Australia, wooden memorial boxes were prepared with glass tops. Inside, were carefully placed medals, coins, and buckles from the airplane, as well as the personal effects of each crewman. Each piece was arranged in an orderly fashion. The boxes were then presented to the four families as memorials to their crewmen. Sqn. Ldr. John Cotterell, Flt. Lt. Mark French and Flt. Lt. Justin Cox had the honor of delivering them. Coincidentally, they learned that John Cotterell's grandfather, Jack Gardiner, had played cricket at State level in Australia against Frank Thorn who had perished on the airplane. One can image John's surprise after hearing that news. Sgt. Frank Thorn's family provided an Air Force photo of Frank wearing an RAAF ring, so the ring that had been found was returned to his family.

One could only imagine the impact the memorial boxes would have had on the families to finally have something of their loved ones and to hear a final report of what had happened to the crew. The officers spent a few hours with each of the families showing them videos and pictures of the recovery effort. The note, below, represents some of the responses from the families.

Dear John and Justin,

I am writing to you on behalf of Dora Dance & family. (The sister of Bill Coutie) Thank you for the presentation on Wednesday of the results of your explorations of the crash site of Bill Coutie. I think everybody appreciated the obvious efforts you went to to recover the artifacts from the site and the sensitivity which you brought to bear whilst doing so. The story you told was fascinating, illuminating, and sure brought a feeling of closure for those who actually knew Bill when he was alive.

We also wish to thank Mark Reichman for his explorations in finding the wreck and the others involved in the subsequent expeditions.

We are sure the medals and artifacts will remain in a place of pride in the Coutie households for years to come.

Dr. Sandy Dance

By way of explanation, Dr. Sandy Dance was Dora Dance's (maiden name – Coutie) son. Dora was Bill Coutie's sister, making Dr. Dance the deceased Barton (Bill) Irving Coutie's nephew. Dr. Sandy Dance did not sign with his full name, which is Dr. George "Barton" Dance. He too was named after his Uncle Bill Coutie. Dr. Dance was nicknamed "Sandy" because of his blonde hair during his younger years. Sgt. Barton Irving Coutie may have died young (23 years old), but his memory has traveled fairly well.[76]

James Forrester also wrote:

Hi John,

I can only give you a 9.5 out of 10 for all your and the

RAAF's efforts, to give higher would not leave any room for improvement. I cannot thank you and your staff enough for the treatment, kindness and absolute patience extended to myself and the rest of the family. Your little surprises were very big deals to us.

Regards and many thanks, James Forrester

I had always thought that once I had found an airplane with an identified MIA, that that would be the icing on the cake and it would serve as a climax for the finish of the book I had talked about writing for so many years. But the experience of helping families to find closure was personally rewarding in many ways. I now truly believed that there were families longing for closure. I personally knew of several sites that were yet to be explored, including one on which the airplane was "teetering on its wings over a large hole …."

Motivated by this belief, I persisted with my searching, and, working off the lead I had received from Leo, who claimed to have seen this "teetering airplane" in 1994. I went to the village of Akam, East of Gasmata, and began to inquire. The village was quite empty, but people slowly gathered as I explained the reason for my visit and what I wanted to accomplish. A lady passed by and said that her husband had seen it, but he was not here now. Another man said that someone he knew had seen it, but he was not present either. After they deliberated among themselves, they said that they would go look for it and send a message to me once they had found it. That message never arrived before I moved away from PNG in May of 2009.

Dorsel turret w/machine gun from wreckage of Hudson A16-126.

Mr. Tony Gibson, Mrs. Roy Eyres, Sqn. Ldr. John Cotterell, Flt. Lt. Mark French

Memorial Award for Sgt. Barton "Bill" Coutie.

Chapter 36

CAVES AND BONES

As I continued to search for crash sites, I made various connections. One of those acquaintances was with a Japanese historian. He became my e-mail friend. He has been passionate about finding lost soldiers and had heard about six Japanese remains that had never been properly recovered. Since those remains were purportedly in the area where I was living, he contacted me and asked if I would assist him by investigating the rumors. Coincidentally, I had in my possession an eyewitness account of the battle in the Arawes by L. Bell of the RAAF, in which he mentioned the cave on Pililo Island where a skirmish took place between the Japanese and American soldiers. What follows is the text of his report:

It wasn't long before the barge was headed to the nearby coral island of Pililo where I thought Captain Laird would be waiting for us after having cleared out the Japanese. James and I were walking towards an old storage shed that had been built by Catholic missionaries at Mission Beach landing when the crack of a rifle rang out, followed by a series of revolver shots. There was shouting in both Japanese and American voices.

Laird and his party were coming down the track in the cliff; Mexican scout, Little Willy, was ahead. As they turned to walk behind the storage shed a sniper's bullet killed Willy. A Japanese, left to guard the shed had made a foxhole for himself and was probably as surprised to see Willy as we all were at his presence.

In front of the shed I was yelling my head off, calling to Laird to keep his men from shooting our way. They could just as easily have mistaken us for Japanese. Then we followed a trench along the cliff which brought us to the main Japanese foxhole. That's when the battle between the Japanese and Captain Laird's B Company really began.

The enemy had dug a deep cave in the cliff and barricaded the entrance with sandbags and coconut logs. They were firing at anything that moved but it was almost impossible for us to see anything over the barricade. The top was packed with sandbags and only a rifle and the top of a head were momentarily visible when a shot was fired. There was little show of American bullets finding their mark.

As the battle raged, LAC James and I were checking out what was in the shed. There were several 20-kilogram bags of rice packed in rubber waterproof sacks along with packets of dried shrimps and fish. This and local foods made up Japanese rations. I told James not to let anyone touch those supplies and I went back to where the fighting was still going on. Captain Laird and his men were bogged down. A flamethrower was brought up and it stopped the enemy for a while. An American then crawled along the front of the cave and threw a grenade. Unfortunately it hit the top of the coconut logs and burst outside. Finally they brought in a bazooka which demolished the centre coconut log of the protecting line.

Captain Laird's sergeant and I were first into the cave. The Japanese commander had been hit in the chin by a ricocheting bullet. The others, with their rifles were lying on the sloping sandbank, faces buried. It was as though they were hiding their faces. 'They might be playing possum', I said to the sergeant. 'You start one end and I'll start the other'. Whether they were already dead or our bullets killed them I will never know. We had to be sure. We searched the bodies for anything that might be of interest to Intelligence.

With that report in hand, Jared and I went to Pililo and talked with the locals about that skirmish. We sat in the cave with a few men in their twenties as I read the account by L. Bell. It really came to life as we could look out and see exactly where the shed was that was mentioned in the story. A shed was still there! We clearly visualized the entire battle to the end and realized that we were sitting in the exact spot where soldiers had been shot.

One of the men informed me that while he was digging post holes for his house he had dug up some bones. We then went to his house and dug down about two feet; we found a pelvis and some upper leg bones. Could those have been the Japanese soldiers from the cave? As we were digging, an older man came by and told us that the bones were from a woman they had buried years ago. We then carefully placed the bones into a plastic bag and respectfully reburied them.

I later received a message from my friend that he had received word from the Department of Defense that six remains were recovered from Pililo Island on October 9, 1970. That set him at ease, for the time being, although he was somewhat upset that that report had never been properly circulated.

HEAD TO HEAD WITH *SAN ANTONIO ROSE*

We were still very interested in the B-17 named *San Antonio Rose* (SAR). To some, it was the holy grail of lost aircraft, from which Brigadier General Kenneth Walker had disappeared. E-mails with his son, Douglas Walker, and other researchers had been ongoing for quite awhile. I acquired nearly 500 messages in my in folder which related to the missing B-17. An entire book could be written just on the correspondence that flew around about that aircraft. Since the airplane was declared missing, many years have been spent trying to determine the location where it went down. An article by Michael John Claringbould and a book, *Kenneth N. Walker: Airpower's Untempered Crusader,* by Martha Byrd have been written, but no one had yet gone on the ground in the jungle to ask the PNG locals what they knew about it. In my opinion, regardless of which theory had the most speculation, it was time to get started on the groundwork. The area I believed the wreckage to be was quite a distance from where I lived and funds were limited so it was not possible for me to go there and ask villagers what they knew of the missing aircraft. Contacting a philanthropist, or starting a website where people could donate was considered, but those ideas never came to fruition.

Because of my past experience, I believed that the locals had seen the wreckage, or they knew something of the story. That seemed particularly plausible, since two men were reportedly taken captive after they had parachuted from the airplane. One man received care for 20 days by the natives before he tried to make his way to the coast where, in the end, he was captured. I felt that certainly someone (or many) knew that story, because in an oral culture, stories would have been told over and over again. It might be a story about how a white man had fallen from the sky from a warplane and had lived with their people.

Since I had offered assistance to my Japanese friend, I felt justified to ask him for a favor, so I mentioned to him the needs I had as I planned the search for the *SAR*. He politely, and with zeal, began investigating Japanese archives, newspaper articles, interrogation reports and even pilot diaries. He was an excellent source of information and a tremendous help, and he found, in the archives, two reports from Japanese pilots who were involved in the air battle against the B-17s on Jan 5, 1943. That was the day Douglas Walker's father went missing. One report, which I noted in chapter 11, focused on the location of the airplanes while the Japanese fighters attacked them. From research at the National Institute of Defense Studies in Tokyo came the following account from a Japanese fighter pilot. It is this pilot who I believe was directly involved in the shooting down of the *SAR*.

...On 5 January (1943), while (I was) in air patrol at the altitude of 4,000 meters in the sky over Rabaul, B-17 and B-24, a dozen of them in all, raided, bombing ships in the harbor. On this occasion, we caught, at about 3,000 meters, one B-17 on home-bound flight, falling behind the rest in formation. Led by Miyabayashi Taichyo (leader or commander), at appropriate intervals, we successively delivered concentrated attack on the B-17 from forward and up. Shishimoto's plane, belonging to the second Hentai (unit), determined not to let the opportunity slip away, caught the plane in the gun sight from about 1,000 meters from forward and up, as had been trained. At that time, one of the engines of the B-17 had already been shot, stopping the propeller. This is the chance!," jubilant, I dashed, delivering concentrated fire aimed at the cockpit starting at about 500 meters from the plane. By the skin of the teeth, we avoided crashing at each other. Disengaging, I turned and saw the plane flying as before. Soon, I saw the plane gradually losing altitude, with black smoke trailing. Probably the plane would not be able to make it back to base. One after another, friendly planes kept attacking the enemy. It could go down soon. Suddenly, I somehow felt and pitiful for the enemy pilot who must have been seriously injured. In the air above, Miyabayashi Chutaicho was signaling us to assemble. Time to assemble! I later heard that the results by the 11th Sentai for the day were two B-17 shot down and two B-24 shot down with one uncertain.[77]

That report of American airplanes shot down did not match with what the Americans had reported; they noted that there were only two B-17s that had failed to return to their base; *SAR* and another one with the Serial Number: 41-24538.[78] By all accounts, it was severely damaged. The ball turret had been shot out, one engine had failed, and it leaked fuel from the wing. Thus, the pilot chose to ditch in Milne Bay with no loss of crew. The Japanese would not have witnessed those events, so their report of two B-17s having been shot down may have been based upon their observation that one had gone down and they had inflicted major damage on another. They must have felt that they had damaged a couple of B-24s, so they claimed that another aircraft had been shot down as well.

To the date of this writing, and as far as I was able to ascertain (although JPAC personnel had told me they were aware of it), no person or government agency has ever searched for the *San Antonio Rose* other than a couple days after it initially went missing. Had I had about US $3,000 for expenses, I believe I could have solved the SAR mystery or at least gleaned some information that might have been useful to its discovery. To fly back now and begin a search would cost at least four or five times that amount so I feel we have missed an opportunity but hopefully there will be more.

David Billings, who had diligently been looking for Amelia Earhart's airplane in Wide Bay (even though some believe he is way off track), said that he had spoken with a gentleman who told him of his sighting a large and a small airplane. Could it have been SAR and the Japanese airplane that did not return to its base?

Author/Historian Bruce Petty stirred up some commotion among fellow historians after he read *East Wind, Rain*, by Brig. Gen. Elliot R. Thorpe, published in 1969. Thorp had spent the war in PNG and the Philippines. He was an intelligence officer under Gen. MacArthur. In his book he talks about not only U.S. intelligence efforts, but also Japanese. On page 144 he writes that, "...when an air corps general was lost over Rabaul, it was determined from captured documents that he had not been killed in the air, but had been murdered by the Japanese after his interrogation." Was that source documentation available? Was this referring to Walker? We may never know.

Cave at Pililo Island. WNBP, PNG

Remains at Pililo Island. WNBP, PNG

Chapter 37

FOREVER LOST

We discovered that we were unable to stop looking for airplanes even though our time was limited; we were scheduled to leave PNG in May of 2009. There was little time to waste (and fortunately our missionaries in Gasmata needed supplies), so in February of 2009, we returned to Gasmata. We fully intended to find that airplane "20 yards from the tip of Umbo Island at the mouth of the Logom River," as stated in Rundle's report to the Americans and supposedly witnessed by a local man as he sat in his canoe. We picked up our guide and proceeded to the site. On the way, I asked the guide where the Logom River was located. To my confusion, he said it was the river on the west side of Umbo Island. That was not what the map had shown or what some of the locals had said. I repeated the question; he was an older man, so I felt that he certainly knew the rivers' names. Again he said the Logom River was on the west side of the island. So instead of going to the east side of Umbo Island, which also has a river on the mainland that exits there, we went to the west side of Umbo.

Rundle's report had indicated that something "appeared to be an airplane 50 yards NE of Umbo Island and 25 yards from the mainland and in 20 feet of water." Once those coordinates were located on the west side of the island, they began to make sense. But it was not 50 yards NE of Umbo, but rather, NW. That confusion in the information called for a further examination to determine, with precision, exactly what he had recorded. The west side of the island where I found myself on this trip actually fit the description better. I also had to assume that the map was wrong regarding the name of the river, at least according to my guide. I was initially confused, but this revised location, other than the discrepancy which indicated a position *NE* of Umbo, was more feasible. Had he said *NW* of Umbo, all would have been better understood.

So we drove the boat back and forth making a grid pattern of the entire area at the mouth of the river. As we motored slowly, we watched the depth sounder, and on each pass, when I saw something sticking up from the bottom, I made a mark on the GPS. As we covered the entire area, there were two areas that had at least 20 marks in them. One area was approximately 18 meters (20 yards) from the tip of Umbo and in about 12 meters (40 feet) of water, the way it had appeared in Rundle's report to the Americans. The other area that had many marks was the first location Rundle had reported, although the water was a bit deeper; it was 11 meters (37 feet) instead of Rundle's reported six meters (20 feet).

We anchored the boat on the edge of the marks according to the GPS. The plan was to swim in a grid pattern while skimming the bottom. We descended closer to the mainland, to begin our search, and as it had been at other times, the water was murky near the bottom. We came prepared with a tether line five feet long, and we still could not see each other even from that distance under the water surface. In order to overcome that situation, I held on to Jared's belt buckle as he navigated with the compass, and I counted flipper strokes as we moved along. We swam 100 strokes, then turned 90 degrees and swam ten strokes, then turned another 90 degrees and swam 100 strokes. We did that for seven long passes. As we swam along, we were just skimming the bottom, but we were unable to see anything. Even Jared's lime green snorkel was difficult to see, and we were touching shoulders!

It was no exaggeration to say that it was uncomfortably scary to dive like that, but we endured it and we tried to stay focused on our system. Our minds did wander a couple of times, because we knew that saltwater crocs have been known to inhabit the area. I had hoped that, if they were around, they could not see us in the murky water. I did not know with any certainty how their vision compared to ours, but they do have pretty big eyes and they do thrash around in mud. I tried not to think about how they might have seen us if they had been in that area! Yikes! I had expected to run into something, but we came up empty again. The bottom was flat and silty from river deposits. It was the same, soft, gooey mud covering the bottom that we had previously encountered in other areas.

We surfaced, and our guide said that he could see where we had been by following our air bubbles. I wanted to make another grid to abut this first one, so we dived down again. On this dive we made nine long passes and were in deeper water, up to 17 meters (57 feet). Still, we saw nothing sticking up from the bottom other than some flower-like plants. They were white and stood about a foot high; it was quite scary when they suddenly appeared!

After our second dive, I found it necessary to run the boat over the area again to see what the depth sounder was revealing. I went back over the GPS marks and, sure enough, there was a reading that indicated something was sticking up sometimes as high as seven feet above the bottom level, while the bottom depth indicated it never changed. I considered that truly perplexing. We moved to the other location where my depth sounder had shown something, and we repeated our procedure in making the grid. Again, there was something there, although we now knew the bottom to be flat in both areas. It seemed that this discovery would have to wait for another time.

On the next day, we attempted to find a guide to take us to the airplane which seemed to be "teetering on its wings." A guide was not to be found, so we went to the village close to where Leo said he had seen it, and I had had a meeting with at least 30 men. When we told them about the rumor of the airplane seen tittering on a cliff, all of them became interested, but none of them had ever seen it. After a long discussion, it was decided that they would make contact with the guy who claimed to have seen it and go find it with him at a later date. They stated that if they were unable to locate him, they had a general idea as to the location of the aircraft and they would take it upon themselves to conduct a search.

I was skeptical that they would do it by themselves, but they seemed genuinely eager, for some reason, to find this airplane. Maybe they were merely humoring me. It was supposedly in an area they would not normally pass through. I was not surprised that I never heard from them again.

We departed from the village, and I told my son that I *had* to dive the area we originally had set out to investigate. It was necessary that I get it out of my system, or it, too, would have haunted me for the rest of my life. We returned to where that old man's supposed eye witness report of the airplane had been. By that time, my son was used to this kind of muck diving, and he seemed to enjoy navigating under water when it was such a challenge. In these conditions, we had to have some idea of our relative position or location in relation to the boat at all times, since the swimming was done in the dark for 45 minutes. Surprisingly, he agreed to go for another dive. That's my boy!

We dived near the south tip of Umbo Island, but this time we were on the east side (opposite our first dive which was on the west side). When we had completed the third exploratory dive, we would have covered both sides of the island and there would be no more sides of the island to investigate. To our disappointment, which by now had become our expectation, we did not find anything but muck and another flat bottom.

After the third dive, I re-read my depth sounder owner's manual and, unfortunately, it did not teach me anything I did not already know. I did believe that the spots I had marked were real echoes of a signal going to the bottom and coming back to the transducer after hitting something solid. The area was entirely covered with muck, yet I do think that the sounder had seen something. It could not register it as a change in the bottom depth because the bottom was flat, as verified by our on-site dive. To anyone looking at all the dots on my screen, it would have generated thoughts that we had found pieces of airplane scattered around.

There were no other readings like that in the entire mouth of the river. It was only those two separate areas that showed something. The face of the instrument did not look as if a school of fish were on the screen. So where had that airplane actually come to rest? The only sense I could make of the readings and our lack of seeing anything while in the water was that the airplane is there but it is *buried* under the bottom muck.

I had worn out some of the locals with these search efforts. My faithful dive buddy and son Jared was also growing weary. Others, no doubt, were getting suspicious of my determination to locate *this* airplane. But some were interested and understood how much I had wanted to find the airplane. They had devised a plan as to how it could be found. Their plan consisted of appeasing the spirit at the crash site and asking it to reveal the airplane so I could find it. I thought that was nice of them to offer to do that, although I personally did not believe that plan was going to work.

None of these negatives, barriers or failures had stopped me up to this point. My next plan, if I were ever to get up there again, was to take a grappling hook and drag it behind the boat. There remained questions, of course, as to which airplane I was seeking. Some have said that it was a B-25, but I thought it might be the B-24, serial number 42-41043, piloted by 1st Lt. James J. Harris. That crew of ten is listed MIA as of December 16, 1943.[79]

I also thought that it might be the Douglas DB-7/Boston A28-16 which disappeared after a bombing raid of Gasmata on September 12, 1943. It was last seen leaving the target area, but it never returned to base. The crew members were as follows: P/O Eric George Turton Riley, 411522 and F/Sgt Lindsay Kenneth Wilson, 413921. The aircraft was one of four detailed to carry out a sweep to destroy barges along the South West coast of New Britain. Since no barges were sighted, a secondary target, Gasmata, was attacked. A28-16 was observed by an accompanying aircraft to carry out the attack and leave the target area in a normal manner, but was not seen again. Air searches were conducted unsuccessfully for two days.

The following is an extract from a report submitted by Sqn. Ldr. Rundle dated April 4, 1946, referring to this airplane:

> Numerous enquiries were made during March 1946, but was unable to obtain any details as to the whereabouts of the aircraft, or the fate of the crew. Wide searches have been conducted in the area surrounding GASMATA and also along the South coast of New Britain. Interrogation of natives and Japanese failed to produce any evidence whatsoever, nor was there any reference found in Japanese documents which were perused at Rabaul.[80]

Daniel Leahy commented that,

> Accordingly, it must be assumed that this aircraft crashed into the sea during its return flight and that the crew had lost their lives on September 12, 1943. On the same mission, two more of the four Bostons were lost, A28-15 ditched off Gasmata and the crew survived. They boarded a dinghy, but that was the last anyone ever saw of them; and, finally, A28-8 crash landed at Vivigani.

Douglas/Boston A20/ DB-7 *Havoc,* San Diego Air/Space Museum.

B-24 *Liberator.*

Chapter 38

RETURN TO PNG

Our departure date of May 4, 2009 finally arrived. It was one day short of the anniversary of our discovery of the lost Hudson. Having supplied missionaries for 23 years, it was time to say good-bye to Papua New Guinea. On one hand, I felt I had completed the task I was called to PNG to do. I had a peace about leaving. On the other hand, I was saddened to leave so much unfinished work of finding more airplanes and the evidence of more MIAs. As we flew back to America, we stopped in Sydney, Australia, and our family had a memorable time meeting David, James and Janet Forrester. They were the great-nephews and a great-niece of Bill Coutie from the Hudson A16-126. What a nice time we had with them as we became more acquainted with each other and shared (in person) the story of our discovery of the wreckage of Bill Coutie's aircraft. I had kept a pair of pliers and a monkey wrench from the wreckage, which I presented to them before we departed.

The following year, on May 5, 2010, the second anniversary of our discovery of the Hudson, Barbara Forrester wrote:

Dear Mark,

Once again I would like to say a big thank you to you for finding the Hudson aircraft two years ago. I was speaking to Dora yesterday; she was saying how pleased she was that the plane had been found. It happened that yesterday, May 4, I was doing tests as part of research into aging. Elizabeth and I are taking part as a twin study. As part of the test I was asked to speak for 5 minutes on a subject. One of the subjects suggested was a relative in the war, so of course I chose that and talked about you and your son finding the plane. I mentioned it was the date of the discovery.

We think of you and your family often and hope all is going very well for you all. Kind regards, Barbara[81]

Three years later, I organized a short-term mission team to go to Hoskins, West New Britain, PNG. Joan's sister Liz and her husband Steve Butler went to cook at the annual missionary conference. Jared wanted to go as well and stay after the conference to assist missionary families in any way that he could. Because I had been in contact with the Forrester family, I wrote and told them that Jared would be in PNG. If they wanted to go see the wreck site, that would be a good time to do so.

They replied that they would like to do that, but asked what it would take for me to come and be their escort. As a result of that communication, some of the Forrester family offered to purchase my airfare to go to PNG. How could I refuse that?! I was so humbled. So, on May 22, 2011, I met Barbara, her daughter Ann and sons David and James at the Hoskins, West New Britain airport in Papua New Guinea. The following day, I had the honor and privilege of escorting Bill Coutie's family to the actual site where he had lost his life; we flew there by helicopter.

As I had predicted, the timber company had been in the area, and the bulldozers had made a road straight through the helicopter landing site we had cut. Actually, there were now many roads in the area, and that made it most difficult to ascertain the actual site of the wreckage. The helicopter circled several times over the general area. During the dizzying loops, I spotted the wreckage through the trees. But for some reason, the helicopter pilot landed quite a distance away from it. He probably thought we could just "walk" the rest of the way on the road. That proved to be more difficult than expected. Because of all the new roads, we quickly became disorientated, even though I had my trusty GPS. We had the family return to the helicopter as the pilot and I wandered aimlessly; at times, we waded through knee-high mud that, of course, sucked my shoes off. Eventually, we came upon a couple of local young men who graciously escorted us to the crash site. The pilot returned to the helicopter to retrieve the family, while I collected logs and made a large "H" in the middle of the road marking a safe place for him to land. He soon landed with the Forrester family.

Again, as I had predicted, the bulldozer operators had knocked over many trees onto the crash site area. Thankfully, they had not run directly over the wreckage with the 'dozers. We spent nearly an hour examining the wreckage and taking photographs. I was able to recover a spent bullet casing, which I gave to Barbara Forrester, the niece, who had named her son after Barton "Bill" Coutie. Although it had to have been an emotional time for the family, they did not express their sorrow at that time, possibly because of the ordeal in locating the wreckage. Barbara later commented that upon first seeing the wreckage it took her voice away, and the others were impressed at how well preserved it was. The family expressed their deep appreciation in messages sent after they had returned to Australia. Cliff Forrester, Barbara's husband, wrote:

> I have had a very excited family come through in the last week. They had an absolutely amazing time with you and were so appreciative of your efforts on their behalf. I hope you enjoyed the time as well. Cliff Forrester[82]

James Forrester wrote:

> I hope you had as good a time as we did. It seemed everywhere we went, no matter how remote, someone knew you as a long unseen friend.[83]

Dr. Barton David Forrester also wrote:

> Thank you for making this such a memorable trip. We could not have done it without you.[84]

And Barbara Forrester, who used to check the phone books when she traveled, hoping to see her favorite Uncle Bill's name; wrote:

> We had a wonderful time with you, thank you so much for accepting our offer and coming to be with us. It was great to meet and spend time with you.

> Thank you so very much for all your organization and help to get us to the crash site. It was a once in a life time experience and such a wonderful feeling to be where Bill ended his days and to understand a little more about their last minutes. We could not have done this without you. Many thanks again for your and Jared's initial discovery of A16-126. It was a miracle that you found it; and clever of you to find it again.

Many thanks for enabling us to go to the crash site; it has been an ambition for many years. We hope to see you again one day.

All the best and kind regards, Barbara Forrester

A PROPER FUNERAL

During the war, there had been four Lockheed Hudsons lost in the Gasmata area. In the postwar period, three had been located but one of them had never been positively identified. That was the one that we had seen on the reef in Gasmata. Sqn. Ldr. Rundle had previously searched for human remains at that site. I never knew whether he actually searched under the water surface with a diving mask or whether he may have used a grappling hook. I never found out, but I do know that he did report that he had not found any human remains. Rod Pearce believes that the remains could have been found if extensive dredging had been done. At the time, it was unclear as to whether this wreckage was A16-101 or A16-126. When we found A16-126 in the jungle, by process of elimination the Hudson on the reef had to be A16-101.

In April of 1947, the Japanese commander Norio Kondo was interrogated and revealed that he was the officer in charge when two airplanes were shot down on the same night by machine gun fire from a minesweeper. It was the night that A16-165 and A16-101 went missing. On the next morning, he personally went to the crash site on the reef. He examined the wreckage and found "all occupants to be dead and so tightly wedged-in that it was not possible to extricate them." Although not officially identified, Rundle, myself, and others believe that the Hudson on the reef was A16-101.

Operating on that assumption, Justin Taylan posted on the *Pacific Wrecks* website the photographs I had taken of the wreckage with the report of A16-101. In October of 2010, I received the following e-mail message:

Dear Mark,

I found on the internet your photos from Lockheed Hudson Mark IVa Serial Number A16-101.[85]

I am so grateful to you and your son for finding this wreck, taking this photo and making it available so that I can find it on the internet. My Nanna was married one week to William Coppin before he was shipped out to active duty. She was pregnant with my Aunty when she received the news that his plane went down and he was missing presumed dead. She went to her grave never knowing for sure what had happened. She told me how for years as a young mum with a daughter that had never met her father she would sit at Fremantle Harbour watching the ships coming in hoping that he was on one of them. No remains have ever been found. Your pictures are the only thing our family has ever had that could resemble a grave. He never had a funeral.

My father has never given up hope that one day we would find out more information about him. (and has hoped that they would find his remains.) So thank you SO MUCH for making this effort – you have no idea the closure it gives us. I just wish my Nanna were alive to see your photos.

I am a pastor myself so as a thank you for the hard work you and your son have done for my family, I will be sure to pray passionately for God's favour upon the excellent ministry that you and your family are doing in Papua New Guinea. May God truly bless you. I think of Bill (William) in that plane, knowing that men in his position were lasting about 3 weeks in the air at that time and place – I know that he would have had opportunity to consider Jesus. My prayer is that he would have grasped that opportunity and received Christ as his Saviour. Signed by, Renae Matich[86]

When the Forresters knew they were coming to PNG, they had contacted Raewyn Pianta (the aunty of Renae Matich), who wanted to come to PNG at the same time and also wanted to contribute to my airfare. So, on the day after I had escorted the Forrester family into the jungle to see the wreckage of A16-126, I accompanied Raewyn Pianta and her son, Drewe Vincent, to the crash site of the Hudson on the reef believed to be A16-101. Rae was the daughter of Sgt. Bill Coppin, the gunner on that airplane who was married one week before he went away to war never to return. It was her mother, Beverley, who watched the ships come into the harbor hoping that her husband was on board. Bill died at the age of 22 not knowing that he was a father. One could not make clear the emotional outburst when his daughter first saw the wreckage on the reef. It was an immensely somber moment for us all on the boat as Rae wept for the father she never knew. Even though Rae was 69 years old, we spent four hours snorkeling around the reef looking at bits and pieces of airplane parts with hopes of possibly finding human remains. Before we left, flowers were laid, the hymn, *Eternal Father Strong to Save* was played and a prayer was lifted up to the heavens. Bill Coppin had finally had his proper funeral, and, it had been officiated by his daughter.

Mrs. Barbara Forrester

Mark & Mrs. Barbara Forrester at wreck site of Hudson A16-126.

Relatives of Sgt. Bill Coutie at wreck site of Hudson A16-126.

James Forrester & Raewyn Pianta at Gasmata. WNBP, PNG

Raewyn Pianta searching for father's remains at Gasmata. WNBP, PNG

Raewyn Pianta and son Drewe Vincent with undercarriage of A16-101.

Chapter 39

JPAC AND JAPAN

While in PNG in May, 2011, I heard a report that the timber company had found another airplane in the jungle near Gasmata. The contact man of the Avio-Amgen timber camp would have been Beven Saile. I wondered if it could have been the other airplane we had hoped to find, Beaufort A9-186. I regret that I did not have the time to fully check out that story. I have remained curious as to whether anyone ever will?

Also on this same trip, I traveled to Rabaul and met up with Rod Pearce. He showed me photographs of human remains (arm bones) that he had found in a TBF/TBM Avenger that had crashed in Simpson Harbor, Rabaul. Research conducted by Rod, Justin Taylan, David Flinn and Dr. David Forrester revealed that it could have been one of three airplanes. There was a slim possibility that it could have been a New Zealand Air Force aircraft, NZ2541. I wrote the NZAF and told them that I had information regarding human remains from an Avenger in Rabaul's Simpson Harbor and suggested it may be NZ2541. They never replied to my e-mail message. I had also sent a message to the Archives New Zealand.[87] To my delight, I did get a reply from a man who worked there, and he said that the brief report stated "Aircraft dived into sea at Creet Harbour off the end of Lakunai Strip, New Britain, following damage by enemy A/A" (anti-aircraft guns). That reported location proved not to be the same area where the Avenger's position was in question and eliminated the New Zealand aircraft as a possibility.

There was an even greater possibility that it could be a United States airplane, TBF-1 Avenger Bureau Number 24264 which was piloted by 1st Lieutenant James W. Boyden,[87] or it could have been TBF-1 Avenger Bureau Number 25316, which was piloted by 1st Lieutenant Alonzo N. Hathway, Jr.[89] Both of those airplanes, along with their three-man crews, were lost on Valentine's Day, February 14, 1944, while attempting to drop aerial mines into Simpson Harbor. The airplane Rod had found apparently crashed violently, as the engine had come to rest 18 meters (60 feet) away from the fuselage and was almost completely buried in silt. The tail had yet to have been found. The outer wing tips, which were beyond the hinge where they folded, were either disintegrated or buried in silt. The main fuselage was intact with one landing gear retracted and the other extended. It lay on a flat bottom at a depth of approximately 20 meters (65 feet). Human remains were found in the upside-down fuselage under the pilot's seat. It is possible that the other two crew members' remains may be in the wreckage as well – even to this day.

Rod had already contacted the American Embassy in Port Moresby, PNG, but there had been no response. He asked me if I could possibly assist him, so I sent an e-mail to JPAC (Joint Prisoner of War, Missing in Action Accounting Command) in Hawaii, to which they immediately replied with interest. I then sent photographs of the pilot's two arm bones, his "May West" life vest, and a photograph of the Avenger's dash board. That evidence reinforced the report, and later, I had an informal meeting with a man from JPAC. I gave him more photographs and also schematics of the wreckage and the location of the wreckage in relation to the Rabaul airstrip. A couple of months later, we again met, along with a lady who was an underwater archeologist. I gave them a compact disc with 21 underwater photographs of the wreckage.

Although the evidence was compelling, from a reliable source, and caused many to be "interested," they could not reveal if or when JPAC would ever go there to investigate the crash site because of official procedures. To my utter surprise, in December of 2011, I was encouraged to have another meeting with a couple of JPAC personnel who were preparing to go to PNG to investigate the report. From that meeting, I was convinced that people and governments *do care* about their Missing in Action (MIA) and do take steps, within their own time frame, to investigate reports they have received.

In January of 2012, a recon team did go to Rabaul. They met with my friend Dave, but instead of thanking him and giving him gifts of pins and pens or a ball cap from the American government, from his point of view he was "grilled," as they questioned him in detail regarding the crash site. No doubt, they were probably disappointed that he and Rod had disturbed the crash site, which was actually a war grave and should have been respected as such. In his defense, he explained that the site has been known by divers since the '60s, and ships have anchored over it ever since it crashed. So, although they did dredge and find human remains, they were surely not the first ones to disturb the site.

There obviously was some misunderstanding during the meeting. The problem may be that when individuals disturb a site, those actions cause more work on behalf of the recovery teams which then adds to the expense. From the individual's viewpoint, as with my experience with the Japanese, unless human remains can be produced, it seems no action is taken. One would think that when human remains are found there would be immediate reactions to the report, but that is not always the case. Governments are dealing with MIA issues on a global scale, and the recovery needs to be planned and budgeted, all of which takes time. Some opinions favor letting the governments worry about finding the remains as it is *their* job. Others contend that the locations of some remains are known, but the governments take too long to act. Obviously there is frustration on both sides.

My friend was informed that, unfortunately, it is not JPAC's policy or obligation to pay outside contractors, even though that person may have found, researched, dredged, recovered and reported the remains discovery. They were grateful for the valuable assistance. But, they were constrained by established procedures which have been developed over the years from much experience in dealing with such reports, some of which have been bogus.

The plan instead was to bring a 12-meter (40-foot) boat, complete with crew and equipment from Hawaii, by way of an airplane flying approximately 8,047 kilometers (5,000 miles), and launch it themselves. This seemed excessive, but they have flown that way regularly for other MIA cases. There were also issues that needed to be ironed out with the Papua New Guinea government, as they consider WWII wreckage to be their property, and in some cases the US Navy considers wreckage to be US property.

The main reasons for the first recon trip were to see if there was a launching pad wide enough, long enough and with the proper angle to launch a large vessel and to see if the airstrip could handle that large an airplane. If the facilities were inadequate, a Navy ship might have to be sent there to do the remains recovery. One can image the preparation for such an exercise, and understandably, JPAC would not want to jeopardize a Navy ship. It would need to be confirmed that the harbor did not have any leftover mines from the war in it. The thought of having to send a minesweeper in first was unimaginable! These are just some of the issues that needed to be dealt with. It was apparent that JPAC had different policies and procedures to follow than the RAAF.

In the event there is no report of human remains, the process of finding MIAs includes obtaining information of lost airplanes or battles in an area and scrutinizing the data from every angle, which in itself is a lengthy process. After much discussion, everyone involved would then need to agree to conduct the search. Once everyone saw eye to eye they would have to wait even longer for the funding.[90] Sometimes, the process takes up to two years and in some cases, even longer. I have heard of cases where the process has taken ten years. This explanation does not even touch on changes that may take place in diplomatic clearances and the possibility some governments may hope to profit from such undertakings. For me, all that bureaucracy was exasperating, and at times it seemed a miracle if anything was actually investigated and recovered.

I had found when going into an area that it is better to have a lower profile. Nice, new equipment and clothes reeks of wealth and the locals get dollar signs in their eyes. Unfortunately, just wearing clean clothes, sporting a wrist watch and tennis shoes is considered high profile. But, the more money it appears you have, the more money the locals want to get. This mentality is called "Arawe thinking" on the south coast.

In spite of all the challenges they have to overcome, to their credit, the Joint POW/MIA Accounting Command (JPAC) has identified nearly 2,000 Americans from an estimated 74,000. Reports conflict as to the actual number of MIAs from WWII. For all wars, the estimate is close to 84,000 missing, with 35,000 potentially recoverable, according to the Pentagon[91] since the accounting started in the 1970s.[92] Once their new 62-million-dollar facility is completed in Hawaii,[93] they should become even more efficient in their efforts to coordinate recoveries and identify remains.

In August of 2010, the Japanese recovery team, which I had long hoped for, finally sent a team to search for the remains of the Val in the water that we had found in 2001. It appeared my reports had not fallen on deaf ears, and the Japanese government, like others, does care about their MIAs. They hired Rod Pearce to assist them. Rod had found the human remains underneath the wreckage in 2003 and reported them to the Japanese Embassy in Port Moresby. The recovery team was escorted by the police and a PNG museum representative to insure there would be no trouble with the locals or demands for compensation. The remains of the pilot and crew were recovered and taken to shore for ceremonial cremation.[94] What remains did not get consumed by the fire I assume were taken to Chidorigafuchi cemetery near Tokyo. That is the national cemetery that houses 352,297 unidentified war dead from the Second World War.[95] I do not know if any attempt to find the families affected had ever been made.

They also diligently investigated the Val site by Wako village where we thought we had found human remains. As it turned out, the recovered pieces we thought were human remains were actually, I am embarrassed to say, corroded aluminum piping. That was determined through the use of a metal detector. Even though we had previously found a rubber shoe sole and a belt buckle along with two harness buckles, the two-to-three-hour effort of excavation at that site by the officials of the Japanese Ministry of Health revealed no human remains. It was communicated to me by Rod that during that trip, they did not hire him to investigate the remaining six Val sites that we had reported.

The Japanese have been searching for MIAs since 1952. To give some idea as to the magnitude of their daunting task, in the Philippines alone they have nearly 370,000 remains yet to be recovered from the more than 500,000 believed to have died there.[96] According to the Japanese Government Ministry of Health, Labour, and Social Welfare, as of 31 March 2011, of the 2,400,000 that were killed during the war, 1,265,000 remains have been recovered, with another 1,135,000 still missing.[97]

To this day, I continue to ponder whether anyone will find that mysterious airplane in the water at Gasmata. My friend Rod Pearce visited Gasmata in 2011 and scanned the area for the mystery airplane. He, too, had readings on his scanner screen, but before he could investigate further, the locals discouraged him from continuing his search. I also wonder if the crash site of the *San Antonio Rose* with Brig. Gen. Kenneth Walker on board will ever be found. And at times I have mused over the possibility that human remains still lie at the crash site of A16-126. Lastly, what about the thousands of other MIAs worldwide whose remains have continued to wait to be found?

How often I have wished that I could return some day to PNG to find more crash sites with human remains or personal items to help even more families to find closure. The confounding thing in my experience has been that the local people have known the location of most of the aircraft wreckage sites. All it required was for someone to go into the villages to ask the people, and they have, for the most part, cooperated with the searchers and led them to the site or sites.

I have gathered more information about other locations that need investigation, as have other historians and Rod Pearce is saying he knows of 19 US and a half dozen Japanese aircraft that could be easily located. Although I have been encouraged by some results I have experienced, the slow response of the governments, seemingly bogged down with bureaucracy or never begun at all and sensing a similar Japanese attitude of, "we have no obligation to find more remains but it is *their* duty" has left me bewildered and others downright upset. In addition, I have seen news reports of how some recovered remains have been lost or have had bad results from sloppy or inappropriate disposal.[98,99] As a result of such actions and responses, many historians have been frustrated and reluctant to pass on information, having done much of the leg work and then reprimanded (or ignored) for their efforts. I was half tempted to agree with my wife and ask the question: besides a handful of enthusiasts, including some who work at the government agencies and the families of the missing, do people really care anymore?

We know the governments have cared, which is reflected in the ramp ceremonies held when MIAs are returned. Also, the families are sincerely grateful. Therefore, I formed the opinion that it was not a matter of caring. It was more a matter of understanding how each government works in relation to recovering remains and then working with their procedures. From my experience, the Australians acted quickly and used local contractors. The Japanese used local contractors but took a much greater amount of time (seven years). The Americans do not act as fast as the Australians but faster than the Japanese – and seem to have a larger budget to work with as they do not employ any contractors. The task seems extremely confusing, overwhelming and enormously expensive, but there are plenty of known sites and others that are yet to be found, waiting for recovery. We must not lose the vision or grow weary in this great cause of leaving no one behind. This is true of the Christian church as well. We too have been commissioned to find those who are lost.

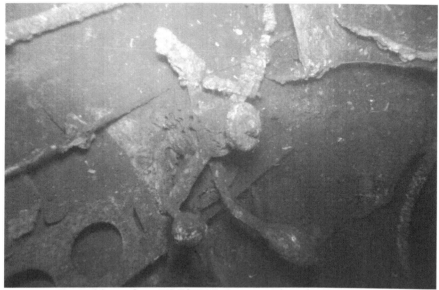

Control lever from TBF/TBM *Avenger*. Photo by Rod Pearce

Dashboard from TBF/TBM *Avenger*. Photo by Rod Pearce

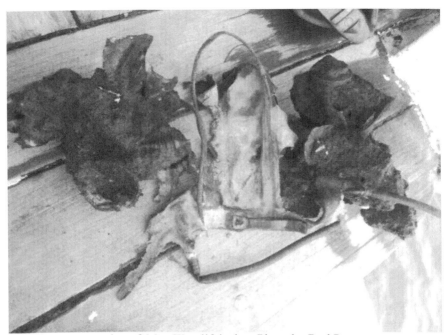

Remains of *Mae West* lifejacket. Photo by Rod Pearce

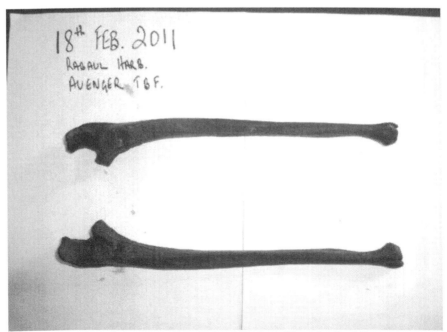

Remains of *Avenger* pilot. Rabaul Harbor. Photo by Rod Pearce

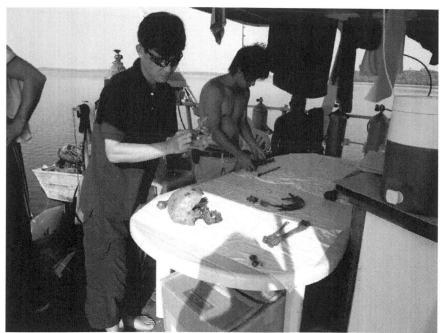

Japanese workers with remains of Arawe *Val*. Photo by Rod Pearce

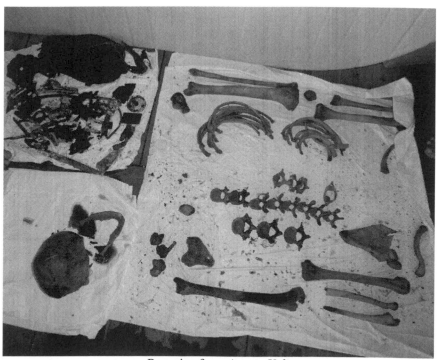

Remains from Arawe *Val*.

Cremation pyre for crew of Arawe *Val*. Photo by Rod Pearce

Cremation of crew of Arawe *Val*. Photo by Rod Pearce

Chapter 40

HEROES

As I have reminisced about all of the wreckage sites we have seen and discovered, the highlight for me, of course, was our discovery of Hudson A16-126. The inner joy I experienced because of our ability to assist the RAAF with the remains recovery operation (although we only found personal effects) and to help a number of families find closure in the loss of their loved ones, has brought to me a satisfaction beyond description. The experience of some of seeing an MIA buried with full honors in view of the wife and relatives, with shots fired over the grave and bugle playing *The Last Post*, only strengthens the urge to find the remaining MIAs.[100] The icing on the cake for me, in addition to having shared these experiences with my children, was the time I was able to meet and escort family members to the crash sites, as they have been so grateful.

On February 11, 2012, I received this copy of a letter that Barbara Forrester had sent out to her relatives:

Hello everyone,

On 11th Feb 1942, Hudson aircraft A16-126 attacked Japanese ships in Gasmata Harbour, was attacked by Japanese planes and went missing. That was 70 years ago today. Sixty six years later the wreck was discovered by Jared and Mark Reichman in the jungle.

Thank you both very much for putting an end to this mystery. It was such a relief to know what happened. Best wishes, Barbara

The gratitude these families have communicated to me repeatedly has made me feel like some sort of hero, if for no other person, at least to them! My sense of pride would like to accept that honor. I have always thought that here was a story worthy of an interview on TV or a write-up in a magazine such as National Geographic, maybe even a movie or documentary of our adventures. If that were to happen, perhaps I would be able to return to PNG and find some of those lingering wreck sites!

But I am not a hero. I am just grateful to God that He has allowed me to have a part in this story. The heroes in this account are the men and women, known and unknown, the found and the missing, who gave their lives and paid the ultimate sacrifice upon the altar of freedom. The least we can do is to continue to find them and bring them home.

There is an old African saying that goes like this: "A man is not truly dead until he is forgotten." For those who are still wondering where their loved ones are, they must never give up hope because there is an enormous amount of effort by governments, professional and amateur historians who are dedicated to finding MIAs. Perhaps one day, someone will be surprised as they are surfing the internet, receiving a telephone call or answering a knock on the door, and learn about their MIA, that the lost has been FOUND!

END NOTE:

The helicopter pilot, Colin Greenwood, who first took us to the crash site of Hudson A16-126, ironically, died in a helicopter crash, July 22, 2011 north of Sydney, Australia in a rugged bushland area. His remains were recovered from the horrific crash site the following day.[101]

In June of 2012, Justin Taylan along with Rod Pearce visited villages along Wide Bay, starting at Tol. They left cameras with the villagers in hopes that they will find and photograph the *San Antonio Rose*.

On November 9, 2012, JPAC posted a News Advisory on their website that they were sending out two teams to Papua New Guinea. One team was to search nine ground sites for approximately 50 individuals unaccounted for. The other team of about 50 people from four organizations including an unmanned underwater vehicle specialist from the Explosive Ordnance Disposal Mobile Unit One on board the USNS *Salvor* was to conduct an underwater investigation at a suspected WWII era aircraft crash site in Simpson Harbor, New Britain.[102]

NOTES

Introduction

1. The Free Encyclopedia. Wikimedia Foundation Inc. Modified on 23 March 2012 at 04:54. Available from http://en.wikipedia.org/wiki/World_War_II_casualties. Internet. Retrieved 4 April 2012.

2. Department of Defense Military Casualties http://siadapp.dmdc.osd.mil/personnel/CASUALTY/castop.htm Internet. Retrieved 3 April 2012.

3. CRS Report for Congress *U.S. Prisoners of War and Civilian American Citizens Captured and Interned by Japan in World War II: The Issue of Compensation by Japan.* Updated 17 December 2002. p. CRS-11.

4. Franklin, H. Bruce (1993) *M.I.A., Or, Mythmaking in America.* Rutgers University Press. ISBN 0-8135-2001-0. pp. 12–13.

5. Japan Ministry of Health, Labor, and Social Welfare. As of 31 March 2011. Provided by my Japanese friend.

6. Sivard, Ruth (1985) *Leger World Military and Social Expenditures.* World Priorities. ISBN-10: 0918281016.

7. Japan Ministry of Health, Labour, and Social Welfare. As of 31 March 2011. Provided by my Japanese friend.

8. The Australian War Memorial reports 39,761.

9. McKernan, Michael (June 1, 2007) *Strength of a Nation: Six years of Australians fighting for the nation and defending the homefront in World War II.* Crows Nest NSW, Allen & Unwin. ISBN: 1-74114-714-X. p. 393.

10. Davis, Paul. Commonwealth War Graves Commission Enquiries Administrator (Names from WWII who are commemorated on the Commission's Memorials to the missing.)

11. Bjij, V. Lal and Kate Fortune (July 2000) *The Pacific Islands- An Encyclopedia*
    University of Hawaii Press ISBN-10: 082482265X. p. 244.

12. Griffith, Christopher J and Duflou, John ALC. *Recovery of Australian service personnel missing in action from World War II p. 47*
    http://www.defence.gov.au/health/infocentre/journals/ADFHJ_a pr00/ADFHealthApr0 0_1_2_47-53.pdf.
    Internet. Retrieved 3 April 2012.

Chapter 1

13. Operations Record Book RAAF Station Headquarters, sheet no. 572, p. 2. Provided by Dr. Barton David Forrester.

14. Vincent, David (2010) *The RAAF Hudson Story Book Two*.
    Vincent Aviation Publications, ISBN 978-9596052-3-5. p. 177.

15. Australian War Memorial, *Lark Force Rabaul Escapee.* Interview of Fred Kollmorgen by Hank Nelson on 21 May 1990 for The Keith Murdoch Sound Archive of Australia in the War of 1939-1945.
    http://www.awm.gov.au/transcripts/kmsa/s00911_tran.htm.
    Internet. Retrieved 27 July 2011 8:37 pm.

16. Lerew, John, *Pearl Harbor Down Under.* Tape 4 side A National Archives. p. 31. http://naa12.naa.gov.au/scripts/Imagine.asp.
    Internet. Retrieved 14 January 2011 12:00 am.

17. Jillett, Leslie (1945) *Moresby's Few: Being an account of the activities of No. 32 Squadron in New Guinea in 1942.* North Western Courier. ASIN: B0007JUP3G. p. 44.

18. Pacific Wrecks "Lockheed *Hudson* Mark IV Serial Number A16-126"http://www.pacificwrecks.com/aircraft/hudson/A16-126.html. Internet. Retrieved 3 April 2012.

19. Vincent, David (2010) *The RAAF Hudson Story Book Two*,
    Vincent Aviation Publications, ISBN 978-9596052-3-5. p. 177.

20. Testimony of Dora Dance, Sister of Bill Coutie, MIA gunner on A16-126.

Chapter 2

21. US Navy, Naval History B Heritage Command, *Dictionary of American Naval Fighting Ships*, Vol. V, p. 65.

22. Eyers, Jonathan (2011) *Don't Shoot the Albatross!: Nautical Myths and Superstitions.* A&C Black, London, UK. ISBN: 978-1-4081-3131-2. Navy Tradition when crossing over the Equator for the first time.

23. Stone, Peter (1995) *Hostages to Freedom: The Fall of Rabaul*, Oceans Enterprises, Publication, ISBN: 0-646-24124-9. p. 91. Australian Dictionary of Biography http://adb.anu.edu.au/biography/robinson-alfred-lambton-11547 Internet. Retrieved 3 April 2012.

24. Information provided by Sgt. Michael Wanyio, Royal Papua New Guinea Constable, Senemsi Village, WNBP Papua New Guinea.

25. Information provided by Jack Lisio, Ais Village, Kandrian, WNBP Papua New Guinea.

26. Information provided by Daniel Leahy of Pacific Wrecks.

27. "The Turtle Song" translated by Mike Hashimoto (Provided by Pastor Seki Shinji) Sung by John Leskit, Ais Village, WNBP Papua New Guinea and Henry Kela, Akanglo Village, WNBP Papua New Guinea.

28. Information provided by Tom Malis, Headmaster, Yumielo Village, WNBP Papua New Guinea.
    Additional information provided by Langa, Aviklo Village, WNBP Papua New Guinea.

29. *Attack! Battle of New Britain* (1944) Documentary/propaganda film produced by the US military http://www.youtube.com/watch?v=WxBHD0sjW90 /

http://www.alluc.org/movies/watch-attack-battle-of-new-britain-1944-online/356018.html.
Internet. Retrieved 4 April 2012.

30. Barbey, Daniel (1969) *MacArthurs Amphibious Navy: 7th Amphibious Force Operation.* (1943-1945) United States Naval Institute; First edition. ASIN: B0006BZ1D4.
Extract provided by John Douglas.

31. US Army, Engineer Special Brigade, 2nd (1946) *History of the 2nd Engineer Special Brigade, United States Army WWII.* Harrisburg, Pa., Telegraph Press. ASIN: B006U1PS6E.
Extract provided by John Douglas.

32. Hough, Frank O and Crown, John A. *The Campaign of New Britain* Chapter 9 Flashback: Action at Arawe: Concept of Mission: http://www.ibiblio.org/hyperwar/USMC/USMC-M-Brit/USMC-M-NBrit-9.html. Internet. Retrieved 4 April 2012.
Extract provided by John Douglas.

33. The Free Encyclopedia. Wikimedia Foundation Inc. Modified on 23 March 2012 at 04:54. Available from http://en.wikipedia.org/wiki/Battle_of_Arawe#cite_note-58.
Internet. Retrieved 4 April 2012.
Miller, John, Jr. (1959). *CARTWHEEL: The Reduction of Rabaul. United States Army in World War II: The War in the Pacific.* Washington, D.C: Office of the Chief of Military History, United States Department of the Army. OCLC 569056928.

Chapter 3

34. Technical information on the Val provided by Brian Bennett.

35. Stone, C.S. (September 1, 1977) *Pearl Harbor: The way it was – December 7, 1941.* Island Heritage Publishing; First Edition. ISBN-10: 0896100391. p. 52.

Chapter 4

36. Information provided by Justin Taylan, Historian, Webmaster of Pacific Wrecks www.pacificwrecks.com est. 1995.

Chapter 5

37. Information provided by Dr. Barton David Forrester.

38. Gamble, Bruce 1st edition (December 15, 2006) *Darkest Hour: The True Story of Lark Force at Rabaul-Australia's Worst Military Disaster of World War II.* Zenith Press; Torture and Execution of Capt. Gray. ISBN-10: 0760323496. p. 281
    Bowman, Alice M. *Not Now Tomorrow.* Daisy Press. ISBN-10: 0646203606. p. 70.
    Australian Archives, Statement by Father Joseph Reischl of Catholic Mission, Bitagalip, Kokopo relative to manner of death of Captain Gray of Rabaul force.
    All above research provided by Dr. Barton David Forrester.

Chapter 6

39. Breuer, William B. (June 1, 1995) *Devil Boats: The PT War Against Japan.* Presidio Press ISBN-10: 0891415866.
    Provided by WWII PT boat crewman, John "Jack" Hopkins.

40. Information provided by Justin Taylan, Historian, Webmaster of Pacific Wrecks. www.pacificwrecks.com est. 1995.

Chapter 9

41. Stanaway, John (January 1, 2004) *Possum, Clover & Hades: The 75th Fighter Group in World War II.*
    Schiffer Publishing, Ltd. ISBN-10: 0887405185.
    By Permission from John Stanaway.

42. Dunn, Richard "248 th Hiko Sentai: A Japanese "Hard luck" Fighter Unit" part 3.
    http://www.j-aircraft.com/research/rdunn/248th/248th-3.htm.
    Internet. Retrieved 4 April 2012.

Chapter 10

43. External Source Catholic Encyclopedia: "Regina Coeli. (Queen of Heaven)" Wikipedia: The Free Encyclopedia. Wikimedia Foundation Inc. Modified on 13 March 2012 at 12:19.

http://en.wikipedia.org/wiki/Regina_Coeli.
Internet. Retrieved 4 April

44. Jeakle, 1st. Lt. William, Pilot *Regina Coeli*. Video interview transcribed by Justin Taylan. Used by permission of William Jeakle III.

45. Information provided by Justin Taylan, Historian, Webmaster of Pacific Wrecks www.pacificwrecks.com est. 1995.

Chapter 11

46. Fresch, Fred, Dictates Reminisces of WWII (He was in another airplane on the mission when *San Antonio Rose* was lost.)

47. Pacific Wrecks "B-17F-10-BO *San Antonio Rose* Serial Number 41-24458." http://www.pacificwrecks.com/aircraft/b-17/41-24458.html. Internet. Retrieved 4 April 2012.

Chapter 12

48. Bradley, James (September 30, 2003) *Flyboys: A True Story of Courage.* Little Brown and Company; 1st edition. ISBN-10: 0316105848. p. 15.

49. Information provided by Justin Taylan, Historian, Webmaster of Pacific Wrecks www.pacificwrecks.com est. 1995.
Information provided by Brigadier General, Jerome T. Hagen.

50. Information provided by Justin Taylan, Historian, Webmaster of Pacific Wrecks. www.pacificwrecks.com est. 1995.
From researching the Japanese defense archives regarding Val manufacturing dates.

Chapter 14

51. The Free Encyclopedia. Wikimedia Foundation Inc. Modified on 12 March 2012 at 04:54. Available from http://en.wikipedia.org/wiki/Bristol_Beaufort. Internet. Retrieved 4 April 2012.

Chapter 18

52. Information provided by Justin Taylan, Historian, Webmaster of Pacific Wrecks. www.pacificwrecks.com est. 1995. From researching the Japanese defense archives regarding Val missions in the Arawes.

Chapter 19

53. GlobalSecurity.org "Caliber .50 Cartridges," Modified: 07-07-2011 at 02:49:39. ZULU http://www.globalsecurity.org/military/systems/munitions/50.htm. Internet. Retrieved 4 April 2012.

54. Pacific Wrecks "B-17E *Texas* #6 Serial Number 41-9207." www.pacificwrecks.com/aircraft/b-17/41-9207.html. Internet. Retrieved 4 April 2012.

55. Piper, Bob. *The Premonition "A Song for Sister Sheah"* Pacific Wrecks Updated October 7, 2011. http://www.pacificwrecks.com/aircraft/c-47/A65-54/index.html. Internet. Retrieved 4 April 2012.

Chapter 20

56. Woodbury, David O. (1946) *Builders for Battle: How the Pacific Naval Air Bases were Constructed.* New York E P Dutton and Company Incp. ASIN: B001QKC51A. p. 163.

Chapter 21

57. Information provided by Richard Dunn.

58. Used by permission of Raewyn Pianta.

59. Report on page 166 of Hudson A16-101 3/3/42 32 Squadron provided by Peter Dunn.

Chapter 22

60. Japanese patriotic song provided by Justin Taylan and Hitoshi Kira. Wikipedia: The Free Encyclopedia. Wikimedia Foundation Inc. Modified 29 March 2012 at 14:25. http://en.wikipedia.org/wiki/Umi_Yukaba. Internet. Retrieved 4 April 2012.

61. National Public Radio, transcribed by Louisa Lim. *War Shrine First Test for New Japanese Premier* (September 26, 2006). http://www.npr.org/templates/story/story.php?storyId=6145772. Internet. Retrieved 4 April 2012.

62. The Free Encyclopedia. Wikimedia Foundation Inc. Modified on 25 March 2012 at 20:29. Yasukuni Shrine http://en.wikipedia.org/wiki/Yasukuni_Shrine. Internet. Retrieved 4 April 2012.

Chapter 28

63. Lewis, Wendy *Events That Shaped Australia*. New Holland. Simon Balderstone and John Bowan (2006) pp. 169–174. ISBN: 9781741104929. Free Encyclopdia. Wikimedia Foundation Inc. Modified on 1 March 2012 at 23:21. http://en.wikipedia.org/wiki/Fuzzy_Wuzzy_Angels. Internet. Retrieved 4 April 2012.

Chapter 29

64. Used by permission from Fiona Thorn.

65. Used by permission from Tony Gibson.

66. Information on Mr. O'Brien provided by Squadron Leader John Cotterell, RAAF.

Chapter 31

67. Pacific Wrecks. "Allied Missions Against Gasmata/ Gasmata Airfield" February 11, 1942 – February 5, 1944.

http://www.pacificwrecks.com/airfields/png/gasmata/missions-gasmata.html. Internet. Retrieved 4 April 2012.

Chapter 34

68. Potocki, John (January 1998) *The Colt Model 1905 Automatic Pistol.* Andrew Mowbray Publication. ISBN-10: 0917218760. Meadows, Edward Scott (1993) *U.S. Military AutomaticPistols, 1894-1920.* Richard Ellis Publications. ASIN: B001TO1OEC.

69. Boorman, Dean K. (2003) *The History of Smith & Wesson Firearms.* Published by Lyons Press. ASIN: B000MZ1I22. p. 46.

70. Military Shooters LLC. Clyde Senior Member Discussion thread on 11-16-2010 http://forums.gunboards.com/showthread.php?196149-Misc-38-S-amp-W-cartridges. Internet. Retrieved 4 April 2012.

71. Information provided by Squadron Leader John Cotterell RAAF.

72. Ibid.

73. Ibid.

Chapter 35

74. Hendrie, Andrew (1999) *Lockheed Hudson in WWII.* First Published by Airlife Publishing Ltd. ISBN: 1 84037 0939. p. 180.

75. Vincent, David (2010) *The RAAF Hudson Story Book Two* Vincent Aviation Publications. ISBN: 978-9596052-3-5. p. 177.

76. Genealogy information provided by Dr. Barton David Forrester.

Chapter 36

77. Senshi, Kanko Kai, Tokyo, (1984) A *memoir by Army pilot Shishimoto Hironojyou of 11th Sentai.*

78. Pacific Wrecks "B-17F-20-BO *Flying Fortress* Serial Number 41-24538." http://www.pacificwrecks.com/aircraft/b-17/41-24538.html. Internet. Retrieved 4 April 2012.

Chapter 37

79. Pacific Wrecks "B-24D-125-CO *Liberator* Serial Number 42-41043."http://www.pacificwrecks.com/aircraft/b-24/42-41043.html. Internet. Retrieved 4 April 2012.

80. Extract of report by Sqn. Ldr. Keith Rundle dated 4 April 1946. Provided by Daniel Leahy.

Chapter 38

81. Used by permission from Mrs. Barbara Forrester

82. Used by permission from Mr. Cliff Forrester

83. Used by permission from Mr. James Forrester

84. Used by permission from Dr. Barton David Forrester

85. Reference to picture on Pacific Wrecks taken by Mark Reichman (1 August 2008). http://www.pacificwrecks.com/aircraft/hudson/A16-101/2007/tail-wreckage.html. Internet. Retrieved 6 April 2012.

86. Used by permission of Renae Matich, Generations Centre, P.O. Box 226, Morley, WA. 6943, Australia

Chapter 39

87. "RNZAF [Royal New Zealand Air Force] Accident Reports – Avenger - NZ 2541 –Lakunai Strip - Missing Enemy Action, 3 dead - 10 MAY (R21075723)" http://archway.archives.govt.nz/ViewFullItem.do?code= 21075723. Internet. Retrieved 7 April 2012.

88. Pacific Wrecks "TBF-1 *Avenger* Bureau Number 24264."
http://www.pacificwrecks.com/aircraft/avenger/24264.html.
Internet. Retrieved 7 April 2012.

89. Pacific Wrecks TBF-1 *Avenger* Bureau Number 25316.
http://www.pacificwrecks.com/aircraft/avenger/25316.html.
Internet. Retrieved 7 April 2012.

90. CNN *U.S Troops Killed in Action Have a Last Ally* by Misty
Showalter, updated 8:33 AM EST, Thursday, January 26, 2012.
http://www.cnn.com/2012/01/26/us/wus-us-identifymia/index.
html?iref=allsearch. Internet. Retrieved 7 April 2012.

91. New York Times *Teams Seeking Remains Dig Back to World War
II* by Elisabeth Bumiller. Published September 5, 2009. A
version of this article appeared in print
on September 6, 2009, on page A1 of the New York edition.
http://www.nytimes.com/2009/09/06/world/europe/06search.ht
ml?_r=2. Internet. Retrieved 7 April 2012.

92. Joint POW/MIA Accounting Command News Release Sept. 7,
2011. Release # 11-19.
http://www.jpac.pacom.mil/index.php?page=press_center&size
=100&ind=0&fldr=PressReleases2011&file=PR2011-9-7
Internet. Retrieved 7 April 2012.

93. Hawaii News Now J*PAC Celebrates Groundbreaking for New
Multi-million Dollar Facility.* Updated: Aug 30, 2011 6:15 PM
by Stephanie Lum.
http://www.hawaiinewsnow.com/story/15364111/jpac-
celebrates-groundbreaking-for-new-multi-million-dollar-
facility. Internet. Retrieved 7 April 2012.

94. Information provided by Rod Pearce
Pacific Wrecks "D3A Val off Arawe." Photo Archive. Photos
by Rod Pearce, August 2010.
http://www.pacificwrecks.com/aircraft/d3a2/arawe/index.html.
Internet. Retrieved 7 April 2012.

95. The Free Encyclopedia. Wikimedia Foundation Inc Modified on 2
April 2012 at 11:20. Chidorigafuchi National Cemetery.

http://en.wikipedia.org/wiki/Chidorigafuchi_National_
Cemetery. Internet. Retrieved 7 April 2012.

96. The Japanese Times - Online. *New Rules Set for Retrieving War Remains in Philippines.* Tuesday, March 13, 2012. http://www.japantimes.co.jp/text/nn20120313f1.html. Internet. Retrieved 7 April 2012.

97. Information provided by a Japanese historian.

98. Los Angeles Times *Partial 9/11 remains cremated, dumped in landfill, Pentagon Says.* by David S. Cloud, Washington Bureau February 29, 2012. http://www.latimes.com/news/nationworld/nation/la-na-dover-mortuary-20120229,0,5950153.story. Internet. Retrieved 7 April 2012.

99. U.S. News on MSNBC.com *Pentagon Admits it Dumped Some 9/11 Remains in Landfill.* By M. Alex Johnson, msnbc.com Updated at 8:38 P.M ET. February 28, 2012. http://usnews.msnbc.msn.com/_news/2012/02/28/10531237-pentagon-admits-it-dumped- some-911-remains-in-a-landfill. Internet. Retrieved 7 April 2012.

Chapter 40

100. Comment provided by an anonymous RAAF officer.

101. ABC News *Two dead in Sydney Helicopter Crash* Updated July 22, 2011 19:24:49 http://www.abc.net.au/news/2011-07-22/helicopter-crash-in-sydney/2805896 Internet. Retrieved 7 April 2012.

102. Joint POW/MIA Accounting Command News Release Nov. 7, 2012. Release # 12-28 http://www.jpac.pacom.mil/index.php?page=press_center&size =100&ind=0&fldr=PressReleases2012&file=PR2012-12-28 Internet. Retrieved 9 November 2012.

BIBLIOGRAPHY

Barbey, Daniel (1969) *MacArthurs Amphibious Navy: 7th Amphibious Force Operation.*(1943-1945) United States Naval Institute; First edition. ASIN: B0006BZ1D4.

Bjij, V. Lal and Kate Fortune (July 2000) *The Pacific Islands-An Encyclopedia* .University of Hawaii Press. ISBN-10: 082482265X.

Boorman, Dean K. (2003) *The History of Smith & Wesson Firearms.* Lyons Pr. ASIN: B000MZ1I22.

Bowman, Alice M. (1996) *Not Now Tomorrow.* Daisy Press. ISBN-10: 0646203606.

Bradley, James (September 30, 2003) *Flyboys: A True Story of Courage.* Little Brown and Company; 1st edition. ISBN-10: 0316105848.

Breuer, William B. (June 1, 1995) *Devil Boats: The PT War Against Japan.* Presidio Press. ISBN-10: 0891415866.

Cross, John R. (2010) *By this NAME.* Goodseed International. ISBN: 978-1-890082-80-2

Eyers, Jonathan (2011) *Don't Shoot the Albatross!: Nautical Myths and Superstitions.* A&C Black, London, UK. ISBN: 978-1-4081-3131-2.

Franklin, H. Bruce (1993) *M.I.A., Or, Mythmaking in America.* Rutgers University Press. ISBN: 0-8135-2001-0.

Gamble, Bruce (December 15, 2006) 1st edition. *Darkest Hour: The True Story of Lark Force at Rabaul-Australia's Worst Military Disaster of World War II.* Zenith Press. ISBN-10: 0760323496

Happell. Charles (2008) *The Bone Man of Kokoda.* Pan Macmillan Australia Pty. Limited. ISBN: 9781405038362

Hendrie, Andrew (1999) *Lockheed Hudson in WWII.* First Published by Airlife Publishing Ltd. ISBN: 1 84037 0939.

Jillett, Leslie (1945) *Moresby's Few: Being an account of the activities of No. 32 Squadron in New Guinea in 1942.* North Western Courier. ASIN: B0007JUP3G

Lewis, Wendy (2006) *Events That Shaped Australia.* New Holland. Simon Balderstone and John Bowan. ISBN: 9781741104929.

McKernan, Michael (June 1, 2007) *Strength of a Nation: Six years of Australians fighting for the nation and defending the homefront in World War II.* Crows Nest NSW, Allen & Unwin.

ISBN: 1-74114-714-X.

Meadows, Edward Scott (1993) *U.S. Military Automatic Pistols, 1894-1920*. Richard Ellis Publications. ASIN: B001TO1OEC.

Miller, John, Jr. (1959) *CARTWHEEL: The Reduction of Rabaul. United States Army in World War II: The War in the Pacific*. Washington, D.C: Office of the Chief of Military History, United States Department of the Army. OCLC 569056928

Potocki, John (January 1998) *The Colt Model 1905 Automatic Pistol*. Andrew Mowbray Publication. ISBN-10: 0917218760.

Sivard, Ruth (1985) *Leger World Military and Social Expenditures*. World Priorities. ISBN-10: 0918281016

Stanaway, John (January 1, 2004) *Possum, Clover & Hades: The 475th Fighter Group in World War II*. Schiffer Publishing, Ltd. ISBN-10: 0887405185.

Stone, C.S. (September 1, 1977) *Pearl Harbor: The way it was – December 7, 1941*. Island Heritage Publishing; First Edition. ISBN-10: 0896100391.

Stone, Peter (1995) *Hostages to Freedom: The Fall of Rabaul*. Oceans Enterprises, Publication. ISBN: 0-646-24124-9.

US Army, engineer Special Brigade, 2nd (1946) *History of the 2nd Engineer Special Brigade, United States Army WWII*. Harrisburg, Pa., Telegraph Press. ASIN: B006U1PS6E.

Vincent, David (2010) *The RAAF Hudson Story Book Two*. Vincent Aviation Publications. ISBN: 978-9596052-3-5.

Woodbury, David O. (1946) *Builders for Battle: How the Pacific Naval Air Bases were Constructed*. New York: E P Dutton and Company. ASIN: B001QKC51A

Memorial Monument to all who sacrificed their lives, Rabaul. ENBP, PNG

ABBREVIATIONS

A/A = Anti-Aircraft.

Ack, ack = Flak from anti-aircraft guns.

AKC = American Kennel Club showing pure bred certification.

A5M = Japanese fighter aircraft built by Mitsubishi. Code named, *Claude*.

A6M-2 = Japanese fighter aircraft built by Mitsubishi. Referred to as, *Zero*.

B-17 = American four-engine bomber designed by Boeing named, *Flying Fortress*.

B-24 = American four-engine bomber designed by Consolidated Aircraft named, *Liberator*.

B-25 = American twin-engine medium bomber by North American named, *Mitchell*.

BP = Burns, Philp & Co, Limited (Operated coconut plantations).

CILHI = The Central Identification Laboratory, Hawaii. Disbanded, November 2003.

Flt. Lt. = Flight Lieutenant.

F/O = Flying Officer.

F/Sgt. = Flight Sergeant.

GPS = Global Positioning System. Satellite-based navigation system.

JPAC = Joint Prisoner of War, Missing in Action Accounting Command.

Kgs = Kilograms.

Kts = Knots. A unit of speed equal to 1.151 mph.

MACR = Missing Air Crew Reports.

MM = Millimeter.

MN = Manufacturer Number.

MRE = Meals Ready to Eat. Self-contained field rations.

Mph = Miles Per Hour. Unit of speed expressing number of miles covered in an hour.

NAS= Naval Air Station.

NTM = New Tribes Mission.

NZAF = New Zealand Air Force.

P-38 = American twin-engine fighter manufactured by Lockheed named, *Lightning*.

PNG = Papua New Guinea.

POM = Port Moresby.

POW = Prisoner Of War.

P/O = Pilot Officer.

Psi = A unit of measurement of pressure, Pounds per Square Inch.

PT boat = Patrol Torpedo. Torpedo-armed, fast-attack, plywood craft used by the US Navy.

Pvt. = Private.

RAAF= Royal Australian Air Force.

RAF = Royal Air Force of British Commonwealth.

SAR = Abbreviation for B-17 serial number 41-24458 named, *San Antonio Rose.*

Sgt. = Sergeant.

SIL = Summer Institute of Linguistics. Wycliffe. A non-profit Bible translation organization.

S/Sgt. = Staff sergeant.

Sqn. Ldr.= Squadron Leader.

TBF = American single-engine torpedo bomber by Grumman named, *Avenger.*

TBM = American single-engine torpedo bomber manufactured by General Motors.

USAAF = United States Army Air Force.

USS = United States Ship.

VAQ = Tactical Electronics Warfare Squadron.

W/Cdr = Wind Commander.

WWII = World War Two.

Micah, Sam and Mark at Yasukuni Shrine, Tokyo (2005).

NOMENCLATURE

Aft = Portion of ship behind the middle area of a ship.

Airdrome = Airport or military air base.

Akolet = Language group in West New Britain, PNG.

Alligator = A small amphibious landing craft used to transport supplies and men.

Amidships = Nautical term for at, near or towards the center of a ship.

Amtrack = Small amphibious landing craft used for transporting supplies and men.

Arawe = Area on the south coast of New Britain approx. 200 miles west of Rabaul.

Avenger = American single-engine torpedo bomber designed by Grumman.

Axis = Alliance nations of Germany, Italy and Japan that fought against the allies.

Balus = Pidgin English for, "airplane."

Banyan tree = A type of fig tree that grows around a host tree.

Baret = Pidgin English for, "ditch."

Baskets = Purses of various sizes made from coconut palms used by men and women.

Beauforts = British twin-engine torpedo bomber built by Bristol.

Bends = Decompression sickness associated with depressurization events.

Bettys = Allied code name for Mitsubishi G4M twin engine bomber.

Bigmen = Term of respect for older men in Papua New Guinea.

Bita Paka = War cemetery in Rabaul, Papua New Guinea.

Boston = A-20 Havoc, American light twin-engine bomber built by Douglas.

Buai = A mixture of beetle nut, mustard seed and lime that is chewed.

Buffalo = A small amphibious landing craft used to transport supplies and men.

Bush = Jungle or interior.

Catalina = PBY, American twin-engine flying boat built by Consolidated Aircraft.

Chidorigafuchi cemetery = Japanese cemetery for unidentified WWII war dead.

Choppered = Helicopter transport.

Coast Watchers = Allied military intelligence operatives during World War II.

Copra = Dried coconut used for soaps and oils.

Cyclone engine = American 9-cylinder radial engine developed by Curtiss-Wright.

Davits = Steel structure for lowering small boats over the edge of a ship.

Decompression = A period of time in which a diver stays at a specific depth.

Digger = Australian military slang term for soldiers from Australia.

Dinghy = A type of small boat.

Dozer = Short for bulldozer.

Drome = Short for aerodrome, airport.

Dugout canoe = Canoe made from hollowing out the insides of a tree.

Fin flash = Tail striping on an aircraft.

Flybridge = An open deck on a cabin cruiser usually with navigation equipment.

Flying Fortress = B-17, American 4-engine heavy bomber built by Boeing.

Fore = Nautical term for toward the bow of a ship.

Hapkas = Individual of mixed races.

Haus boi = Literally, "house boy." House for men and boys to sleep.

Hayabusa = Nakajima Ki-43 single-engine Japanese Army Air Force fighter.

Helo pad = Helicopter landing area.

Helm = A ship's steering mechanism.

Hentai = Section of 3 aircraft of an Air Company (Chutai) consisting of nine aircraft.

Hiko Sentai = Japanese air combat group.

Hudson = American twin-engine bomber built by Lockheed Aircraft Corporation.

Kami = Japanese word for the spirits in the Shinto faith.

Kamikaze = Literally, "Divine Wind." Name given to Japanese suicide pilots.

Karanas = Pidgin English name for gravel made out of limestone.

Kina = Papua New Guinea currency name with the one Kina being a round coin with a hole in the middle.

Kinsei engine = Bomber aircraft engine manufactured by Mitsubishi

Klostu = Pidgin English expression for "close to" or "near."

Knots = A unit of speed equal to 1.151 mph.

Kokoda trail = Overland trail in Papua New Guinea through the Owen Stanley Range.

Kol = Indigenous group in East New Britain of Papua New Guinea.

Kulau = Half ripened coconuts used for drinking and eating.

Kunai grass = Commonly known as blady grass and can grow 2 to 10 feet tall.

Kutins = Pidgin English word for small trees trunks that had been cut.

Lapun = Pidgin English for an elderly person.

Mag = Alloy wheel made out of magnesium.

Mangrove = Trees that are found in tropical and subtropical tidal areas.

Mankies = Pidgin English name for young boys.

Maru = Japanese for "circle." Suffix used on Merchant Ships for good luck.

May West = Nickname, after the actress Mae West, for first inflatable life preserver.

Mumiangru = Kaul language meaning, "reef."

Myu = Indigenous group in West New Britain province of Papua New Guinea.

Narcosis = A condition similar to alcohol intoxication.

New Guinea Volunteer Rifles = Infantry battalion of the Australian Army.

Odontologist = One who has studied forensic dentistry.

Oscar = Allied reporting code name for Nakajima Ki-43 single-engine fighter.

Paul Guut = Kaul language literally, "down finish" or "fell down."

Pidgin English = Simplified language developed to communicate basically as in trade.

Pislama = Sea cucumber considered a delicacy in East and South East Asia.

Polywog = Nickname for Sailors who have not crossed the Equator.

Port = Nautical term for left side of a ship.

Roundel = National insignia used on military aircraft generally circular in shape.

Sake = Japanese alcoholic beverage made from fermented rice.

Samurai sword = Long, single-edged curved sword.

Shellback = Nickname for Sailors who have already crossed the Equator and gone through an initiation.

Singsing = All night singing/dancing ceremony used to appease dead ancestors.

Sked = Scheduled time for radio communication.

Starboard = Nautical term for right side of a ship.

Stockade = Military prison camp.

Tabunas = Pidgin English term for ancestors.

Telikom = Papua New Guinea Telephone Company.

Toea = Papua New Guinea coins 1,2,5,10 and 20 toea.

Tol Massacre = Japanese atrocity on February 4, 1942, at Tol Plantation.

Tok Pisin = Literally, "Talk Pidgin" meaning "Pidgin English."

Tony = Allied reporting code name for Kawasaki Ki-61 single-engine fighter.

Transom = The verticle, rear cross section at the back of a boat.

Val = Allied reporting code name for Aichi D3A single-engine attack bomber.

Vitiaz Straits = Strait between New Britain and mainland of Papua New Guinea.

Vivesection = Torturous surgery on a living human being.

Wantok = Pidgin English for, "one talk" meaning, "same language."

West New Britain = Province in Papua New Guinea.

Wirraway = Australian training aircraft built by Commonwealth Aircraft Corporation.

Wrasse = Fish able to reach up to 8.2 feet long.

Yasukini shrine = Shrine in Tokyo, Japan for the souls of the war dead from all the war dead after Meiji Restoration.

Zeke = Official Allied reporting name for Mitsubishi A6M single-engine fighter.

Zero = Allied referred name for Mitsubishi A6M single-engine fighter.

Grave of martyr, Father John Frederick Barge, Kandrian. WNBP, PNG

RESOURCES

In the event one were ever to find a crash site, they should contact:

AUSTRALIA: raaf.enquiries@defence.gov.au

JAPAN: www-admin@mhlw.go.jp

NEW ZEALAND: http://www.airforce.mil.nz/contact-us/

USA: http://www.jpac.pacom.mil/index.php?page=sitereport_l
ist&size=100&ind=5

To have a part in this honorable endeavor:

PacificWrecks is a free website dedicated to preserving the legacy of the Pacific War by documenting and sharing information about veterans, locations, airfields, remaining wreckage and MIA cases. Pacific Wrecks is a 501c3 non-profit charity established in 1995 by Justin Taylan. http://www.pacificwrecks.com/

New Tribes Mission, is dedicated to reaching those who have never heard the Gospel of Jesus Christ. They are a 501c3 non-profit charity established in 1942 and also are in need of short and long term personnel. www.ntm.org

Other groups who look for MIA:

Malaysia Historical Group searches the jungles of Malaysia.
mhg.mymalaya.com
http://www.asianage.com/international/malaysian-jungle-adventurers-solve-wwii-mysteries-639

The Bent Prop Project searches in Palau, Philippines.
http://www.bentprop.org/

Rabaul and Montevideo Maru Society represent the interests of the families of the soldiers and civilians captured in Rabaul and the New Guinea Islands after the Japanese invasion in January 1942. http://memorial.org.au/

For information on POW/MIA:

Defense Prisoner of War/Missing Personnel Office
http://www.dtic.mil/dpmo/

Vietnam Veterans of America
http://www.vva.org/Committees/POW_MIA/index.html

Australia Commonwealth War Graves Commission
http://www.cwgc.org/

For information on Australian and New Zealand military aircraft:

ADF Serials
www.adf-serials.com

For information and color photos of the crash sites visited in this book:

http://www.pacificwrecks.com/people/visitors/reichman/
http://www.mia-missinginaction.com

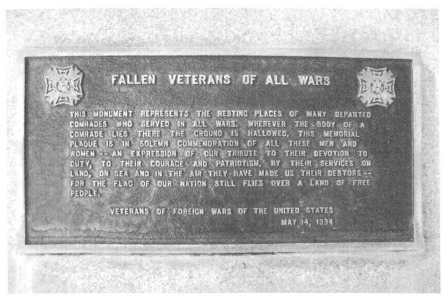

Monument to Fallen Veterans, Punchbowl Cemetery, Hawaii.

EPILOGUE
By Dr. Richard Perez

People needing to know about the fate of their loved ones who have gone to war is a natural consequence of the human condition. Many men have gone to war and never returned. They have left wives and children, parents and grandparents, aunts and uncles, siblings and extended families. It is for their honor and courage that a story such as this is told. These men went to war because of a common bond of loyalty, patriotism and friendship. Their love of country was beyond reproach, and their belief in God and Country surmounted all other concerns. Such dedication and valor is reflected in John 15:13 which reminds us that:

"Greater love has no one than this, than to lay down one's life for his friends."

The stories of war have been fraught with pain and agony for those who were left behind to wait for the reports of the fate of their loved one who was sent off to war. The histories of families become more complete when they can realize that some one cared enough (as described in this documentary) to go into the jungles and into the seas of PNG to seek to recover remains. Although only God knows of the whereabouts of every MIA, it is the grieving families who have been compelled by their grief to seek answers to the mystery that has surrounded the disappearance of the many loved ones who perished on those tragic days and who have remained lost.

There are formal organizations, specifically, JPAC (Joint Prisoner of War, Missing in Action Accounting Command) which have been established to locate and retrieve the remains of wartime American and Allied dead heroes. There are also a handful of independent people (some missionaries), who have cared enough to continue the search until all soldiers have been found or accounted for. It is as if God has appointed a few good men to continue this precious work. They are dedicated searchers who have risked life and limb to attempt to find answers. The coordination and travel through the jungle has been a difficult life for all who have experienced it and one which requires communication with the local population – and, believe it or not, many of them have retained memories of the war which they had

337

actually witnessed as it raged over their country so many years ago. Of course, those native men have aged and they have passed their knowledge over to the youth, who have begun to assist searchers on their treks into the jungle.

Life in the jungle is a continual challenge for people who have never had that opportunity – the challenges range from assuring that water was available and telephone/computer contact was in place, to locating food and obtaining transportation and fuel – even a sheltered home and the constant threat of malaria. In addition, one should not assume that all of the nationals were comfortable with Americans, Australians, etc., taking up residence on their lands. Many have retained the idea that they owned the land as well as the waters that surround it. Their acceptance of "foreign intruders" requires a great deal of diplomacy and tact on the part of the visitors. It was a God-directed process that has allowed the Missionaries to obtain favor among these people. It did not take long to realize that successful treks and guidance through the jungle were a vital contribution that the searchers could get from the nationals. Therefore, the development of camaraderie with them was vital.

The dedication to the cause of the searches was also vital. The teams in this documentary had precisely as their goal to locate and extract any human remains that may have survived the many years of exposure and souvenir hunting by travelers who may have passed. The all-encompassing philosophy of the independent searchers was based upon a genuine belief in the idea that our men had been lost and it was someone's task to find them and bring them home. It was a difficult task to convince some of the national people that the teams were not searching for gold or other items of value, which may have existed; they considered any items found to be locally owned. That, again, added to the degree of difficulty incurred with such searches.

The elation of reunions of family members with the remains of their long lost relatives has been experienced and documented by those who have searched the wilderness and who have successfully united families. It has served as a motivating factor, and so the searches continue.

As citizens of free countries, we have always honored those who have given the supreme sacrifice in the defense of them. It behooves us to continue to honor their memories, but also to continue to properly seek and find their remains so as to dispose of them properly and close the doors of concern and "unknowing" for the families of those who were lost.

It is our love for our fellow man that has united us over time immemorial, and we give our heartfelt appreciation to those who were lost in the war, but also to those who have dedicated their time, their efforts and, in essence, their lives to the search for solutions of a great mystery.

This book has been offered as a remembrance of those who fought for us and, in their effort to serve their country, were lost. The searchers identified in this book, specifically Mark Reichman and his son, Jared, his wife Joan and the other children, Micah, Mariko and Mieko who survived 23 years in the jungle as missionaries, have also given honorably to their respective countries and their efforts should be applauded with sincere appreciation from grateful nations.

We can rest in the assurance that these men, for whom they have searched, have not died in vain, since the countries involved owe a debt of gratitude to honor their courage and dedication to the lost airmen and to the Missionary cause.

Dr. R. L. Perez
Lt. Col, United States Air Force (Ret)

Memorial of the Army and Navy Union, USA Inc. Punchbowl, Hawaii.

Mark J. Reichman was born in Joliet, Illinois. Upon graduation from Lockport Central High School, he served four years in the US Navy from 1973 – 1977 as an Aviation Mechanic working on jet engines for the EA6B Prowler. He received his B.A. in intercultural ministries with New Tribes Mission. In 1986, along with his wife Joan, and five-month-old baby, Micah, he moved to Papua New Guinea.

During their 23 years of service in Papua New Guinea, his family grew to four children, and for family outings, they would trek the jungles and scuba dive the seas in search of WWII relics. With PNG locals as their guides, they have discovered eight Japanese dive bombers code-named Val, of which one was in 21 feet of water with the remains of the pilot and crew. They also discovered a U.S. P-38 named *Regina Coeli* and a U.S. B-17 named *Texas #6*.

They have dived on two sunken Japanese Merchant ships and scoured the Arawe battlefield with its remnants of U.S. tanks, bombs and caves full of dumped rations. After visiting one Australian Beaufort and three Lockheed Hudson crash sites, they discovered a fourth Hudson with its four-man crew that had been Missing In Action for 66 years. Mark is available for lectures and interested in hearing your MIA story. For contact information, visit: www.mia-missinginaction.com.

Made in the USA
Charleston, SC
11 March 2013